Facts
about Germany

Facts
about Germany
The Federal Republic
of Germany

BERTELSMANN
LEXIKOTHEK VERLAG

Published by Lexikon-Institut Bertelsmann

Editors: Heinz Dieter Bulka M. A. (responsible), Hans-Georg Michel,
Claudia Wullenkord
Layout: Günter Hauptmann
Pictorial editor: Elisabeth Franke (†)
Graphics: HTG-Werbung Tegtmeier + Grube KG., Bielefeld
Maps: Kartographisches Institut Bertelsmann, Gütersloh,
and Karl Wenschow GmbH, Munich

English: Diet Simon, 5000 Cologne 51

Fifth revised edition
Editorial deadline: 31 December 1985

Production:
© Verlagsgruppe Bertelsmann GmbH
Bertelsmann LEXIKOTHEK Verlag GmbH, Gütersloh, 1979, 1986 E

Mohndruck Graphische Betriebe GmbH, Gütersloh
Printed in the Federal Republic of Germany

Contents

Preface

There are many reasons for taking an interest in the Federal Republic of Germany. Many people see it first and foremost as a modern, efficient industrial country whose products are spread throughout the world. Others tend to associate it more with the great German traditions in the arts and sciences. Still more have in mind the country attracting the tourist, with its green rolling hills and romantic old towns. Those interested in politics will be aware that there is still an unsolved "German question" and will want to know its origins. And those convinced of the importance of social questions will want to learn about the major transformations which the Federal Republic of Germany has undergone in recent decades. And then there will be those who simply want to know more about the country whence the Germans one meets the world over as tourists, technicians or businessmen come.

This book is designed to help all those who, for whatever reasons, seek information about the Federal Republic of Germany. In 68 short chapters it deals with the country's geography and demography, its history, the political system and practical politics, the economy with all its branches, the social structure and the cultural life. We have tried to assemble as much reliable information as possible in a limited space in order to help readers broaden their knowledge and understanding of the country. In doing this, however, it was also necessary to include some statistical information though this has, whenever possible, been presented in a graphic form to ease comprehension. Although we would, of course, be pleased if the reader were to be enticed from time to time to read on, each chapter is self-contained, but as some subjects are treated under various aspects in several chapters, it is advisable to refer to the index when seeking particular information as cross references are only occasionally given.

Readers may also wish to direct an inquiry to an organisation or office in the Federal Republic. For this purpose, addresses of associations, institutions and authorities are given at the end of relevant chapters.

A book like this needs the cooperation of its readers and we would be grateful to receive any suggestions. Please send them to

Lexikon-Institut Bertelsmann
Postfach 5555
D-4830 Gütersloh 1
Federal Republic of Germany

Many experts and institutions, too numerous to list, have helped us in the making of this book. We thank them all.

Lexikon-Institut Bertelsmann

Country
People
History

The country

Germany lies in the centre of Europe, between the Scandinavian countries to the north, the Alpine countries to the south, the countries in Atlantic Western Europe and in continental East Europe. It ranges from the high southern Alps to the North and Baltic Seas. There are no natural barriers to the west, east and north, which is why Germany has always been a region of migration, seeing the exchange of peoples, cultures, economic, social and intellectual forces and ideas, as well as political clashes.

Germany has been divided since the end of World War II. A frontier 1,378 kms long separates the two states in Germany: the Federal Republic of Germany in the West and the German Democratic Republic (GDR) in the East. On the Eastern side the frontier is hermetically sealed off by various installations and is tightly guarded (see p. 72).

The sovereign territory of the Federal Republic of Germany comprises 248,706 sq. kilometres. The longest north-south distance is 867 kms, the longest west-east 463 kms. At its narrowest place the Federal territory measures 225 kms between France and the GDR. The circumference of all the border lines totals 4,231 kms on land and 572 kms on sea.

Landscapes. The German landscapes are extraordinarily varied and attractive. In a small area abound low and high mountain ranges, upland plains, terrace-country, hill, mountain and lake terrains and wide, open lowlands.

The are three main topographical regions, the North German Plain or Lowland, the Central German Uplands and the Alpine Foothills. The present Federal Republic comprises parts of all three.

The German share of the Alps is limited to the Allgäu (Mädelegabel, 2,645 m), the Bavarian Alps (Zugspitze, 2,962 m) and the Berchtesgaden Alps (Watzmann, 2,713 m). Genuine high alpine features with sharply jagged peaks, deep valleys and fast-flowing streams give them their character. In this alpine mountain world lie picturesque lakes, such as the Königssee near Berchtesgaden, and popular tourist resorts such as Garmisch-Partenkirchen, Berchtesgaden or Mittenwald.

Running up to the Alps is a wide, hilly upland, the Alpenvor-

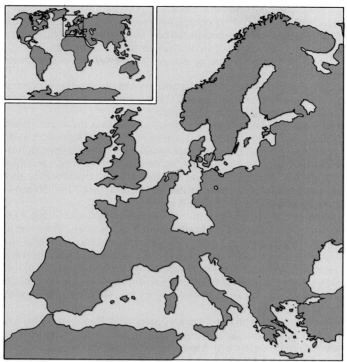

The location of the Federal Republic of Germany in Europe and the world

land. It has average elevation of 500 metres and gradually slopes away to the River Donau (Danube). The main characteristics of this landscape are moors, lake-studded ranges of rounded hills (Chiemsee, Starnberger See, Ammersee) and small villages.

The Central Uplands contain high plains, undulating hills, volcanic formations, troughs and basins. Nowadays, roads through mountain gaps and depressions and along river courses, which over millions of years have carved deep, broad valleys, make the Central Uplands easily accessible to traffic.

In south-west Germany, and rising along the climatically favoured Upper Rhenish Lowlands, is the Black Forest (Schwarzwald). This ascends to 1,493 metres in the rugged southern part (Feldberg) and contains many health resorts.

Extending eastwards of the Black Forest like the steps of a staircase is the Swabian-Franconian terrace country. This consists of usually fertile, densely populated basins and the rough highlands of the Swabian-Franconian Alb, which protrude with an impressively high steep terrace of about 400 metres out of the lower zone.

To the east, this landscape is bounded by the frontier ranges of the Bavarian-Bohemian Forest (1,456 m high at the Grosser Arber) and the Upper Palatinan Forest.

In a narrow valley between Bingen and Bonn the River Rhein (Rhine), the most important German north-south transport axis, slices through the Rhenish Slate Mountains (Rheinisches Schiefergebirge) whose low-fertility highlands and mountain terrains of Hunsrück, Taunus, Eifel and Westerwald are considerably less densely populated than the protected left and right-Rhenish wine-growing and tourist-frequented valleys.

Between the Rhineland in the west and Thuringia in the east lies the Hesse Central Upland, which has a variety of scenery, from hill areas averaging 500 to 600 metres in altitude to river basins and valleys. Old trade routes (e. g. the Salt Road) circumvent the once volcanically active heights of Vogelsberg and Rhön, run through the Hessische Bergland and through the Leine Trough (Leinegraben), known respectively as the Weserbergland, into the North German Lowland.

At the frontier with the German Democratic Republic (GDR) the massive Harz mountain range rises up to 1,100 metres. It forms its own climatic region with bleak mountain winds, cool summers and snow-rich winters.

The North German Lowland between the North and Baltic Sea coasts and the fringe of the Central Uplands has a very uniform character, its surface having been graven by Ice Age glaciers.

The North Sea is part of the Atlantic Ocean and has very marked tides and swell. Off the coast many islands rise out of the shallow tidal flats (Wattenmeer). Among the best known are the beach resorts of Sylt and Norderney. For protection from floods the inhabitants of the North Sea coast have put up dikes, behind which spreads a fertile marsh region used for animal grazing and crop growing. Sixty-five kilometres (40 miles) off the North Sea coast lies the impressive red cliff island of Heligoland (Helgoland).

The Baltic Sea coast consists partly of flat sand shore and partly of steep cliffs. Between the North and Baltic Seas lies the low hill country called "Holsteinische Schweiz", a wooded, domed landscape with picturesque lakes such as Plöner See and Ukleisee.

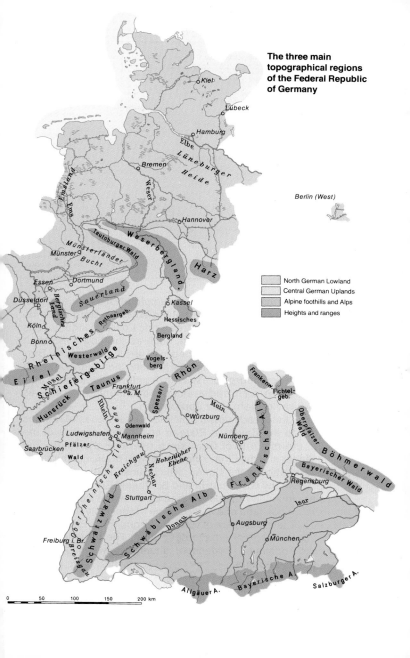

The three main
topographical regions
of the Federal Republic
of Germany

Kiel

Lübeck

Hamburg

Elbe

Bremen

Lüneburger Heide

Ems

Emsland

Weser

Berlin (West)

Hannover

Teutoburger Wald

Weserbergland.

Münsterländer Bucht

Münster

Harz

Essen

Dortmund

North German Lowland

Central German Uplands

Alpine foothills and Alps

Heights and ranges

Düsseldorf

Bergisches Land

Sauerland

Kassel

Köln

Rothaargeb.

Hessisches

Bonn

Rheinisches

Westerwald

Bergland

Eifel

Schiefergebirge

Vogelsberg

Mosel

Taunus

Rhön

Frankenw.

Hunsrück

Frankfurt a. M.

Spessart

Fichtelgeb.

Rhein

Main

Oberpfälzer Wald

Würzburg

Böhmerwald

Ludwigshafen

Odenwald

Saarbrücken

Pfälzer Wald

Mannheim

Nürnberg

Bayerischer Wald

Hohenloher Ebene

Regensburg

Neckar

Fränkische Alb

Oberrheinische Tiefebene

Kraichgau

Stuttgart

Isar

Schwäbische Alb

Donau

Augsburg

Freiburg i. Br.

Breisgau

Schwarzwald

München

Allgäuer A.

Bayerische A.

Salzburger A.

0   50   100   150   200 km

Rivers, lakes, mountains, islands

Rhein (below Konstanz)	865 kms
Donau (as far as Passau)	647 kms
Elbe (below Schnackenburg)	227 kms
Dortmund-Ems Canal	269 kms
Mittelland Canal (inside the Federal Republic of Germany)	259 kms
Edersee (Eder Valley reservoir)	202 mill. m^3
Bodensee (Lake Constance) (total area)	538 sq. kms
(German part)	305 sq. kms
Zugspitze (Bavarian Alps)	2,962 m
Watzmann (Bavarian Alps)	2,713 m
Feldberg (Black Forest)	1,493 m
Grosser Arber (Bavarian Forest)	1,456 m
Fehmarn Island	185 sq. kms
Sylt Island	99 sq. kms

The North German Lowland is not completely flat, however, but is interspersed with hills like that of the Wilseder Berg on Lüneburg Heath which rises to 169 metres. Wide Lowland indentations penetrate into the Central Upland, such as the Lower Rhenish Bight (with the Cologne Bight) between the Eifel and the Bergisches Land, or the Westphalian or Münsterland Bight between Sauerland and Teutoburg Forest. With their fertile loess soils they have always been preferred areas of settlement and trade, as have the entire northern Harz approaches.

Because of the steady upward incline from the coastal regions of the north to the Bavarian Plateau and Alpine regions of the southeast, the majority of Germany's rivers — the Rhein, the Ems, the Weser and the Elbe — flow north and drain into the North Sea. The exception is the Donau, which runs into the Black Sea and links Germany with Austria and Southeast Europe.

Lakes are found in regions covered by ice in the Ice Age in the North German Lowland and in the alpine fringe. Only the circular Eifel Maars (Eifelmaare) are of volcanic origin. In the Eifel, Sauerland and Harz, reservoirs have been built. The largest natural lake is Lake Constance (Bodensee), situated between Germany, Switzerland and Austria.

Climate. Germany is situated in the temperate zone, with precipitation throughout the year. In the north-west the climate is more ocean-determined with moderately warm summers and mostly mild winters. Towards the east and the south-east it becomes continental in character, with warm to hot summers and cold winters. The continental type of climate also strengthens towards the north, in part supported by the rising relief.

Average temperatures of the coldest month of the year (January) range from 1.5° C in lowland areas and below −6° C in the mountains. In high summer, average temperatures of the warmest month (July) lie between 17° and 18° C in the North German Lowland, while in the Upper Rhine trough and protected valleys they rise to 20° C. The annual average temperature is around 9° C. The situation of the Central Uplands varies the climate of the individual regions. The moist, Atlantic air masses always reach the mountains from a southerly to north-westerly direction so that precipitation here can reach up to 2,000 mm a year, while in the basins and depressions and along the eastern mountain fringes it can be as low as 500 mm a year (for example in the Mainz depression).

More characteristic than the regional distribution of climate types is the frequent change between moist-cool (in winter moist-mild) weather with Atlantic low pressure troughs on the one hand and dry-warm (in winter dry-cold) high pressure situations on the other. In winter the warm, dry "Föhnwind" ("snow-devourer") coming over the northern Alps to the Bavarian plateau often makes itself felt. The period between the last frost in spring and the first frost in autumn, which is important for vegetation and agriculture, averages 205 days in Berlin, 212 in Wiesbaden and 250 on Heligoland.

The people

The German nation, comprising some 74 million people, lives in two states: about 57 million in the Federal Republic of Germany (with West Berlin) and 17 million in the German Democratic Republic (with East Berlin). Millions of everyday occurrences testify to the feeling of the inhabitants of the two states that they belong to one people, to one nation.

The population of the Federal Republic of Germany. In 1984 the Federal Republic and West Berlin were inhabited by about 61.2 million people, including around 4.4 million foreigners. Only 100 years previously there were merely 20 million people in the same area. At that time 85 people had to share one square kilometre of land; today it is 247 people. In Europe only the Netherlands and Belgium have higher population densities. The greatest population increase occurred in the years immediately following World War II, when more than 14 million refugees and expellees from Germany's former eastern territories and from the GDR came in (see p. 66, 71/72). The construction of the Berlin wall by the communist GDR regime in 1961 put an abrupt stop to the influx of refugees from the GDR. In the ensuing years 65 % of the population growth was due to foreign workers coming into the Federal Republic, mainly from Mediterranean countries. The largest single contingent were Turks.

Since 1974 the population has been declining. The Federal Republic cannot depend on natural growth since the birthrate has been falling for years and is no longer even able to offset the death rate. At 9.5 births per 1,000 inhabitants per year the Federal Republic has the lowest birthrate in the world. The statistical average number of children per marriage is now only 1.6. The decline in the population is expected to continue.

The population is distributed very unevenly. Major conurbation areas are the Rhein-Ruhr (Essen, Dortmund, Köln [Cologne], Düsseldorf) region, the Rhein-Main area around Frankfurt, the Rhein-Neckar (Mannheim, Ludwigshafen) area, the Swabian industrial belt around Stuttgart and the concentrations around the cities of Bremen, Hamburg, Hannover, Nürnberg (Nuremberg) and München (Munich). Population density is greatest in the Ruhr district, where 9 % of the federal German population live on only

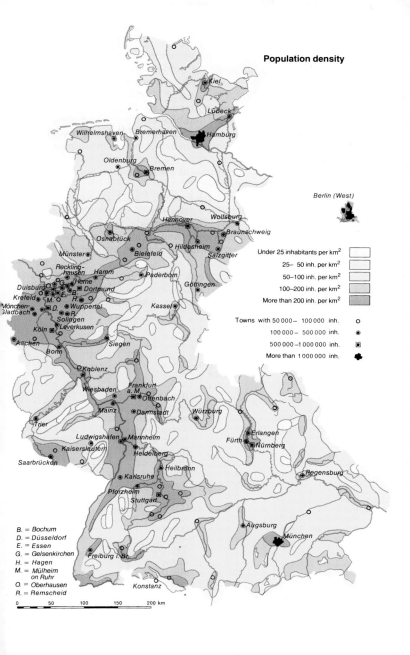

Population density

Berlin (West)

Under 25 inhabitants per km²	
25– 50 inh. per km²	
50–100 inh. per km²	
100–200 inh. per km²	
More than 200 inh. per km²	

Towns with 50 000– 100 000 inh. ○
100 000– 500 000 inh. ◉
500 000–1 000 000 inh. ⊡
More than 1 000 000 inh. ✦

B. = Bochum
D. = Düsseldorf
E. = Essen
G. = Gelsenkirchen
H. = Hagen
M. = Mülheim on Ruhr
O. = Oberhausen
R. = Remscheid

0   50   100   150   200 km

Kiel
Lübeck
Wilhelmshaven
Bremerhaven
Hamburg
Oldenburg
Bremen
Hannover
Wolfsburg
Braunschweig
Osnabrück
Hildesheim
Bielefeld
Salzgitter
Münster
Recklinghausen
Hamm
Paderborn
Göttingen
Duisburg
Herne
Dortmund
Krefeld
Mönchen-Gladbach
Wuppertal
Kassel
Solingen
Köln
Leverkusen
Aachen
Siegen
Bonn
Koblenz
Wiesbaden
Frankfurt a. M
Offenbach
Mainz
Darmstadt
Würzburg
Trier
Ludwigshafen
Mannheim
Erlangen
Fürth
Kaiserslautern
Heidelberg
Nürnberg
Saarbrücken
Heilbronn
Karlsruhe
Regensburg
Pforzheim
Stuttgart
Augsburg
München
Freiburg i. Br.
Konstanz

2 % of its sovereign area. In the central part of this German industrial heartland the extreme population density of 5,500 per square kilometre is reached. Without any clearly recognisable demarcation the cities of this region abut one another and form what is already sometimes referred to as "Ruhr City" (Ruhrstadt), with more than four million inhabitants. Contrasting with these very densely settled areas are a number of thinly populated ones such as the heath and moorland areas of the North German Plain, parts of the Eifel mountain region, the Bavarian Forest, Upper Palatinate and, above all, peripheral areas abutting the frontier between the two German states.

Every third inhabitant of the Federal Republic lives in a large town or city — some 20 million people in 65 towns with more than 100,000 population in 1984. The worldwide process of the rural exodus, that is of fast-growing city and shrinking small town or village populations, is no longer taking place in the Federal Republic of Germany, however.

Nevertheless, many Germans still live in small towns or villages: 25 millions (40 %) in communities with fewer than 20,000 inhabitants, and of these, 3.8 million in villages with fewer than

The largest cities *(1984)*

City	Inhabitants in 1,000s	City	Inhabitants in 1,000s
Berlin (West)	1,855	Bonn	292
Hamburg	1,610	Münster	273
München (Munich)	1,283	Wiesbaden	270
Köln (Cologne)	941	Karlsruhe	269
Essen	632	Mönchengladbach	258
Frankfurt/Main	610	Braunschweig	
Dortmund	590	(Brunswick)	257
Düsseldorf	576	Kiel	248
Stuttgart	567	Augsburg	247
Bremen	540	Aachen	242
Duisburg	536	Oberhausen	225
Hannover (Hanover)	523	Krefeld	221
Nürnberg		Lübeck	215
(Nuremberg)	474	Hagen	211
Bochum	389	Saarbrücken	190
Wuppertal	384	Kassel	188
Bielefeld	305	Mainz	187
Mannheim	298	Freiburg	180
Gelsenkirchen	293	Herne	176

Age structure of resident population on 31. 12. 1983

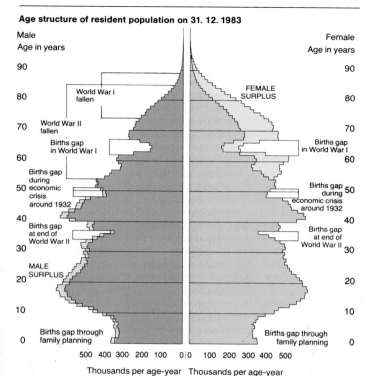

Male
Age in years

Female
Age in years

90

80 — World War I fallen

70 — World War II fallen

Births gap in World War I

60

Births gap during economic crisis around 1932

50

40

Births gap at end of World War II

30

MALE SURPLUS

20

10

Births gap through family planning

0

FEMALE SURPLUS

Births gap in World War I

Births gap during economic crisis around 1932

Births gap at end of World War II

Births gap through family planning

500 400 300 200 100   0|0   100 200 300 400 500

Thousands per age-year   Thousands per age-year

2,000. There are also 16 million people living in medium-sized municipalities (Gemeinden) of 20,000 to 100,000 inhabitants.

The German tribes. The German nation grew out of a number of tribes. There were Franks and Saxons, Bavarians and Swabians before there were "Germans". Indeed, it is safe to say that the differences between them are felt to this day. The old tribes have, of course, long since lost their original character. Tribal duchies had already disappeared by the first few centuries of German history and were succeeded by regional autocracies which, if anything, had no more than their names in common with the old tribal domains. But each in its own way continued the tribal tradition. The German nation has always consisted of larger and smaller units and particularism, which has been a constant factor in German history, continues to have manifold effects in the present, for example in the federal state form of government and in the large number of cultural centres. We shall come across this phenomenon in its positive and negative aspects on many pages of this book.

When speaking of German tribes today one should not try to define them too rigidly. They are historically evolved regional groups, each feeling itself to be quite distinct from the others and leading a vigorous life of its own. In the south of the Federal Republic live Bavarians, Swabians and Franks, in the centre Rhinelanders, Palatinans and Hessians, in the north Westphalians, Lower Saxons, Schleswig-Holsteiners and Frisians. That is only a rough categorisation, for each tribe is, in turn, sub-divided into smaller elements (Upper and Lower Bavarians, for example) which all have marked characteristics.

By no means are the tribes identical with the populations of the individual federal states (Bundesländer) which make up the Federal Republic. To a large extent the states were formed only after World War II with the involvement of the occupation powers and in most cases the boundaries drawn did not take tradition into account. Thus the "Land" of Nordrhein-Westfalen (North-Rhine-Westphalia) unites Rhinelanders and Westphalians, neither of whom can find much in common with the others' perception of history, character traits and temperament. But even those "Länder" which existed before 1945 owe their present territorial status to political events — conquests, hereditary successions, marital pacts — and their frontiers have little in common with the old tribal ones. For example, in Bayern (Bavaria), territorially one of the most stable German regions, one finds not only Bavarians but also Franks and Swabians. Inter-tribal rivalries can be quite an important political factor in such cases. This is why great care is taken to ensure that all the tribes inhabiting a "Land" are adequately represented in its important public institutions.

Beyond politics, tribal idiosyncrasies are the subject of ineradicable stereotyped ideas. Rhinelanders are thought to be easygoing, Swabians thrifty, Westphalians phlegmatic and so forth. There are, of course, traits of behaviour and character which are more typical of one tribe than another, but "tribal character" put in too simple a formula is invariably wrong and unjust when applied to the individual.

The expulsion of millions of Germans from the eastern territories after 1945 and the flight of millions more from the GDR has placed Silesians, East Prussians, Pomeranians, Brandenburg-ers, Saxons and Thuringians in the midst of the other tribes. This mixing was further accelerated by the mobility of modern industrial society. But despite so many differences having been levelled out, marked peculiarities in styles of building and settlement, customs and folklore remain. Then, of course, there is the cuisine, with each German tribe proudly laying claim to many tasty specialities of its own!

The German language. What really distinguishes German tribes from one another are their dialects. Even though the great postwar migrations and the impact of radio and television have resulted in much adaptation and blurring the dialects remain very much alive. Except for those who have learned the standard language at school, people as a rule can be identified as Hessians, Hamburgians, Thuringians and so forth by the dialect colouring of a particular region, even though they may be trying to speak the purer "High German" (Hochdeutsch). And those who give their dialects free rein can run into quite a bit of bother trying to understand people of other tribes. If, say, an Upper Bavarian and a Lower Saxon were both to speak pure dialect they would probably need an interpreter to converse. It's the same with dialects as it was with the tribes. There was Franconian, Saxon and Bavarian before there was German. For a long time the German language existed only in the form of its various regional vernaculars. Written German has evolved through a long process concluded only in the 18th century. Martin Luther's widely disseminated translation of the bible from Greek and Hebrew into the vernacular German in the 16th century was an important, although not the only milestone.

The oldest known record of written German dates from about 770. It is a small Latin-German dictionary, the so-called "Abrogans". Texts from that early time and following centuries up to about 1500 can no longer be understood by present-day Germans without specialised study. They would have to learn the older forms of German like foreign languages.

Today, German is the mother tongue of more than 100 million people. As well as being spoken in the two German states it is also the official language in Austria and Liechtenstein and one of the official languages in Switzerland. In international political and economic usage German plays a lesser role than English, French, Russian and Spanish. Its importance is greater in the cultural field: every tenth book in the world is published in German; among the languages most frequently translated into others it

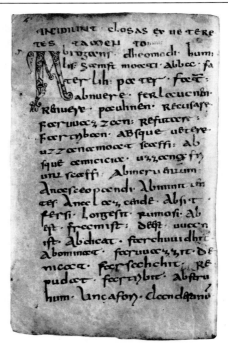

Abrogans handwriting (8th centruy; Stiftsbibliothek St. Gallen)

comes third after English and French, and it is the language into which most translation is done.Some 20 million people around the world learn German as a foreign language.

A fear sometimes expressed that the division of Germany will ultimately also split the language into "West German" and "East German" does not stand up to close scrutiny. It is true that some vocabulary in the two states varies and that in each new words have been created to describe new institutions which are not always immediately understandable in the other. Under the influence of the communist ideology in the GDR some words and concepts have taken on completely different meanings. On occasions, although the same language is being used in East and West, utterly different things may be expressed. Apart from this, though, there have always been regional differences in German without its unity having suffered. The basic vocabulary and grammatical construction remain the same in East and West. There is no "growing apart" linguistically. On the contrary, the language common to both is one of the strong clasps holding the two parts of the divided nation together.

The federal states

The Federal Republic of Germany consists of the "Länder" (states) of Baden-Württemberg, Bayern (Bavaria), Bremen, Hamburg, Hessen (Hesse), Niedersachsen (Lower Saxony), Nordrhein-Westfalen (North-Rhine Westphalia), Rheinland-Pfalz (Rhineland-Palatinate), Saarland and Schleswig-Holstein as well as the "Land" of Berlin which has a special status but is fully integrated in the legal and economic system of the Federal Republic.

This chapter contains thumbnail profiles of the federal states. In this context, the 1,000-year German history can be dealt with only peripherally.

Germany always consisted of small states, but the map looked different from century to century. The major changes in most recent history came with the Napoleonic wars in the early 19th century, the Prussian-Austrian war of 1866 and the German defeat in World War II. It resulted in the occupation and division of Germany and the dissolution of Prussia, the largest German state. Most of the present federal states came into being after 1945 in what were then occupation zones. From 1946 to 1953 they gave themselves democratic constitutions.

Baden-Württemberg

Baden-Württemberg lies in the southwest of the Federal Republic. It borders on France and Switzerland, the Rhein (Rhine) River forming most of the frontier. Along the Upper Rhenish Lowland rises the Black Forest, a densely wooded Central Upland whose healthy highland climate makes it a popular recreation area. In

The Bundesländer
(Federal States)

Schleswig-
Holstein

Kiel

Hamburg

Bremen

Niedersachsen

Hannover

Berlin
(West)

On Berlin's
special status
see p. 76–80

Nordrhein-Westfalen

Düsseldorf

Bonn

Hessen

Rheinland-

Pfalz

Wiesbaden

Mainz

Saarland

Saarbrücken

Baden-

Stuttgart

B a y e r n

Württemberg

München

0   50   100   150   200 km

Black Forest farmhouse

the south Baden-Württemberg extends to Lake Constance (Bodensee), the "Swabian sea". Apart from the Rhein and the Donau
(Danube), the Neckar is Baden-Württemberg's major river. The
state capital, Stuttgart, lies in the middle of the Neckar basin.

Baden-Württemberg's economic and financial strength is
above the federal average. It is the most industrialised of the federal states. Industrial centres are Mannheim, Karlsruhe, Pforzheim, Heilbronn, Stuttgart and Ulm. A number of products are
world-renowned, such as cars from Daimler-Benz (Mercedes),
jewelry from Pforzheim, Black Forest (Schwarzwald) clocks, but

Area: 35,751 km²
Population: 9.2 million
Inhabitants per km²: 259
Capital: Stuttgart
Parliament: Landtag, elected for 4 years
Executive: State Government (Landesregierung)
Administrative structure: 4 government districts (Regierungsbezirke),
    9 town-counties (Stadtkreise), 35 land-counties (Landkreise)
Gross Domestic Product per capita: DM 27,082

also electronics, fine-mechanics, chemicals and optics. Agriculture is also a major economic factor in the state. Many farmers specialise in cattle raising. Cereals, fruits, vegetables, tobacco and wine are grown. Badish and Württembergish wines are much appreciated by connoisseurs.

Baden-Württemberg is the only federal state which came into being as the result of a popular referendum. At war's end the occupation powers first formed three states of the old states of Baden and Württemberg, but in 1951 a large majority of the population voted for their merger. The strongest political party has long been the Christian Democratic Union (CDU) which has provided the state premier (Ministerpräsident) since 1953. The German southwest having traditionally been a stronghold of liberalism, the Liberal Free Democratic Party (FDP) had a very strong position in the beginning; in the meantime its share of votes has levelled out to that in the other states.

Bayern (Bavaria)

Bayern is the biggest federal state in area, about the size of Belgium and the Netherlands together. It occupies the entire eastern half of southern Germany. To the south it borders on Austria and in the east on Czechoslovakia. Its landscape attractions — the mountain world of the Alps, the lakes in the hilly Alpine uplands, the Bavarian Forest with the first German national park — as well as its rich heritage of cultural monuments make Bayern one of the most popular tourist regions.

In the midst of the Alpine uplands lies the state capital of Bayern, München (Munich) whose population has swelled to more than a million since the war. Many call it "Germany's secret capital". The Donau (Danube) valley separates the alpine uplands

Garmisch-Partenkirchen and Zugspitze mountain

from the Franconian Alb. Apart from München, south of the Donau cultural and economic life is dominated by the old imperial city of Augsburg.

North of the Donau, the former imperial free city of Regensburg, the bishops' residences of Würzburg and Bamberg, the Wagner town of Bayreuth and above all the metropolis of Franconia, Nürnberg (Nuremberg), call the cultural and economic tune.

The northern parts of Bayern are more strongly industrialised than the southern, disregarding München, Augsburg and Ingolstadt for the moment. Processing and refining industries domi-

---

Area: 70,553 km²
Population: 11 million
Inhabitants per km²: 155
Capital: München (Munich)
Parliament: 1. Landtag, elected for 4 years, 2. Senate as representation of social, economic, cultural and municipal corporations
Executive: State Government (Staatsregierung)
Administrative structure: 7 government districts (Regierungsbezirke), 25 town-counties (Stadtkreise), 71 land-counties (Landkreise)
Gross Domestic Product per capita: DM 25,078

---

nate. Other important branches are electrical engineering and textiles, mechanical engineering and vehicle manufacture and chemicals. Much of Bayern lives on agriculture and forestry. Hundreds of breweries make the famous Bavarian beer.

Bayern is one of the oldest and most constant German states. It was ruled by the Wittelsbach dynasty for almost three quarters of a millennium. Full of pride over their long history, the Bavarians tenaciously defend their independence vis a vis the central power. For example, the "Free State of Bavaria" is the only federal state which puts up its own frontier markers. Since the war the strongest political party in Bayern has been the Christian Social Union (CSU). It has had an absolute majority in the state parliament (Landtag) since 1962 and has ruled alone since 1966.

Bremen

The "'Free Hanseatic City of Bremen'", the smallest federal state, consists of the cities of Bremen and Bremerhaven, located 60 kilometres from each other along the mouth of the Weser River. Bremen is the Federal Republic's second largest and one of the world's leading sea ports. The "'Norddeutsche Lloyd'" and other large shipping companies are based in Bremen. Bremerhaven has grown from Bremen's outport into one of mainland Europe's largest fishing ports. Industry is closely linked with the port. Many imported raw materials, including coffee, tobacco, cotton and jute, to name but some, are processed and refined.

Area: 404 km²
Population: 677,000
Inhabitants per km²: 1,675
Capital: Bremen
Parliament: Bürgerschaft, elected for 4 years
Executive: Senate
Administrative structure: 2 town-counties
Gross Domestic Product per capita: DM 35,698

The Great Hall of Bremen Rathaus

Bremen was founded in the 8th century. In the late Middle Ages — together with Hamburg and Lübeck — it became one of the leading members of the Hanseatic League, an association of towns which dominated trade in the North and Baltic Sea region from the 14th to the 16th centuries. This era is still recalled by the official name. The city was able to keep its independence. throughout the turmoils of history. Since World War II the Social Democratic Party (SPD) has had the strongest following. In several legislative periods it had an absolute majority in the state parliament, the "Bürgerschaft", and ruled alone.

Hamburg

The "Free and Hanseatic City of Hamburg", "Germany's gateway to the world" before the division, lies some 120 kms above the mouth of the Elbe River at the North Sea. Hamburg is the Federal

Area: 755 km^2
Population: 1.61 million
Inhabitants per km^2: 2,133
Parliament: Bürgerschaft, elected for 4 years
Executive: Senate
Administrative structure: 7 districts
Gross Domestic Product per capita: DM 48,319

Republic of Germany's main trading port and can handle large ocean-going ships. The harbour area comprises 75 km^2, of which 16 km^2 are a free port zone. In addition to industrial branches typical of ports, such as shipyards, refineries and imported raw material processing enterprises, Hamburg has a wide range of consumer goods industries.

Like Bremen, Hamburg still proudly calls itself "Hanseatic" and has undergone a very similar development. It was founded in the early 9th century, so is a little younger than its rival, but over the centuries has vastly outgrown it. In the 19th century it became the second largest German city after Berlin. Since the end of World War II, except for the period from 1953 − 1957, Social Democrats have ruled Hamburg alone or together with junior coalition partners.

Hamburg harbour

Hessen (Hesse)

The federal state of Hessen lies in the centre of the Federal Republic. Between the Odenwald and Taunus uplands lies the Rhein-Main plain where one of the Federal Republic's major economic regions has developed. It includes the metropolis of Frankfurt. Here motorways, railways and inland waterways run together and Frankfurt airport is the turntable of European civil aviation. The focus of industrial production lies in the fields of chemistry, electro-technology, rubber and leather goods, machinery and cars. Another industrial centre has grown up around Kassel in north Hessen.

In the scenically attractive upper Lahn valley between the Taunus and Westerwald areas lie the university towns of Marburg and Giessen as well as Wetzlar, known for its optical industry. On

Frankfurt on Main

the periphery of the Taunus upland rise many mineral springs, around which spa resorts have developed, the state capital of Wiesbaden being the major one. In the partly loess-covered fertile lowlands north of the Main, cereals, vegetables and sugar beet are grown; stock raising and forestry dominate in the higher regions. The "Bergstrasse" south Darmstadt and the "Rheingau" rank with the best German wine growing areas.

In German history Hessen only briefly played an important role as a state, namely in the 16th century, when the Hessian count Phillip the Benevolent became one of the political leaders of the Reformation. Previously and subsequently it was almost always territorially fragmented. Only after World War II the old Hessian areas were reunited as the federal state of Hessen. Since 1950 the Social Democratic Party has had the largest following.

Area: 21,114 km^2
Population: 5.4 million
Inhabitants per km^2: 264
Capital: Wiesbaden
Parliament: Landtag, elected for 4 years
Executive: State Government (Landesregierung)
Administrative structure: 3 government districts (Regierungsbezirke),
    5 town-counties (Stadtkreise), 21 land-counties (Landkreise)
Gross Domestic Product per capita: DM 29,313

Niedersachsen (Lower Saxony)

The federal state of Niedersachsen occupies the northwest of the Federal Republic, extending from the North Sea coast with the East Frisian islands to the central German uplands with the "Weserbergland" and the western "Harz" in the south, from the "Emsland" at the Dutch border in the west to the Lüneburg Heath and Elbe River in the east. Next to Bayern (Bavaria), Niedersachsen is the major agricultural region ot the Federal Republic, particularly as a supplier of cereals, sugar beet, feed maize and potatoes. Stock keeping is highly developed. Along the lower Elbe and south of Emden fruit and vegetables are grown.

Industry is concentrated in the densely inhabited areas between low and uplands (Hannover conglomeration and Harz plains) and the port towns of Emden (vehicle assembly), Wilhelmshaven (the biggest German oil-landing port) and Cuxhaven(fish processing). Of big economic importance is the extraction of petroleum and natural gas in the Emsland and the German North Sea sector. The state capital of Hannover has made a name for itself all over the world as an industrial and fair city. Wolfsburg, located between the Heath and the Harz, is the seat of the Volkswagen company. The main tourist resorts are the East Frisian islands, the Harz mountains and the Lüneburg Heath.

Niedersachsen comprises nearly all of the area of the powerful

---

Area: 47,447 km^2
Population: 7.2 million
Inhabitants per km^2: 153
Capital: Hannover
Parliament: Landtag, elected for 4 years
Executive: State Government (Landesregierung)
Administrative structure: 4 government districts (Regierungsbezirke),
   9 town-counties (Stadtkreise), 38 land-counties (Landkreise)
Gross Domestic Product per capita: DM 22,862

Mills in Greetsiel, East Friesland

medieval Duchy of the Saxons, which broke up already in the 12th century. The name "Saxons" wandered up the Elbe with dynastic changes and remained with a central German region which now belongs to the German Democratic Republic. To distinguish from this, the name "Lower Saxony" came to be used for the old Saxonian core area.

The present federal state was formed in 1946 of the Prussian province of Hanover and the states of Braunschweig, Oldenburg and Schaumburg-Lippe. In the early years rightwing parties and parties of a regional character had strong positions in the state. Since the early 1960's parliamentary representations in Lower Saxony have become similar to those in other Länder. Both the CDU and SPD, the large parties, have ruled the state both alone and in coalition with other parties. Since 1986 Lower Saxony is governed by a coalition of the CDU and FDP.

Nordrhein-Westfalen (North-Rhine Westphalia)

Nordrhein-Westfalen lies in the west of the Federal Republic and borders on Belgium and the Netherlands. It is the most populous federal state. Almost a third of the population of the Federal Republic lives there. The core area of the Rhenish-Wesphalian industrial landscape is the Ruhr region, one of the richest bituminous coalbearing areas of the world and long one-sidedly characterised by mining, steel and iron-making industries. Meanwhile other industries have come, such as electronics, chemicals, synthetic fibres, paints, aluminium smelting and petroleum processing. There are also textiles and automobile manufacture, mechanical engineering, cement and glass works and large breweries. Between Köln (Cologne) and Bonn, in the Ville upland, the Federal Republic's largest brown coal deposit is mined.

Northeast of the Ruhr region, stretching to the Teutoburg Forest, lies the Münsterland Bight with the university town of Münster as the central point. Here, as in neighbouring areas, agriculture is the main pursuit, with wheat, barley and sugar beet growing, beef cattle raising, pig fattening and horse breeding. The forest-rich highlands of the "Sauerland", "Siegerland", "Bergisches Land" and northern "Eifel" in the south of Nordrhein-Westfalen are popular recreation areas and vitally important drinking water

Area: 34,062 km^2
Population: 16.8 million
Inhabitants per km^2: 494
Capital: Düsseldorf
Parliament: Landtag, elected for 5 years
Executive: State Government (Landesregierung)
Administrative structure: 5 government districts (Regierungsbezirke),
   23 town-counties (Stadtkreise), 31 land-counties (Landkreise)
Gross Domestic Product per capita: DM 26,506

Power station in the Ruhr region

sources for the industrial conurbations along the Rhein and Ruhr rivers. Nordrhein-Westfalen's lively economic activity is reflected in its densely knit network of transport facilities linking the many cities: Köln, Essen, Dortmund, Düsseldorf, Duisburg, Bochum, Wuppertal, Bielefeld, Gelsenkirchen, Solingen, Leverkusen and Paderborn, to name but some. South of Köln on Rhine lies Bonn which up to 1949 was a medium-sized university town and since then has been the capital of the Federal Republic.

The state of Nordrhein-Westfalen was formed in 1946 mostly of areas which had belonged to Prussia since the early 19th century but had formed no political unit. Party-political power relationships in the state have changed frequently. Both Christian Democrats (CDU) and Social Democrats (SPD) have ruled partly in coalition with the Free Democrats (FDP) and alone. From 1958 to 1962 the CDU had the majority in the state parliament (Landtag), the SPD has had it since 1980.

Rhine valley grape harvest

Rheinland-Pfalz (Rhineland-Palatinate)

The federal state of Rheinland-Pfalz borders on Belgium, Luxembourg and France. In the mountainous Eifel landscape a conspicuous feature are the small, almost perfectly circular volcanic lakes. The valleys of the Rhein and Mosel (Moselle) are preferred habitation and economic areas. Centres are the old Roman towns of Koblenz (Coblence), Trier, Mainz and Worms as well as the cities of Ludwigshafen and Kaiserlautern. The mid-Rhenish valley

Area: 19,848 km^2
Population: 3.6 million
Inhabitants per km^2: 183
Capital: Mainz
Parliament: Landtag, elected for 4 years
Executive: State Government (Landesregierung)
Administrative structure: 3 government districts (Regierungsbezirke),
    12 town-counties (Stadtkreise), 24 land-counties (Landkreise)
Gross Domestic Product per capita: DM 24,350

with its many castle ruins is one of the most beautiful German landscapes; many in the world may see it in front of their mind's eye when they think of Germany.

With two thirds of the German vineyards, Rheinland-Pfalz is the Federal Republic's main wine-growing region. The best-known wine-growing districts are Rheinpfalz, Rheinhessen, Mosel-Saar-Ruwer, Nahe, Mittelrhein and Ahr. Rheinland-Pfalz also has industry; chemical works in Ludwigshafen; mechanical engineering in Kaiserslautern, Frankenthal, Mainz and Koblenz; shoe factories in Pirmasens; jewelry making in Idar-Oberstein.

The state of Rheinland-Pfalz was formed in 1946 of Bavarian, Hessian and Prussian lands which previously had never belonged together. The Christian Democrats (CDU) have been the strongest political party uninterruptedly since 1947. They have ruled in coalition with the Social Democrats, Free Democrats or alone.

Saarland

Apart from the city-states, Saarland is the smallest federal state. It lies in southwest Germany and borders on France and Luxembourg. The economic centres lie in the Saar Valley around Saarlouis, Neunkirchen and the state capital of Saarbrücken. The Saarland's coal is smelted with iron ore from the neighbouring French Lorraine (Lothringen) to iron and steel.

Saarbrücken

There are also metal processing, mechanical engineering, chemical, ceramic and glass industries. France is the main trading partner for the Saarland's economy.

Saarland was formed as a political unit in 1920 by the Versailles peace treaty, separated from Germany and placed under the administration of the League of Nations. France obtained preferential economic rights and great political influence. In a 1935 referendum the Saarland population voted to return to Germany. After World War II France made a new attempt to annex the Saarland step by step. The population resisted these strivings and also rejected an interim "Europeanisation" of their land. On the ba-

---

Area: 2,571 km²
Population: 1.0 million
Inhabitants per km²: 409
Capital: Saarbrücken
Parliament: Landtag, elected for 5 years
Executive: State Government (Landesregierung)
Administrative structure: 6 land-counties (Landkreise),
Gross Domestic Product per capita: DM 24,417

sis of an unmistakeable expression of the will of its inhabitants, Saarland became a federal state of the Federal Republic of Germany on January 1, 1957. From 1957 to 1985 the leading governing party was the Christian Democratic Union (CDU); since then the Social Democratic Party (SPD) has governed.

Schleswig-Holstein

The northernmost federal state lies between the North and Baltic Seas and in the north borders on Denmark. In the west the state consists of fertile marshland, in the centre it is dry and sandy and in the east it has a hilly lake landscape. Off the west coast lies a 15 to 30 km wide tidal flat zone in which lie the north Frisian islands of Sylt, Amrum and Föhr and the Halligens. Also part of Schleswig-Holstein is the red-stone cliff island of Heligoland rising steeply from the North Sea.

The eastern seaboard region is strongly featured with excellent natural harbours, notably Flensburg, the state capital of Kiel and the old Hanseatic city of Lübeck. From the Baltic Sea ports there are ferry connections to Denmark, Sweden and Finland. The shortest transport route between the Federal Republic and Scandinavia is the socalled "birds flight line" over the island of Fehmarn. The "Nord-Ostsee-Kanal" ("Kiel Canal") links the lower Elbe with the Kiel Bay. It is the most-used waterway in the world.

Area: 15,721 km^2
Population: 2.6 million
Inhabitants per km^2: 166
Capital: Kiel
Parliament: Landtag, elected for 5 years
Executive: State Government (Landesregierung)
Administrative structure: 4 town-counties (Stadtkreise), 11 land-counties (Landkreise)
Gross Domestic Product per capita: DM 22,415

Baltic coast near Kiel, Schleswig-Holstein

Schleswig-Holstein is still predominantly agricultural, with the emphasis on cattle and pig raising. The agricultural produce are the basis for a food industry. The Baltic Sea ports are dominated by shipbuilding. In the south of the state, where access to the Elbe and the proximity of Hamburg offer favourable site conditions, other industries have been growing up in recent years. The North and Baltic Sea bathing resorts and the "Holsteinische Schweiz" cater to tourists. Of special importance to Schleswig-Holstein are land reclamation and coastal protection along the North Sea.

Schleswig-Holstein was a subject of contention between Germany and Denmark for a thousand years. After two German-Danish wars it finally came to Germany in 1864 and became a Prussian province in 1866. The predominantly Danish population in northern Schleswig voted in a 1920 referendum to join Denmark. South Schleswig, where there is a small Danish minority, stayed with Germany. In 1946 Schleswig-Holstein was made an independent federal state. Since 1950 the Christian Democrats (CDU) have been the leading government party. The Danish minority are organised in a South Schleswig Voters' Association, which sends one deputy to the state parliament (Landtag).

Berlin (West)

The Land of Berlin has a special status amongst the federal states in every respect. Like Bremen and Hamburg it is a city-state, but comprises only half a city, the Western part of Berlin, and is not geographically connected with the rest of the federal area. The history of the Berlin problem and the city's special political status are dealt with in detail in the chapter "The division of Germany", pages 76 — 80.

Before World War II the Reich capital of Berlin was a transport turntable and centre of European trade. The division cost it this role. Even so, West Berlin is still Germany's largest industrial city. The major products are electrical appliances, machinery, garments, optical goods, pharmaceutical and printed goods. Many of the large enterprises based in the Federal Republic have branches in Berlin (West). Berlin (West) is also one of Europe's major congress and fair cities. As a city of the arts and theatre it enjoys international renown. Part of the city area are large forests and lakes.

Founded in the 13th century, Berlin became the residence of the margraves of Brandenburg in the 15th century. With the rise of Brandenburg-Prussia its importance grew. A metropolitan development began when Berlin became capital of the German empire in 1871. In the 1920s Berlin was the third largest city of the world. It suffered severe destruction in World War II. After the divi-

Area: 480 km^2
Population: 1.9 million
Inhabitants per km^2: 3,863
Parliament: Abgeordnetenhaus (House of Deputies), elected for 4 years
Executive: Senate
Administrative structure: 12 districts
Gross Domestic Product per capita: DM 32,988

Memorial Church and Kurfürstendamm, Berlin (West)

sion of the city, largescale reconstruction of the western part, aided by funds from Bonn, was begun. A 1950 constitution gives Berlin (West) the status of a federal state. For decades the Social Democrats (SPD) were the strongest party, governing with changing coalition parties. After severe losses of votes in 1981, the SPD had to cede the city's government to the Christian Democrats (CDU) which has been governing together with the FDP since 1983.

The reader will come across references to the federal states at many other places in this book. More information is to be found particularly in the chapters "The people", "A brief German history" and "Federal, regional and local government".

A brief German history up to 1945

Up to last century it was a widely held belief that German history began in the year A.D. 9. That was when Arminius, a prince of a Germanic tribe called the Cherusci, vanquished three Roman legions in the Teutoburg Forest (south-east of modern-day Bielefeld). Arminius, about whom not much else is known, was regarded as the first German national hero and a huge memorial to him was built near Detmold in the years 1838 — 1875.

Nowadays historical concepts are no longer thought to be so simple. The fusing of a German nation was a process which took hundreds of years. The word "deutsch" (German) probably began to be used in 8th century and initially defined only the language spoken in the eastern part of the Francocian realm. This empire, which reached the zenith of its power under Charlemagne (Karl der Grosse), incorporated peoples speaking Germanic and Romance dialects. After Charlemagne's death (814) it soon fell apart. In the course of various inheritance divisions, a west and an east realm developed, whose political boundary approximately coincided with the boundary between German and French speakers. Only gradually did a feeling of cohesion develop among the inhabitants of the eastern realm. Then the term "deutsch" was transferred from the language to its speakers and ultimately to the region they lived in, "Deutschland".

The German western frontier was fixed relatively early and remained fairly stable. But the eastern frontier moved to and fro for hundreds of years. Around 900 it ran approximately along the Elbe and Saale rivers. In subsequent centuries German settlement, partly peaceful and partly by force, expanded far eastward. This expansion stopped only in the middle of the 14th century. The ethnic boundary then made between Germans and Slavs remained until World War II.

High Middle Ages. The transition from the East Franconian to the German "Reich" is usually dated from 911, when, after the Carolingian dynasty had died out, the Franconian duke, Conrad I was elected king. He is regarded as the first German king. (The official title was "Frankish King", later "Roman king", from the 11th century the name of the realm was "Roman Empire", from the 13th century, "Holy Roman Empire", in the 15th century the words "of the German Nation" were added.) It was an electoral monarchy, that is to say that the high nobility chose the king. In addition, "dynastic right" also applied and so the new king had to be a blood relation of his predecessor. This principle was broken several times. There was also a number of double elections. The medieval empire had no capital city; the king ruled roving about from place to place. There were no imperial taxes; the king drew his sustenance mainly from "imperial estates" he administered in trust. His authority was not always recognised by the powerful tribal dukes unless he was militarily powerful and a skilful forger of alliances. Conrad's successor, Henry I (919 − 936), was the first to succeed in this, and to an even greater extent his son, Otto I (936 − 973). Otto made himself the real ruler of the realm. His great power found obvious expression when he was crowned Emperor in 962 in Rome.

From then on the German king could claim the title Emperor. The emperorship was conceived as universal and lent its incumbent the rule over the entire Occident. However, this notion never became full political reality. For the coronation as emperor by the Pope the king had to make his way to Rome. With that began the Italian policy of the German kings. For 300 years they were able to retain control of upper and central Italy but because of this were diverted from important tasks in Germany. And so Otto's successors inevitably suffered big setbacks. However, under the succeeding Salian dynasty a new upswing occurred. With Henry III (1039 − 1056) the German king and emperorship reached the zenith of its power, maintaining above all a supremacy over the Papacy. Henry IV (1056 − 1106) was not able to hold this position. In a quarrel with Pope Gregory VII over whether bishops and other influential church officials should be appointed by the Pope or the temporal ruler he was superficially successful. But Gregory retaliated by excommunicating Henry, who thereupon surrendered his authority over the church by doing penance to the pope at Canossa (1077), an irretrievable loss of power by the emperorship. (To this day Germans use the phrase "A walk to Canossa" for someone having to eat humble pie.) From then on emperor and pope were equal-ranking powers.

In 1138 the century of rule by the Staufer or Hohenstaufen dynasty began. Frederick I Barbarossa (1115 − 1190), in wars with the pope, the upper Italian cities and his main German rival, the Saxon duke, Henry the Lion, led the empire into a new golden age. But under him began a territorial fragmentation which ultimately weakened the central power. This weakening continued

*Emperor Charles IV and the seven elector princes
(heraldry book, around 1370, Bibliothèque Royale Albert Ier, Brussels)*

under Barbarossa's successors, Henry VI (1190 – 1197) and Frederick II (1212 – 1250) despite the great power vested in the emperorship. The religious and temporal princes became semi-sovereign "land dukes". The end of Hohenstaufen rule (1268) practically meant the end of the universal Occidental emperorship, too. Internal disintegrative forces prevented Germany from becoming a national state, a process just beginning then in other west European countries. Here lies one of the roots for the Germans' becoming a "belated nation".

Late Middle Ages to modern times. Rudolf I (1273 – 1291) was the first Habsburg to take the throne. Now the material foundation of the emperorship was no longer the lost imperial estates but the "house estates" of the dynasties and house power politics became every emperor's main preoccupation. The "Golden Bull" (imperial constitution) issued by Charles IV in 1356 regulated the election of the German king by seven electors privileged with special rights. These sovereign electors and the towns, because of their economic power, gradually gained influence while that of the small counts, lords and knights declined. The towns' power further increased when they linked up in leagues. The most important of these, the Hanseatic League, became the leading Baltic power in the 14th century. To this day the city-states of Hamburg and Bremen proudly call themselves "Hanseatic cities".

From 1438 the crown — although the empire nominally was an electoral monarchy — practically became the property of the Habsburg dynasty which had become the strongest territorial power. In the 15th century demands to reform the empire increased. Maximilian I (1483 to 1519), the first to accept the imperial title without a papal coronation, tried to implement such a reform but without much success. The institutions newly created or reshaped by him — Reichstag (Imperial Assembly), Reichskreise (Imperial Counties), Reichskammergericht (Imperial Court) — lasted until the end of the Reich (1806), but were not able to halt its continuing fragmentation. Consequently, a dualism of "Emperor and Reich" developed: the head of the Reich was offset by various institutions — electoral princes, princes and municipalities. The power of the emperors was curtailed and increasingly eroded by "capitulations", which they negotiated at their election with the electoral princes. The princes, especially the powerful among them, greatly expanded their rights at the expense of imperial power. But the Reich continued to hold together, the glory of the imperial idea had remained alive and the small and medium territories were protected in the Reich system from attack by powerful neighbours.

The towns became centres of economic power, profiting above all from growing trade. In the burgeoning textile and mining industries, forms of economic activity grew which went beyond the guilds system of the craftsmen and, like distant trading, were beginning to take on early capitalistic traits. At the same time an intellectual change was taking place, marked by the Renaissance and Humanism. The newly risen critical spirit turned above all on church abuses.

Age of religious schism. The smouldering dissatisfaction with the church broke out, mainly through the actions of Martin Luther from 1517, in the Reformation which quickly spread. Its consequences went far beyond the religious. The entire social structure began to stir with change. In 1522/23 the Reich knights rose up and in 1525 the Peasants' Revolt broke out, the first larger revolutionary movement in German history to strive for both political and social change. Both uprisings failed or were bloodily quelled. The dukes profited most from the Reformation. After changing fortunes of war they were given the right to dictate their subjects' religion by the 1555 Peace of Augsburg. This accorded the Protestants equal rights with those of the Catholics. With that, the religious division of Germany was established.

Farmers in revolt (woodcut by Hans Burgkmair, 1525)

On the imperial throne at the time of the Reformation was Charles V (1519 – 1556), heir to the biggest realm since the time of Charlemagne but also the last Holy Roman emperor to aspire to the medieval ideal of universal empire. His world-political interests were too demanding for him to be able to assert himself within Germany. After his abdication the empire was split up. The German territorial states and the west European national states together now formed the new European system of states.

At the time of the Peace of Augsburg, four fifths of Germany were Protestant but the struggle between the faiths had not ended with it. In following decades the Catholic church was able to recapture many areas (Counter-Reformation). The differences between the faiths sharpened, religious parties – the Protestant Union (1608) and the Catholic League (1609) – were formed. A local conflict in Bohemia then triggered off the Thirty Years War which widened into a European conflict over religious and political differences. Between 1618 and 1648 much of Germany was devastated and depopulated. The 1648 Peace of Westphalia ceded territories to France and Sweden and confirmed the withdrawal of Switzerland and the Netherlands from the Reich. The Reich institutions were accorded all major sovereign rights in religious and temporal matters and the right to enter alliances with foreign partners.

Age of Absolutism. The almost sovereign principalities took over the absolutist form of government modelled on the French. Absolutism gave the ruler limitless power while at the same time allowing tight administrations to be built up, an organised fiscal policy to be introduced and new armies to be mobilised. Many princes aspired to making their residences cultural focal points. Some of them − representatives of "enlightened absolutism" − encouraged learning and philosophy, albeit within the confines of their power interests. The policy of state control of all economic life also allowed the absolutistically ruled states to gain in economic strength. Thus lands such as Bavaria, Brandenburg (the later Prussia), Saxony and Hanover were able to develop into power centres in their own right. Austria, which repelled the attacking Turks and acquired Hungary as well as parts of the formerly Turkish Balkan countries, rose to a large power. A rival to it developed in the 18th century in the form of Prussia which, under Frederick the Great (1740 − 1786), grew into a first rank military power. Both states pursued European big power policies.

Age of the French Revolution. The nudge which brought the crumbling Reich crashing down came from the West. Revolution broke out in France in 1789. Under pressure from the middle classes, the feudal social order which had existed since the early middle ages was swept away, a division of powers and human rights were to assure the liberty and equality of all. The attempt by Prussia and Austria to intervene by force in the events in the neighbouring country failed ignominiously and triggered a counter-thrust by the revolutionary armies. Under the stormy advances of the forces of Napoleon who had assumed the revolutionary heritage in France the Reich finally collapsed. France took the left bank of the Rhine. To compensate the former owners of these areas for their losses, an enormous territorial reshuffling took place at the expense of the smaller and particularly the religious principalities. By the "Reichsdeputationshauptschluss" of 1803 some four million subjects had changed rulers. The middle states were the beneficiaries. In 1806 most of them grouped together under French protection in the "Rheinbund" (Rhenish League). In the same year Emperor Franz II laid down the crown and with that the Holy Roman Empire of the German Nation ceased to be.

The French revolution did not spread into Germany. Although there, too, various individuals had over the years tried time and again to do away with the barriers between the aristocracy and the common people and although leading thinkers welcomed the overthrow in the west as the start of a new era one major reason why the spark could not catch easily was that in contrast to the

Fireworks at the court of Dresden
(copper etching by Johann August Corvinus, 1719)

centrally oriented France, the federalistic structure of the Reich
hampered the spread of new ideas. Another big reason was that
France, the motherland of the revolution, opposed the Germans
as an enemy and an occupying power. Indeed, the struggle
against Napoleon forged a new national movement which culminated in wars of liberation. But Germany did not remain unaffected by the forces of social change. First in the "Rheinbund" states
and then in Prussia (in the latter connected with names like Stein,
Hardenberg, Scharnhorst, W. von Humboldt) reforms were begun, aimed at breaking down feudal barriers and creating a society of free, responsible citizens. The objectives were abolition
of serfdom, freedom of trade, municipal self-administration,
equality before the law, general conscription. But many reform
moves were pulled up short. Participation by the populace in
legislation was refused almost everywhere. Only hesitantly did

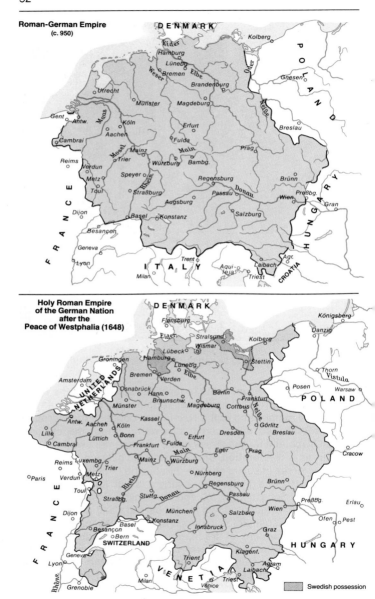

Roman-German Empire
(c. 950)

DENMARK

Kolberg

P O L A N D

Eider
Hamburg
Lüneburg
Weser Bremen Elbe
Brandenburg
Gnesen
Utrecht
Münster Magdeburg
Elbe
Gent Antw. Maas
Köln
Erfurt
Breslau
Aachen
Fulda
Cambrai
Mainz Main
Prag
Reims
Moser Würzburg Bambg.
Verdun Trier
Metz Speyer Rhein Regensburg Brünn
Toul Straßburg Donau Passau Wien Preßbg.
Dijon Augsburg Gran
Basel Konstanz Salzburg
Besançon HUNGARY
Geneva
Lyon ITALY Trent Aqui-leja Laibach Agr.
Milan Triest CROATIA

FRANCE

**Holy Roman Empire
of the German Nation
after the
Peace of Westphalia (1648)**

DENMARK
Flensburg
Königsberg
Danzig
Eider Stralsund
Wismar Kolberg
Lübeck
Groningen Hamburg Lünebg. Stettin Thorn Vistula
Amsterdam Bremen Verden Elbe
UNITED NETHERLANDS Osnabrück Berlin Posen
Hann. Braunschw. Magdeburg Frankfurt Warsaw
Münster Cottbus Neiße POLAND
Antw. Aachen Köln Kassel
Lille Lüttich Bonn Erfurt Görlitz Breslau
Cambrai Frankfurt Fulda Dresden
Reims Luxembg. Mainz Würzburg Eger Prag Cracow
Paris Trier Main
Verdun Metz Nürnberg
Toul Rhein Regensburg Brünn
Straßbg. Stuttg. Donau Passau
Dijon München Wien Preßbg. Erlau
Basel Salzburg Ofen Pest
Besançon Konstanz Innsbruck Graz
Bern SWITZERLAND Klagenf. HUNGARY
Geneva
Lyon VENETIA Trient Agram
Rhône Laibach
Grenoble Milan Venice Triest

FRANCE

Swedish possession

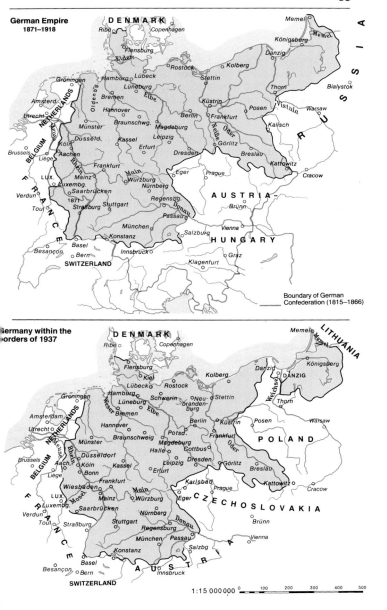

German Empire
1871–1918

DENMARK

Ribe • Copenhagen
Flensburg
Eider
Memel
Königsberg
Danzig
Rostock Kolberg
Hamburg Lübeck
Lüneburg Elbe Stettin Thorn Bialystok
Groningen Bremen Küstrin Posen
Amsterd. Oldenburg Hannover Berlin Frankfurt Kalisch Warsaw
NETHERLANDS Münster Braunschwg. Magdeburg Neiße Oder
Utrecht Maas Düsseld. Kassel Leipzig Görlitz
Brussels Aachen Erfurt Dresden Breslau
Liège Köln Rhein Kattowitz
BELGIUM Frankfurt Main Eger Prague Cracow
LUX. Mainz Würzburg
Verdun Luxembg. Nürnberg AUSTRIA-
Saarbrücken Regensbg.
1871 Stuttgart Donau Brünn
Toul Straßburg Passau
München Vienna
Konstanz Salzburg HUNGARY
Basel Innsbruck
Besançon Bern Graz
SWITZERLAND Klagenfurt

RUSSIA
Vistula
FRANCE

———— Boundary of German
Confederation (1815–1866)

**Germany within the
borders of 1937**

DENMARK LITHUANIA

Ribe • Copenhagen
Memel
Memel
Flensburg Kiel Danzig Königsberg
Lübeck Rostock Kolberg DANZIG
Weser Schwerin Neu- Stettin Weichsel
Groningen Hamburg branden- Thorn
Lüneburg Elbe burg
Amsterdam Bremen Berlin Küstrin Posen POLAND Warsaw
NETHERLANDS Hannover Potsd.
Utrecht Maas Münster Braunschweig Magdeburg Frankfurt Oder
Brussels Düsseldorf Halle Cottbus
BELGIUM Aach. Köln Kassel Leipzig Dresden Görlitz
Liège Bonn Rhein Erfurt Breslau
Frankfurt Karlsbad Kattowitz
Wiesbaden Main Eger Prague CZECHOSLOVAKIA Cracow
FRANCE LUX. Mainz Würzburg
Verdun Luxembg. Mosel Nürnberg
Toul Saarbrücken Brünn
Straßburg Stuttgart Donau
Regensburg Vienna
München Passau A U S T R I A
Konstanz Salzbg.
Basel Innsbruck
Besançon Bern
SWITZERLAND

1:15 000 000 0 100 200 300 400 500

some princes grant their states constitutions, especially in southern Germany.

The "German Confederation". After the victory over Napoleon the Congress of Vienna (September 1814 to June 1815) redrew the map of Europe. The hopes of many Germans for a free, unitary national state were not fulfilled. The "Deutsche Bund" (German Confederation) which replaced the old Reich was a loose association of the individual sovereign states. Its sole organ was the "Bundestag" in Frankfurt, not an elected but a delegated diet. It was able to act only if the two great powers, Prussia and Austria, agreed. It saw its main task in the ensuing decades in suppressing all aspirations and efforts aimed at unity and freedom. Press and publishing were subject to rigid censorship, the universities were under close supervision and political activity was virtually impossible.

Meanwhile a modern economic development which worked against these reactionary tendencies had begun. In 1834 the "German Customs Union" (Deutscher Zollverein) was founded, creating a unitary inland market. In 1835 the first German railway line went into operation. Industrialisation began. With the factories there grew the new class of factory workers. At first they found better incomes; but the rapid growth of the population soon led to a labour surplus. And since there were no social welfare provisions, the mass of factory workers lived in great misery. Tensions exploded violently, for example in the 1844 uprising of the Silesian weavers, which was harshly put down by the Prussian military. Very hesitantly at first, a workers' movement began to form.

The 1848 revolution. In contrast to the revolution of 1789, the French February revolution of 1848 found immediate response in Germany. In March there were uprisings in all states, and these forced many concessions from the shocked princes. In May the National Assembly (Nationalversammlung) convened in Frankfurt's Paulskirche (St. Paul's Cathedral). It elected Austrian archduke Johann Imperial Administrator (Reichsverweser) and set up a Reich Ministry which, however, had no powers or authority. The tune was called in the National Assembly by the Liberal centre, which strove for a constitutional monarchy with limited suffrage. The splintering of the National Assembly from Conservatives to Radical Democrats which already indicated the spectrum of parties to come made it difficult to draw up a constitution. But not even the Liberal centre could overcome the differences between

National Assembly in Frankfurt, 1848 (lithograph)

the protagonists of "greater Germany" and "smaller Germany" concepts, that is a German Reich with or without Austria. After hard bargaining a democratic constitution was drawn up which attempted to combine old and new ideas and required a government responsible to parliament. But when Austria insisted on bringing into the future Reich its entire realm, encompassing more than a dozen different peoples, the "smaller Germany" concept won the day and the National Assembly proffered Friedrich Wilhelm IV (Frederick William) of Prussia the hereditary German imperial crown. The king turned it down, not wanting to owe imperial majesty to a revolution. In May 1849 popular uprisings in Saxony, the Palatinate and Baden which aimed at enforcing the constitution "from below" failed. That was the seal on the failure of the whole revolution. Most of the achievements were rescinded, the constitutions of the individual states reactionarily revised. In 1850 the German Confederation was refounded.

The rise of Prussia. The 1850s were years of great economic upswing. Germany became an industrial country. Although its production output still lagged far behind England's it outpaced it in growth rate. Pacemakers were heavy industry and machine manufacture. Prussia also became the predominant economic power of Germany. The economic power strengthened the political self-confidence of the liberal middle class. The German Progress Party (Deutsche Fortschrittspartei), set up in 1861, became the strongest party in the Prussian diet and denied the government the funds when it wanted to make reactionary changes in the structure of the army. The newly appointed Prime Minister (Ministerpräsident), Otto von Bismarck (1862), took up the challenge and for some years governed without parliamentary approval of the budget which was required by the constitution. The Progress Party dared offer no further resistance than parliamentary opposition, however.

Bismarck was able to offset his precarious position on the domestic front by foreign policy successes. In the German-Danish war (1864) Prussia and Austria forced the Danes to cede the duchies of Schleswig and Holstein (now forming Federal Germany's northernmost state) which they initially administered jointly. But Bismarck had from the outset pursued the annexation of the two duchies and steered for open conflict with Austria. In the "German War" (1866) Austria was defeated and had to leave the German scene. The German Confederation was dissolved and replaced by the North German Federation (Norddeutscher Bund) of states north of the River Main, with Bismarck as Federal Chancellor (prime minister).

The Bismarck Reich. From then on Bismarck worked towards "smaller German" unity. He broke France's resistance in the war of 1870/71, triggered off by a diplomatic conflict over the succession to the Spanish throne. Defeated France had to cede Alsace-Lorraine and pay huge reparations. In the patriotic enthusiasm of the war, the southern German principalities joined up with the northern federation to form the German Empire (Deutsches Reich). At Versailles near Paris, on the vanquished enemy's territory, King Wilhelm (William) I of Prussia was proclaimed German Emperor on January 18, 1871.

German unity had not come about by popular decision "from below" but by a treaty between princes, "from above". Prussia's predominance was stifling. To many the new Reich seemed like a "Great Prussia". The Reichstag (Imperial Assembly) was elected

Proclamation of Wilhelm I as German emperor in the Versailles Hall of Mirrors, 1871 (painting by Anton von Werner)

by general and equal suffrage. Although it had no say in the formation of the cabinet, it could influence government by its participation in lawmaking and its budgetary right. Although the Reich Chancellor (chief minister) was accountable only to the Kaiser (emperor) and not to parliament he did have to try to get majorities for his policies in the Reichstag. Suffrage in the Länder (states) still varied. In eleven it was still class suffrage, dependent on tax paid; in four there was still the old division into estates. The south German states, with their longer parliamentary tradition, reformed their electoral laws after the turn of the century and Baden, Württemberg and Bavaria made theirs the same as the Reich laws. Although Germany's becoming a modern industrial country strengthened the influence of the economically successful middle class, the people who still called the tune in society were the aristocrats, above all in the army officer corps where they predominated.

Bismarck ruled as Reich Chancellor for 19 years. Through a consistent peace and alliance policy he tried to give the Reich a secure position in the new European power relationships. In contrast to this farsighted foreign policy was his home policy. He had no understanding for the democratic tendencies of his time. To him, political opposition was "hostility to the Reich". Bitterly, but ultimately vainly, he fought the left wing of the liberal middle class, political Catholicism and especially the organised labour movement which for 12 years (1878 − 1890) was practically under a ban by an Anti-Socialists Act. Hence the vastly growing working class, despite progressive social legislation, were alienated from the state. Bismarck ultimately became a victim of his own system when he was dismissed in 1890 by the young Emperor Wilhelm II.

Wilhelm II wanted to rule himself but he lacked the knowledge and staying power. More by speeches than by actions he created the impression of a peace-threatening dictator. Under him there took place a transition to "Weltpolitik" (world policy), with Germany trying to shorten the lead of the great imperialist powers and thereby becoming more isolated. In his home policies Wilhelm II soon took a reactionary course after his attempt to win the working class over to a "social emperorship" failed to bring the quick success he had hoped for. His chancellors had to rely on changing coalitions of conservatives and national liberals. Social Democrats, although one of the strongest and, from 1912 the strongest party in the Reichstag, were continually prevented from participating.

World War I. The assassination of the heir to the Austrian throne on June 28, 1914, triggered off the outbreak of World War I. The question as to who was to blame for this war remains in dispute. Certainly, Germany and Austria on the one side, France, Russia and Britain on the other, did not consciously seek it but they were prepared to risk it. From the start, all had definite war aims for which military action was at least not unwelcome. The Germans failed in their aim quickly to vanquish France. The fighting in the west after the defeat of Germany in the Battle of the Marne soon froze into trench warfare, ultimately peaking in senseless material attrition with enormous losses on both sides. With the outbreak of war, the Kaiser receded into the background. As it progressed, the weak Reich Chancellors had to submit more and more to the will of the army supreme command, whose nominal chief was Field Marshal Paul von Hindenburg, and whose real head was General Erich Ludendorff. The entry into the war of the United

States in 1917 brought the decision which had long been developing and which could no longer be changed by the revolution in Russia and the peace in the east. Although the country had bled dry, Ludendorff, completely misjudging the situation, continued until September 1918 to insist on "peace through victory" but then surprisingly demanded an immediate armistice. Hand in hand with the military collapse went the civilian. Unresisting, the Kaiser and the princes yielded their thrones in November 1918. Not a hand stirred to defend a monarchy which had lost all credibility. Germany became a republic.

The Weimar Republic. Power fell to the Social Democrats. Their majority had long since abandoned the revolutionary notions of earlier years and saw its mission as securing an orderly transition from the old to the new form of state. Private ownership of industry and agriculture remained untouched. The mostly anti-republican civil servants and judges were taken over without exception. The imperial officer corps retained command of the armed forces. Attempts by radical leftists to drive the revolution on in a socialist direction were quelled militarily. In the National Assembly elected in January 1919, which convened at Weimar and drew up a new Reich constitution, three unconditionally republican parties — Social Democrats, German Democratic Party and the Catholic Centre — had the majority. But through the 1920s the parliamentary parties and popular forces which were more or less hostile to a democratic state went from strength to strength. The Weimar Republic was a "republic without republicans", rabidly fought by its opponents and only half-heartedly defended by its supporters. Especially the postwar economic misery and the oppressive terms of the peace of Versailles Germany had to sign in 1919 bred deep skepticism towards the republic. Growing domestic instability was the result.

In 1923 the confusion of the postwar era reached its peak (inflation, Ruhr occupation by France, Hitler coup, communist overthrow attempts). This was followed by economic recovery and with it some political pacification. The foreign policy of Gustav Stresemann regained political equality for defeated Germany through the Pact of Locarno (1925) and accession to the League of Nations (1926). The art and sciences experienced a brief, intensive flowering in the "golden 20's". After the death of the first Reich President, the Social Democrat Friedrich Ebert, the former Field Marshal Hindenburg was elected head of state in 1925 as the candidate of the Right. Although abiding strictly by the consti-

Gustav Stresemann addressing the League of Nations in Geneva in 1926

tution, he never developed a personal commitment to the republican state.

The ultimate collapse of the Weimar Republic began with the world economic crisis in 1929. Left and right-wing radicalism exploited unemployment and the general deprivation to their ends. No more majorities capable of government could be found in the Reichstag, the cabinet being dependent on the support of the constitutionally very strong Reich President. From 1930, the up to then insignificant National Socialist movement of Adolf Hitler which fused extreme anti-democratic tendencies and a raging anti-Semitism with pseudo-revolutionary propaganda gained strength in leaps and bounds and by 1932 had become the strongest party. On January 30, 1933, Hitler became Reich Chancellor. Apart from members of his own party his cabinet included politicians of the right and non-partisan specialist ministers, so that it was hoped that sole rule by the National Socialists could be prevented.

The Hitler dictatorship. Hitler soon rid himself of his allies. An Empowering Act, approved by all the middle class parties, gave him practically limitless power. He banned all parties but his own. The trade unions were smashed, basic rights virtually removed and press freedom abolished. The regime exercised ruthless terror and violence against anyone who stood in its way. Thousands disappeared without trial in hastily constructed concentration camps. Parliamentary institutions at all levels were abolished or made powerless. The "Führer" (Leader) principle advanced everywhere. When Hindenburg died in 1934, Hitler united in his person the offices of president and chancellor. By this he gained control as commander in chief of the armed forces which up to then had still had a certain inner life of their own.

In the few years of the turbulent Weimar Republic the majority of Germans had not acquired any deep-rooted affinity to freedom and democracy. More than anything else, years of political turmoil, violence between the various camps — including bloody street battles — and the mass unemployment engendered by the world economic crisis had shattered confidence in government. Hitler, on the other hand, succeeded with job-creation and armament production programmes to reinvigorate the economy and quickly reduce unemployment. He was favoured in this by the world depression coming to an end. His position was also bolstered by foreign policy successes.

In 1935 the Saar region, until then administered by the League of Nations, returned to Germany and the same year the Reich regained its defence sovereignty. In 1936 German troops moved into the up to then demilitarised Rhineland. In 1938 Austria was joined to the Reich and the Western powers allowed Hitler to annex the Sudetenland. All this helped him quickly to achieve his political ends, although in all classes of society there were people who courageously resisted the dictatorship.

Immediately after taking power, the regime began to carry out its anti-Semitic programme. Step by step the Jews were stripped of all human and civic rights. Those who could, tried to escape the persecution by fleeing abroad. The persecution of political opponents and the suppression of freedom of opinion also drove thousands out of the country. Many of the best German writers, artists and scientists fled the country — an irredeemable loss to German culture.

World War II and its consequences. Hitler was not to be satisfied. From the outset he prepared for a war he was willing to wage to

Frankfurt, 1945

subjugate Europe. With his attack on Poland on September 1, 1939 he unleashed World War II, which lasted five and a half years, devastated much of Europe and killed 55 million people.

The German armies defeated Poland, Denmark, Norway, Holland, Belgium, France, Yugoslavia and Greece. In the Soviet Union they advanced to a position just short of Moscow and in North Africa they threatened the Suez Canal. Harsh occupation regimes were set up in the conquered countries. They were fought by resistance movements. In 1942 the regime began the "Final Solution of the Jewish Question": all the Jews the regime could lay its hands on were taken to concentration camps in occupied Poland and murdered. The total number of victims is estimated at six million. The year this inconceivable crime began brought the turning point in the war. From then on Germany and its allies, Italy and Japan, suffered setbacks in all theatres.

The terror of the regime and the military setbacks strengthened resistance against Hitler in all classes of society. A coup attempt on July 20, 1944, carried out mainly by officers, failed. Hitler survived the bomb attack in his headquaters and struck back mercilessly. More than 4,000 people from all walks of life who had been involved with the resistance were executed in the ensuing months. Outstanding figures of the resistance, whose names stand also for many nameless, were General Ludwig Beck, Colonel Count Stauffenberg and the former Leipzig Mayor, Carl Goerdeler.

The war continued, Hitler prosecuting it under enormous losses, until the entire Reich area was occupied by enemies. Then, on April 30, 1945, he killed himself. Eight days later the successor he had willed by testament, Grand Admiral Dönitz, carried out the unconditional capitulation and was arrested shortly afterwards by the victors.

Germany had suffered the greatest defeat in its history. Most towns lay in ruins, a quarter of all houses were destroyed or heavily damaged. The economy and transportation networks were smashed. The most urgent things to sustain life were lacking. Millions of Germans were captives, millions homeless, millions in flight. Germany appeared to have no future.

The division of Germany

While the war was still in progress the allies considered what should be done with defeated Germany. They were determined to make it impossible for it ever to wage an aggressive war again. The surest way of doing this appeared for a while to be splitting the Reich into several states. But as the end of the war approached this plan was abandoned. Germany was to be completely disarmed, militarily occupied and put under the authority of the victors, but remain intact. That it was ultimately divided after all, and remains so to this day, was due to postwar world-political development.

The Potsdam Conference and the eastern territories. After the capitulation of the German forces on May 8, 1945 the victorious powers — the USA, the Soviet Union, Great Britain and France — in line with an agreement reached in September 1944, the so-called "London Protocol", divided Germany into four occupation zones. The military commanders of the four zones together constituted the Allied Control Council which assumed supreme authority in Germany. The capital, Berlin, belonged to none of the zones, being jointly administered by the four powers, each occupying a sector of the city.

The Allied Control Council held its first session on July 30, 1945. At the same time a meeting was taking place at Potsdam, near Berlin, of the heads of government of the United States, the Soviet Union and Great Britain.

The decisions reached at this trilateral conference were summarised in an official "Protocol" signed on August 2, 1945, by J. V. Stalin for the Soviet Union, Harry S. Truman for the USA und C. R. Attlee for Great Britain. This "Protocol" which later became known as the "Potsdam Agreement" contained a number of provisions which decisively influenced Germany's future.

One of the main ones is the declaration by which the three powers "reaffirm their opinion that the final delimitation of the western frontier of Poland should await a peace settlement" but that "pending the final determination of Poland's western frontier" the "former German territories" east of the Oder or western Neisse rivers should come under Polish administration. "Agreement in principle" was also reached at Potsdam on the Soviet proposal

Potsdam conference, 1945. Seated left to right: Attlee, Truman, Stalin

"concerning the ultimate transfer to the Soviet Union of the city of Königsberg (now Kaliningrad) and the area adjacent to it", i. e. all of northern East Prussia. The US President and British Prime Minister pledged their support of the proposal.

These decisions affected about a quarter of the Reich area. Indubitably Poland had a claim for compensation for the monstrous sufferings and losses inflicted on it by the war. That this was to take the form of a westward territorial expansion was due above all to the fact that the Soviet Union annexed about 200,000 square kilometres of east Polish territory in 1939. This had been made possible at the time by an agreement between Hitler and Stalin on the "delineation of mutual spheres of interest in east Europe". In the course of the war the Soviet Union favoured Poland being compensated for this loss by German territory. Poland was "shifted westwards", as it were.

The German eastern territories concerned — totalling 114,000 square kilometres — comprised East Prussia, Silesia and part of Pomerania and Brandenburg. They had been inhabited by Germans for centuries and were diffused with German culture. They were economically important as agricultural surplus areas, producing food for 13.5 million people. Other important economic interests included the Silesian mines which produced almost a fifth of Germany's coal.

Expulsion of Germans and the Oder-Neisse line. The "Protocol"of the tripartite Potsdam Conference also contained the portentous agreement according to which the three signatory powers recognised the necessity of a "transfer" of the German parts of the population from Poland, Czechoslovakia and Hungary to Germany. This agreement, though sounding dry and matter-of-fact, brought a great deal of suffering and misery to millions of people.

Although the agreement did not relate to the German areas put under Polish administration nor those allotted to the Soviet Union, Poland and the Soviet Union achieved a fait accompli. As soon as the Soviet armies came on to German soil, a huge refugee movement to the west began. Up to the time of the Potsdam Conference four million Germans had already left their homelands in the eastern territories. Now, without this being covered by the Potsdam decisions, most of the 5.5 million Germans still living in the German territories east of the Oder and Neisse rivers were expelled by force.

At the same time most of the 3.5 million Sudeten Germans who lived in Czechoslovakia were expelled. On top of that there were about five million Germans who lived in other East and Southeast European states and were either expelled or deported or stayed where they were. Altogether 15 million Germans were refugees, deportees or expellees at war's end and in the immediate postwar years up to 1950. How many of them died can only be roughly estimated; the number is likely to be more than two million. The expellees were distributed to all occupation zones. By far the majority of them came to the area which later became the Federal Republic of Germany. To find them food, clothing and housing in the devastated, starving country was very difficult in the beginning. However, the exiles received help to build new livelihoods, the funds for this being raised through levies on assets which had remained intact ("Lastenausgleich" − "burden-sharing"). The economic recovery which began after the foundation of the Federal Republic eased the integration of the refugees. The exiles have found a new homeland.

Expulsion and severance of the territories east of Oder and Neisse were generally felt in Germany to be unjust. All political parties — initially even the Communists — rejected them. However, the German Democratic Republic (GDR) formed out of the Soviet occupation zone, soon revised its policy: on July 6, 1950, it concluded with Poland the "Agreement of Zgorzelec" (Görlitz) in which it recognised the Oder-Neisse line as the final German-Polish frontier. The Federal Republic of Germany, however, referred to the Potsdam Agreement which deferred settlement of the frontier issue to a peace treaty with all Germany and it insisted that the expellees should not be deprived of the right to their homeland. At the same time it emphasised that it had no intention of changing the border by force. Nevertheless, for a long time the contrasting views on the frontier issue prevented the normalisation of relations with Poland. In the "Charta der deutschen Heimatvertriebenen" (Charter of German Expellees) of August 5, 1950 the expellees foreswore revenge and violence while reaffirming their right to their homeland and equal participation in the reconstruction of Germany and Europe.

The Warsaw Treaty of December 7, 1970 between the Federal Republic of Germany and the People's Republic of Poland opened the way to understanding between the two states. The treaty lays down that the Oder-Neisse line forms Poland's western state frontier. The Federal Government has made clear that it acts only on behalf of the Federal Republic of Germany, that is that does not commit a reunited Germany. The treaty does not impinge on the rights and responsibilities of the four powers in respect of Germany as a whole and Berlin, nor does it replace the still lacking peace treaty. Both sides underlined the inviolability of their existing borders "now and in the future" and declared that "they have no territorial claims whatsoever against each other".

Germany under occupation rule. Another important topic of the Potsdam Conference was what was to be done with defeated Germany. In this respect agreement was reached on the following principles: total disarmament and demilitarisation, destruction of the war potential, destruction of National Socialism, decentralisation of the economy and reconstruction of political life on a democratic basis. No central German government was to be formed until further notice: there could, however, be several German central administrations as support organs for the Control Council.

It soon became apparent that each of the victorious powers interpreted the Potsdam Agreement in its own way and in line with its own interests. France, for example, especially distrustful of all

German strivings for unity, prevented by its veto the establishment of the intended German central authorities. The crassest differences existed from the outset, however, over the question of what the democratisation of Germany was to look like. Despite these differences of opinions on details, however, the Western powers were agreed on the basic principles of the future German order of state and society: parliamentary democracy, legal security, civic liberties, human rights, private property and private enterprise were to them an inseparable whole. For the Soviet Union, however, "democratisation" according to Leninist doctrine was possible only in a socialist order in which the state — and with that the communist party dominating it — controls the decisive means of production.

Fundamental as these differences were, they comprised only one aspect of the overall East-West conflict which assumed world dimensions and soon turned into the "cold war". Under these circumstances the cooperation of the four powers in Germany practically came to an end at the turn of 1947/48. In March 1948 the Soviet Union left the Allied Control Council in Berlin. The relationship between the former allies turned into open hostility, indeed came almost to the brink of war, when in 1948/49 the Soviet Union made the ultimately futile attempt to incorporate the parts of Berlin occupied by the Western powers into its sphere of power (see page 77).

New political beginning in the occupation zones. In the meantime the building up of German political parties and administrative organs had begun in the different occupation zones. This proceeded very fast and under rigid steerage in the Soviet zone where already in the summer of 1945 political parties on a zonal scale were allowed and several central administrations for the zone established. The occupation power favoured the Communist Party (KPD). In April 1946 the Social Democratic Party (SPD) which had a larger following than the KPD was forced to merge with it to form the Sozialistische Einheitspartei Deutschlands (SED, Socialist Unity Party of Germany). A vote among SPD members about the merger was prevented in the Soviet zone. Such a vote did take place in the Western sectors of Berlin; there 82% of those who voted were against merging with the KPD. Although in the 1946 local government and Landtag elections the SED won the most votes in the Soviet zone, the other parties, too, although they were greatly hindered, did well. Since then the SED — except in Berlin (West) — has never again contested free elections.

Germany in 1945

—— Germany within the borders of 1937

Western zones and Western sectors of Berlin* (Federal Republic of Germany from 1949)

Soviet zone and Eastern sector of Berlin* (German Democratic Republic from 1949)

German eastern territories under Polish or Soviet administration

* On special status of Berlin see p. 76 – 80

In the three Western zones the development of political life proceeded from the bottom to the top. Political parties were allowed initially only at local level; after the Länder had been constituted, also at state level. Mergers at zonal level occured only later. In 1946/47 Landtag elections took place in all states. Zonal level administrative organs were only beginning to form. But since the deprivation of the ruined country could only be overcome with largescale planning across state and zonal frontiers and the four-power administration was not functioning, the USA and Great Britain decided in 1947 to unite their two zones in economic matters. This "united economic area", also called "Bizone", was the germ-cell of the later Federal Republic of Germany. The Frankfurt "Economic Council" made up of Länder delegates and the "Administrative Council" it appointed in turn were the first steps towards a future parliament and a future government.

Foundation of the Federal Republic of Germany. In the early summer of 1948, when all hopes of solving the Germany problem together with the Soviet Union had been abandoned, the Western powers gave the signal for the establishment of a West German state. They proposed that a national assembly work out a constitution. The suggestion met with resistance from most German politicians who feared that in this way they would be cementing the division of Germany. After long negotiations it was decided to form a "Parliamentary Council" of delegates from the Länder parliaments to draw up a "Basic Law" (Grundgesetz). The choice of this term instead of the word "constitution" (Verfassung) was to underline the fact that it was not to be the final constitution of a separate state but only a temporary makeshift solution.

The Parliamentary Council convened on September 1, 1948 in Bonn. A leading figure of the Christian Democratic Union (CDU), Konrad Adenauer, the former Chief Mayor (Oberbürgermeister) of Köln (Cologne), was elected its president. In a period of seven months this body wrote the Basic Law for the Federal Republic of Germany. On May 8, 1949 it was adopted by the Parliamentary Council by 53 votes to 12. It then required adoption by the assemblies of two thirds of the participating Länder. In the ensuing weeks 10 of 11 Länder parliaments gave their approval. On May 24, 1949 the Basic Law went into force. Only the Bavarian Landtag refused ratification because it felt the central organs had been given too much power at the expense of the Länder. Despite this, Bayern nevertheless recognised the Basic Law as being legally binding.

The authors of the Basic Law emphasised in several points the provisional nature of their work. The preamble declared (and declares to this day) that the Basic Law had been adopted "to give a new order to political life for a transitional period". The German people in the West German Länder had "also acted on behalf of those Germans to whom participation was denied", that is to say the inhabitants of the Soviet zone. The preamble goes on: "The entire German people are called upon to achieve in free self-determination the unity and freedom of Germany." And the last article of the Basic Law states: "The Basic Law shall cease to be in force on the day on which a constitution adopted by a free decision of the German people comes into force." Restoration of Germany as a united state was the declared supreme objective of all political parties and few were probably so pessimistic at the time to assume that its realisation would still be far off even decades later.

With the coming into force of the Basic Law, the Federal Republic of Germany had come into existence. On August 14, 1949 the first election of its parliament, the Deutsche Bundestag, took place. The great majority of voters gave their support to parties which backed the Basic Law which thus gained democratic approval. Then the federal organs were constituted. On September 15, 1949 Konrad Adenauer was elected the first Federal Chancellor (Bundeskanzler).

When it was founded the Federal Republic of Germany did not have full sovereignty. Supreme authority remained with the three Western occupation powers. In the following years the occupation regime was eliminated step by step. On May 5, 1955, with the coming into force of the Paris Treaties, full sovereignty was restored to the Federal Republic. From a vanquished enemy it had turned into a partner of the Western powers.

The German Democratic Republic. In the Soviet zone the establishment of state organs and changes to the structure of society on the Soviet model had, as mentioned earlier, begun early. But in its propaganda the Socialist Unity Party (SED) always portrayed itself as the pioneer of German unity and accused the West German parties of betraying the national cause. This was also the reason why it allowed the western state foundation to take place first. Only after the creation of the Federal Republic of Germany was the German Democratic Republic (GDR — Deutsche Demokratische Republik) founded on October 7, 1949 in the eastern sector of Berlin. According to its constitution it appeared to be a parliamentary democracy. But in reality the communist SED dominated from the outset all political activity and its leading organ, the Politbureau, to all intents and purposes governed dictatorially.

In the summer of 1952 the SED proclaimed the "building up of socialism". From then on the transformation of the social and state order along communist lines was continued at an accelerated pace and in all openness. Already in 1950 the GDR had become a member of the Council for Mutual Economic Assistance, COMECON, and its accession to the Warsaw Pact in 1955 completed its integration in the eastern bloc.

The political pressures and the economic difficulties aroused great dissatisfaction among the GDR's population. An uprising broke out on June 17, 1953 which was bloodily put down by Soviet troops stationed in the GDR. Day by day people fled from the GDR to the Federal Republic, especially to West Berlin. To prevent

The German Democratic Republic (GDR)

(1984 statistcs. All data include Berlin [East])

Area: 108,333 sq. kms, of which 6.24 million hectares are under agriculture
Population: 16.7 million (154 per sq. km)
Gainfully employed: 8.5 million, of whom 49.4 % are women
Capital: Berlin (East)*
Biggest cities (population): Berlin (East) 1,197,000, Leipzig 556,000,
    Dresden 520,000, Karl-Marx-Stadt (Chemnitz) 317,000
Collective head of state: 25-member Council of State (Staatsrat);
    chairman: Erich Honecker
Government: Ministerial Council (Ministerrat); chairman: Willi Stoph
Parliament: 500-member People's Chamber (Volkskammer), elected for
    5 years; chairman: Horst Sindermann.
Political parties: Socialist Unity Party of Germany (Sozialistische Einheits-
    partei Deutschlands, SED), 2.3 million members; Secretary-General:
    Erich Honecker. In addition there are four other parties and many mass
    organisations which are united together with the SED in the National
    Front of the GDR (Nationale Front der DDR)
Currency: 1 Mark = 100 Pfennig

* Declared capital by the GDR. In the view of the Federal Republic of Germany and the three
  Western powers (USA, Great Britain, France) there still exists the four-power status for all
  of Berlin, that is to say also for Berlin (East).

"flight from the Republic" the GDR authorities from 1952 onwards
constructed along the entire demarcation line with the Federal
Republic extensive barriers with barbed wire fences and mine-
fields — the most heavily guarded frontier in Europe. But for a
long time refugees were still able to go unhindered through East
Berlin to West Berlin and fly from there to the West. In 1961 this escape route was cut off by the construction of the Berlin wall (see
page 77). By then some 3.5 million people had fled from the Soviet
zone, respectively the GDR, to the West. Even to this day, despite
the dangers faced at the frontier, a few hundred GDR inhabitants
risk flight every year, but their chances are slim. Many have died
or been injured in the attempt by gunfire or exploding mines.

The refugee exodus had badly weakened the GDR's economy
because it reduced the important labour force. After the construction of the wall there was a certain amount of consolidation and an
economic recovery began. The standard of living rose considerably, although it remained far behind that of the Federal Republic.
Among the eastern bloc countries the GDR moved up to second
place after the Soviet Union in terms of industrial production and
foreign trade. Internationally, too, it gained in weight. It won influence, especially in a number of ideologically close Third World

The border between East and West Germany

countries. All these successes notwithstanding, the SED leadership has not dared to submit to a free election by the population. To this day voting is by unitary lists which are dominated by the communist SED.

Reunification of Germany. Thus from 1949 there were two states on German soil. The Federal Republic of Germany regards itself as the only legitimised German state. In so doing it can point to its democratic legitimation through free elections which the GDR cannot. This was why in the first few years Bonn responded to the GDR offers of all-German consultations by demanding free elections in all of Germany. The GDR rejected this. But both states continued to declare the restoration of German unity the supreme objective of their policies.

Great dissension developed between government and opposition in the Federal Republic over how this objective was to be achieved. The Christian Democrat government of Konrad Adenauer initially pursued the Federal Republic's integration in the Western alliance system because it wanted to secure the freedom of the Federal Republic and was unable to achieve a solution to the German question without the support of the West against the hegemonial aims of the Soviet Union. The opposition, then mainly comprising Social Democrats, took the contrasting stand, arguing that the integration in the West was disastrous because it barred the way to German unity, a way which had to be kept open under all circumstances.

There appeared to come a chance to solve the German question in March 1952. At that time the Soviet Union sent the Western powers a note with a draft peace treaty with Germany and demanded immediate negotiations. In the ensuing exchange of notes the Western powers for their part declared that before negotiations about a peace treaty could start, internationally controlled free elections for the formation of a German government would have to take place. A United Nations commission formed to this end was refused entry into the GDR. It has remained a point of dispute to this day whether the Soviet note aimed only to disturb the then developing integration of the Federal Republic into the Western defence system or whether its seriousness could and should have been tested further.

In 1955 the incorporation of both German states in their respective Western and Eastern alliance systems was concluded. And with that what has become known for short as "the German question" also moved into a new stage. The GDR dropped its reunification slogans and from then on proposed merely a confederation of both states. The Federal Republic stuck to its stand that reunification could come only out of all-German free elections and that it alone had the right to speak in the name of all Germany. Bonn treated other states' assumption of diplomatic relations with the GDR as an "unfriendly act" — the so-called "Hallstein doctrine" of 1955. By this doctrine it prevented, far into the 1960s, non-eastern bloc countries taking up diplomatic links with the GDR. But in time this policy became more and more difficult to sustain. Given the world-political climate it seemed unrealistic to expect reunification of Germany in peace and freedom in the foreseeable future. And so the attempt had to be made to put the relations between the two German states on a new footing.

"Regulated co-existence." Since 1949 there had always been contacts in practical questions, such as trading matters, between the two German states. But only in the changed climate created by the treaties with the East European states and the Berlin Agreement, the first talks at government level were begun under the Bonn government under Willy Brandt formed in 1969. On December 17, 1971 the two German states signed an agreement on transit traffic of civilian persons and goods between the Federal Republic of Germany and Berlin (West) and on May 26, 1972 a treaty on traffic questions was made whose main purpose was to ease the practicalities of mutual visiting. Following extremely difficult negotiations it was possible to sign on December 21, 1972 a

German-German talks: Chancellor Brandt and GDR Prime Minister Stoph in Kassel, 1970

"Treaty on the Basis of Relations between the Federal Republic of Germany and the German Democratic Republic". The two states committed themselves to developing normal good-neighbourly relations, refraining from the threat or use of force and respecting each other's independence and autonomy in internal and external affairs. The conclusion of the treaty was accompanied by a "Letter of the Federal Government on German Unity" which states that the treaty does not contradict the political goal of the Federal Republic of Germany to work towards a state of peace in Europe in which the German nation regains its unity in free self-determination. So far a health agreement and several other accords have been concluded, e.g. about non-commercial financial transactions, posts and telecommunications, protection and maintenance of border streams and the improvement of transport routes to Berlin (West). Moreover, each of the two states set up a "permanent mission" in the respective centres of government.

Even today, however, relations between the two German states are still far from normal. The border barriers erected by the GDR have lost none of their horror. People trying to get from the GDR to the West are still shot at. The improvements in travel are still mainly one-sided, that is, it has become much simpler for inhabitants from the Federal Republic to visit the GDR. Conversely, inhabitants of the GDR, with few exceptions, are allowed to leave their state to visit the Federal Republic only when they are in retirement. Since the conclusion of the agreements millions of West

Berlin

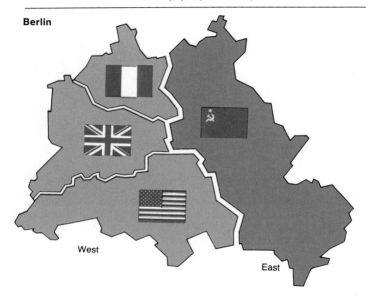

West

East

Germans have made use of the improved travel possibilities and visited the GDR. The GDR leadership looks with distrust on the increased contacts between Germans from west and east, seeing in them a threat to the stability of their system. To deter inhabitants of the Federal Republic from visiting the GDR it drastically raised the obligatory amount which visitors have to convert into East German marks in 1980. The number of visits fell appreciably as a result. The Federal Government has urged the GDR on many occasions to lower the compulsory exchange sum again. But so far it has only been cut a little for pensioners.

In all fields the GDR tries to limit alien ideas and opinions coming in. Newspapers and books from the Federal Republic are let in only exceptionally and after thorough screening. Journalists from the West are subjected to hindrances in the GDR and risk expulsion if its authorities dislike the way they report. However, inhabitants of the GDR are known to be keen watchers and listeners of television and radio programmes from the Federal Republic which are easy to receive.

Divided Berlin. The division of Germany repeats itself on a smaller scale, but no less cruelly for the people concerned, in the division of Berlin. The Reich capital was conquered by Soviet troops in the last few days of World War II. As agreed in the "London Protocol" of 1944, the city was put under the joint administration of the four victorious powers. Each of them — France, Britain, the Soviet Union and the USA — occupied a sector of Berlin which together formed an island, as it were, in the middle of the overall Soviet occupation zone. This "island" location gave rise to the Berlin problem.

As the East-West conflict worsened, the joint four-power administration of Berlin proved as impossible as that of all Germany. Under Soviet pressure, the city was politically and administratively split in 1948. But the Soviet Union did not want to tolerate the existence of a "Western enclave" within its occupation zone and tried to push the Western powers out of Berlin.

In June 1948 the Soviets paralysed all passenger and goods transportation between Berlin and West Germany. The aim was to starve the Western part of the city into submission. But for 10 months the Western powers managed to keep the two million Berliners in the Western part of the city supplied with their most urgent needs by air, through the famous Berlin airlift. Finally, in May 1949, the Soviet Union lifted the blockade. Then, in 1958, followed another attack: the Sovet Union issued an ultimatum to the Western powers to agree to the transformation of West Berlin into a "demilitarised free city". Resolutely the Western powers rejected the demand. Thwarted in achieving its objective in this way, the Soviet Union first set about solving a particularly pressing problem it faced in its own way. This was the flight of hundreds of thousands of GDR inhabitants every year through the open sector boundary in Berlin. On August 13, 1961 the GDR, with Soviet backing, sealed off the sector boundary by constructing a wall right across the city which, in the passage of time, was consolidated into a deep system of anti-escape barriers. Berlin was now also a physically cleaved city.

In 1949 the eastern sector of Berlin, in violation of the city's four-power status, was declared the capital of the just founded GDR. As time went by the eastern sector was increasingly integrated into the GDR system. This violates the "London Protocol" of September 1944 in which initially Great Britain, the USA and the Soviet Union, and later France, agreed that all of Berlin would belong to none of the occupation zones and that hence this area is subject to special status. The West still holds to this legal position.

The Basic Law of 1949 and the Berlin Constitution of 1950 proceeded from the premise that Berlin (West) is a Land of the Feder-

Bellevue Palace, the Berlin residence of the Federal President

al Republic. The Western powers declared that this regulation is irreconcilable with the four-power status of Berlin and retained supreme government authority for themselves. But they permitted West Berlin's integration into the legal, economic, fiscal, monetary and social systems of the Federal Republic of Germany. For years the eastern side raised no objections to this. But after construction of the dividing wall it turned increasingly against West Berlin's ties with the Federal Republic. Almost all Berlin activities of the Federal Republic were claimed to be illegal. The free part of Berlin was to be an "independent political unit" devoid of any ties with the West German state. To underline this demand the GDR persistently obstructed traffic between Berlin and West Germany. Travellers to Berlin had to put up with arbitrariness and chicaneries. More than once the situation on the transit routes through GDR territory assumed crisis proportions.

The Berlin Agreement. Since the Berlin problem had proved a stumbling block to a general policy of detente in Europe, the four powers in March 1970 began negotiations over Berlin. The outcome was in the Four Power Agreement of September 3, 1971 which went into force on June 3, 1972. It brought no final solution of the Berlin problem, the signatories not even being able to agree on its geographical area of application, which in the Western interpretation covers all Berlin, in the Soviet only West Berlin. But the agreement contains practical regulations which have helped the city's situation. The Soviet Union no longer disputes the right of the Western powers' presence in Berlin and accepts the existing ties of the part-city to the Federal Republic of Germany, including the right of the Federation (Bonn) to represent Berlin (West) to the outside world. Traffic on roads, railways and waterways between Berlin and West Germany has been put on a secure legal footing by the Four Power Agreement and subsequent bilateral agreements between the two German states. After years of being prohibited, Berliners of the Western half of the city, after a long time when they could not, were now again able to visit the eastern sector and the GDR at large. Telephone services between the two parts of the city, suspended for years, were resumed.

In line with the unchanged legal standpoint of the Western powers, Berlin (West) is still not a part of the Federal Republic of Germany nor is it governed by it. This is why federal laws are not directly applicable in the Land of Berlin but are taken over in a

Transit routes to Berlin

Border crossing point
from Berlin (West) to Berlin (East)

special procedure. But the existing economic, financial, legal and cultural ties between Berlin (West) and the Federal Republic of Germany are being maintained and developed further. The federal government makes a substantial contribution to the budget of the Land of Berlin.

Berlin (West) sends 22 deputies to the Bundestag in Bonn and three to the European Parliament, though these delegates are not elected by the population at large, but by the city parliament, the Abgeordnetenhaus. They are not entitled to vote in plenary divisions in the Bundestag on legislative matters or in the election of the Federal Chancellor. The same holds for the Berlin representatives in the Bundesrat (Federal Council, the assembly of federal states). In Bundestag and Bundesrat committees and in the European Parliament, however, the Berlin representatives do have full voting powers and in the Federal Convention (Bundesversammlung) they participate in the election of the Federal President. The Governing Mayor (Regierender Bürgermeister) of Berlin (West) is, in rota with the chiefs of government of the federal states (Bundesländer), President of the Bundesrat and thus deputy to the Federal President every 11 years. The Federal President has an official residence in the city and many federal authorities and institutions are based there.

The Four Power Agreement has by no means done away with all points of dispute. There are still periodic frictions with the Soviet Union — and the GDR — over the interpretation of individual provisions. But all in all the agreement has made the future of Berlin (West) more secure.

Since then much thought has been devoted to how this future should look. Berlin (West) had to redefine its role after it was no longer capital nor "front city" in the "Cold War". Much has happened meanwhile in the economic field but much remains to be done. As a result of the years of insecurity the city's economic development has not been able to keep pace with average growth in the Federal Republic. Many people of working age have left, giving the city an unfavourable age structure. Here Bonn tries to help, giving tax advantages for investments in the city and, through financial incentives, trying to encourage young people to settle there. Its isolation notwithstanding, Berlin (West) has remained a major cultural centre, its theatres, orchestras and museums enjoying world renown. Whatever the future may hold in store for Berlin, one thing is certain: nowhere are people as aware of Germany's division as there. Within sight of the wall one cannot forget that the national question is still unsolved.

The national question. In the national question there are incompatible differences between the two states in Germany. The Federal Republic of Germany continues to maintain that Germans in East und West form one nation. There are good grounds for this view. Almost 40 % of the inhabitants of the Federal Republic have relatives or acquaintances in the GDR; leading Federal German politicians were born on what is now GDR territory, leading GDR politicians in what is now the Federal Republic.

That is a degree of personal intertwinement that can rarely occur between alien nations. But above all, the inhabitants of both the Federal Republic and the GDR continue to feel as members of one German nation, linked by a common language and history and many other common heritages which cannot simply be wiped away from one day to the next. This is why it is out of the question for the Federal Republic of Germany to recognise the GDR as a foreign country in terms of international law. According to the Basic Law an inhabitant of the GDR is just as much a German citizen as any inhabitant of the Federal Republic. In trade, the Federal Republic imposes no import duty on products coming in from the GDR. For mail to the GDR, inland postage is charged. From the point of view of the Federal Republic there is a very special relationship between the two German states: as part-states in Germany they are independent of each other, but not foreign countries to each other. The Federal Constitutional Court has confirmed these principles. It has ruled that the Basic Treaty between the Federal Republic of Germany and the German Democratic Republic is compatible with the Basic Law, emphasising at the same time that it is the duty of all organs of the Federal Republic of Germany to work towards restoration of state unity and to avoid any action that would thwart reunification.

The GDR takes a totally different stand on this issue. It refuses to acknowledge any special relationship between the two German states. As far as it is concerned, there is the same international legal relationship between them as between any other two states. In recent years the GDR has even moved away from the concept of a common German nation. Whereas in its 1968 constitution it still saw itself as a "socialist state of the German nation" and proclaimed as an objective "the step by step approaching of the two German states until their unification", its new 1974 constitution struck out all references to the continuing existence of a German nation. Since then the GDR insists that the two are now completely separate nations. This abrupt about-turn has no basis in reality. The brusque demarcation apparently serves the

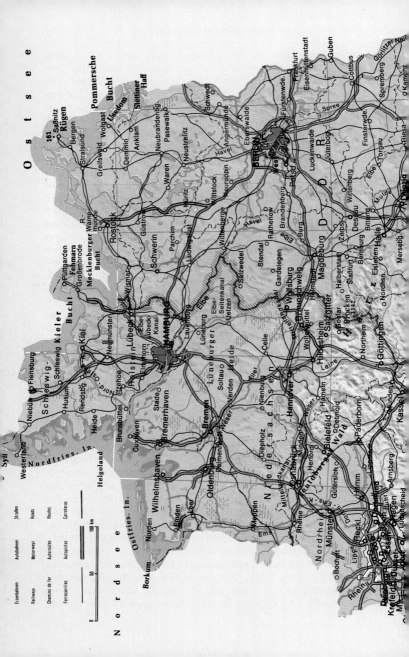

purpose of nipping in the bud newly awakened hopes among the GDR population of reunification, or at least better neighbourliness between the two states.

The "German question", that is the entire complex of issues concerning divided Germany, has of late come back into the headlines not only of the German media. Even if the Eastern side claims falsely that the "Geman question" has long been settled, for many Germans on both sides of the frontier it is still a painful reality and will remain an issue until the entire German nation gets the opportunity to exercise its right to self-determination within the framework of a European peace order.

The Federal Republic
from 1949 to the present

The two major political parties, the conservative Christian Democrats alliance (CDU/CSU) and the Social Democratic Party (SPD), came out of the August 14, 1949 Bundestag election almost equally strong. Together they received more than 60 % of the votes. There was a broad body of public feeling that in view of the country's difficult situation they should go into a "grand coalition" and govern together. But grave political differences and perhaps even more the wilful personalities of the two party leaders, Konrad Adenauer of the CDU and Kurt Schumacher of the SPD, stood in the way. Thus a coalition between CDU/CSU, Free Democrats (FDP) and Deutsche Partei (a small right-of-centre party) which had already been practised in the Frankfurt Economic Council, was continued. This constellation lasted until 1966. The CDU/CSU governed with one or two small partners, the SPD formed the opposition.

Decision for the West. The office of Federal Chancellor was taken by 73-year-old Konrad Adenauer. He remained government chief for 14 years, a period of office longer than the entire Weimar Republic between the two world wars.

When it came into existence the Federal Republic of Germany was no sovereign state. In an Occupation Statute the three Western powers retained supreme authority in many fields. Adenauer saw as his most important objective gradually to regain the freedom of action for the new German state. The best means of achieving this was, to his mind, by the greatest possible integration of the Federal Republic of Germany with the gradually forming Western community.

World-political events favoured this approach. East-West tensions sharpened even more, climaxing in the outbreak of the Korean war in the summer of 1950. That year the Federal Republic joined the Council of Europe, negotiations began over a West European coal and steel community and Adenauer made the Western powers the offer of mobilising German troops for a European Defence Community. In several stages and not without setbacks the integration of the Federal Republic with the Western alliance system proceeded. By the Paris Agreements of 1954 it became a member of the North Atlantic Treaty Organisation

(NATO). With the coming into force of these treaties on May 5, 1955 occupation rule ended. Occupation troops became stationed troops with contractually regulated status. The Federal Republic became sovereign.

The policy of rearmament and Western integration was subject to impassioned dispute. The mainly Social Democrat opposition rejected it, their main argument being that it prevented Germany's reunification (see pages 73/74). Adenauer was, however, able to point to broad popular backing. In the 1953 Bundestag election his party scored enormous gains and in 1957 it even won an absolute majority.

The "economic miracle". But these electoral successes were not, of course, primarily due to foreign policy. What probably swayed most voters was the astounding economic recovery made possible by the economic policies of the Adenauer government. Several factors converged to cause this so-called "economic miracle". Adenauer's economics minister, Ludwig Erhard, energetically promoted private initiative according to market economy principles. The initial spark was provided by the economic aid given by the USA within the framework of the Marshall Plan. Also significant was that the Federal Republic had no military expenditure and that in the refugees from the East it had a large reservoir of people ready to work hard. Production figures and profits rose quickly and so did incomes. In the early 50s full employment was achieved. The standard of living of a broad section of the population rose noticeably and with that there grew the readiness to settle permanently for the West German state system originally conceived as provisional.

Carried by solid majorities, Adenauer continued his Western orientated policy. Apart from the unification of Western Europe, reconcillation with the "hereditary enemy", France, was close to his heart. For its sake he was willing to agree to a "European" settlement for the Saar region which France had taken out of its occupation zone in 1946 and tied closely to itself. But in a 1955 plebiscite the Saar population rejected the intended statute which was to be guaranteed by the Western European Union. In 1957 Saarland became a Land of the Federal Republic of Germany. A big step towards West European unification came with the 1957 Treaties of Rome founding the European Economic Community (EEC). The six founding states have meanwhile been joined by six more.

After Adenauer. Adenauer's star began to sink in the late 1950s. Home policy crises and electoral losses in the 1961 Bundestag poll gave rise to criticism within his own party. In 1963 he resigned at the age of 87. The party chose Ludwig Erhard to succeed him. The legendary man of the "economic miracle" was less successful as head of government. Although winning a convincing electoral victory in 1965, when economic recession set in a year later differences in the coalition government camp over how to deal with it culminated in his resignation.

The political parties entered negotiations which brought a completely new constellation. A grand coalition was formed by the CDU/CSU and the SPD, with the CDU's Kurt Georg Kiesinger as Federal Chancellor and Willy Brandt of the SPD as Foreign Minister. The Free Democratic Party, with only 49 Bundestag seats, became the opposition, no other parties having been represented in the house since 1961.

With a programme of fast-acting measures the grand coalition government quickly overcame the recession. In foreign policy it continued the course of integration with the West which the SPD meanwhile espoused. The main home policy project of the grand coalition was the enactment of legislation for a national emergency, lacking until then in the Basic Law. The drafting of these provisions led to acrimonious public dispute, critics fearing they would curb civil liberties. In the course of the debate the bills were greatly modified. In 1968 the Bundestag adopted the emergency laws (Notstandsgesetze).

The Social-Liberal coalition. After the 1969 Bundestag election there was a reversal of the party-political fronts. Social Democrats (SPD) and Liberals (FDP), who together had only a narrow majority, formed a coalition government, with Willy Brandt (SPD) as Chancellor and Walter Scheel (FPD) as Foreign Minister. For the first time in its history the CDU/CSU alliance had to go into opposition. The new government tackled an extensive programme of domestic reforms. But above all it set new importance on foreign and inter-German policies. While clinging to the Federal Republic's incorporation in the Western alliance system, it strengthened the up to then only hesitant efforts to settle with its eastern neighbours the questions remaining open since World War II. This objective was served by a whole host of treaties concluded from 1970 to 1973. They put relations with the Soviet Union, Poland, Czechoslovakia and the GDR on new foundations and strengthened the viability of Berlin (West) (see pages 74/75 and 137/138).

Government quarter in Bonn

This new "Ostpolitik" (eastern policy) was highly controversial. The disputes over it rank as some of the most dramatic since 1949. In spring of 1972 the SPD/FDP government lost its Bundestag majority, but the opposition could not muster the necessary votes to topple it through a vote of no-confidence. Premature elections that same year strenghened the coalition.

In May, 1974 a close aide of Chancellor Willy Brandt was unmasked as a spy for the GDR. Brandt assumed political responsibility for the affair and resigned. He was succeeded by Helmut Schmidt (SPD) and Hans-Dietrich Genscher (FDP) became the new Foreign Minister. The coalition was also continued after the 1976 and 1980 elections.

Whereas in the first years of the SPD-FDP coalition, foreign policy had been in the foreground, from 1973 onwards public interest turned more and more to economic and social policy. The oil price explosion and the world enonomic recession hit the Federal Republic hard. From 1974 the number of unemployed rose constantly to more than two million in the early 1980s. By then the economic and financial situation had worsened drastically. The Social Product had stopped growing, more and more enterprises were collapsing, it was becoming more difficult all the time to fund the social security system and the public debt assumed menacing dimensions.

Dissension grew between the ruling SPD and FDP parties — and also within the chancellor's SPD — over how to tackle the crisis, as well as over foreign and defence policies. These differences ultimately led to their coalition government's breaking apart.

The coalition of the centre. The withdrawal from the coalition by the FDP Liberals left the Social Democrats unable to govern because on their own they had no parliamentary majority. On 1 October 1982 the allied CDU/CSU Conservatives and most of the FDP MPs in the Bundestag carried a vote of no confidence in the Social Democrat chancellor, Helmut Schmidt, and elected CDU chairman, Helmut Kohl, to take over. He formed a coalition government of his CDU, the Bavarian CSU and the FDP, whose chairman, Hans-Dietrich Genscher, remained vice-chancellor and foreign minister. The new government declared a crash programme focussing on righting the state's accounts, creating jobs, bringing welfare benefits into line with economic potentials and conducting foreign policy on the basis of existing treaties. After putting in train the most urgent measures, the Kohl-led government put these policies to the voters in a premature election on 6 March 1983. It received a clear majority.

This first test for the coalition was the start of the deployment of new medium range missiles on the basis of the NATO twin-track decision of 1979. By sticking to this decision the Federal Government strengthened NATO cohesion. Contrary to fears expressed, relations with East Europe and the GDR did not suffer as a result; negotiations with the GDR even brought further improvements for the people in both states. The social security system was put on a sound basis, whereby some benefits had to be cut; the state debt slowed down clearly. Soon the first successes began to show. The economy grew again, inflation dropped and the number of people in work rose again. One problem remained: although unemployment stopped rising, in 1986 there were still more than two million people without work.

State
Politics
The Law

The Basic Law
The constitutional bodies
The legal system
Political parties and elections
Federal, regional and local government
Regional planning and rezoning
The Federal Republic of Germany in the world
Public finance
Public service
Internal security
Defence

The Basic Law

The Basic Law (Grundgesetz) of the Federal Republic of Germany was created in 1949 "to give a new order to political life for a transitional period". Since then almost four decades have passed. The provisional constitution has become permanent for the foreseeable future and has proved a viable foundation for a stable, democratic system of society.

The authors of the Basic Law had seen under the Hitler dictatorship how the law and human dignity had been trampled underfoot and they remembered how in the final phase of the Weimar Republic a weak democracy had succumbed almost without resistance to the forward-surging tyrants. These were the things uppermost in their minds as they went about their work. Many provisions of the Basic Law testify to the eagerness to avoid the kinds of mistakes which contributed to the collapse of the first German republic.

The basic rights. The first 17 articles of the Basic Law list the main basic rights. It is no coincidence that it begins with them, underlining that the state is there for people's sake and not vice versa, that it is not to rule but to serve.

Part of the basic rights are such classic liberties as freedom of faith and creed, of expression, assembly and movement, postal privacy and the right to property. The authors of the constitution added the right of conscientious refusal of military service and the equality of men and women.

A catalogue always leaves gaps. These are closed by the first three articles of the Basic Law which comprehensively guarantee people's dignity and freedom of action and the equality of all before the law.

The basic rights are directly applicable law. Here lies one of the major advances on earlier German constitutions, whose basic rights catalogues were more in the nature of non-binding programme declarations. The parliaments as lawmakers are just as strictly bound to the basic rights as the governments, the courts, the administration, the police and the armed forces.

The following is a famous example of how respect for a basic right was enforced. Article 6 of the Basic Law stipulates that "illegitimate children shall be provided by legislation with the same

Signing the Basic Law, 1949.
At the table: Reinhold Maier; half-covered by the microphone:
Theodor Heuss; left of him: Paul Löbe, Carlo Schmid

opportunities for their physical and spiritual development and their place in society as are enjoyed by legitimate children". No such legislation had been enacted up to 1969. Thereupon one interested party filed suit with the Federal Constitutional Court which, in turn, ordered the Bundestag to fulfil within a specified time the duty commanded by the Basic Law. Soon afterwards the relevant law was enacted.

Laws may encroach on basic rights only in narrow limits. No law, however, is allowed to contravene the substance of a basic right.

By its accession to the European Convention for the Protection of Human Rights and Basic Rights in 1952 the Federal Republic of Germany committed itself to the principle of international control of human rights. Article 25 of this convention entitles citizens of signatory countries to file complaints, even against their own states, before the European Commission and the European Court. The Federal Republic also ratified the international human rights pacts of the United Nations in 1973.

The foundations of the state order. Four principles govern the state order of the Federal Republic of Germany. It is a democracy, ruled by law, a social welfare state and a federation.

The democratic principle means that the people are the sovereign. The Basic Law has implemented this constitutional principle in the form of a representative democracy: the people exercise state power indirectly through elected representatives. In general, direct, free, equal and secret elections all citizens from the age of 18 elect the deputies of the German Bundestag who in turn elect the Federal Chancellor. At federal level forms of direct democracy, such as popular petition or referendum, no longer apply, although they do in some federal states.

The principle of the law-abiding state implies that all state actions are subject to law and justice. This makes state activity predictable and revisable for the citizen. It is at the same time, however, a commitment to real justice, to which the legislative is also bound. Injustice remains injustice, even if it has become law. Such a law would be unconstitutional and could be invalidated by the Federal Constitutional Court. The exercise of state power is entrusted to legislative, executive and judiciary bodies, independent of each other according to the principle of the division of powers. The legality of all acts of state can be tested by independent judges if the person affected sues. A call against all forms of violent rule is contained in a Basic Law article giving all Germans "the right to resist any person or persons seeking to abolish the constitutional order should no other remedy be possible".

The principle of the social welfare state is a modern supplement to the inherited notion of the state having to be law-abiding. It obliges the state to protect the socially weaker and always to strive for social justice. Social basic rights — e. g. the rights to work, to education and training, to housing, to recuperation and to social security — are not expressly mentioned in the catalogue of basic rights. But with the principle of the social welfare state, constitutional onus to implement social justice is placed on legislation and the judiciary. Numerous federal laws and court judgments bear witness to the success of this endeavour. The authors of the Basic Law deliberately omitted to prescribe any particular social and economic order. By and large, the Basic law is neutral in respect of economic policy.

The principle of federalism enables regional distinctions to be taken into account. It gives room for initiative which, in a centralised state, would hardly have a chance. Finally, it distributes power and thus prevents the possible abuse of it by central bodies.

Federal German coat of arms

Federal German flag

Changes to the Basic Law. The Basic Law can be changed only with the approval of two thirds of the members of\the Bundestag and two thirds of the votes of the Bundesrat. Since a party or a coalition of parties would rarely command two-third majorities in both the Bundestag and the Bundesrat — only the grand coalition from 1966 – 1969 has done so far — very broad consensus is required to change the Basic Law which as a rule has to include part of the opposition. In most cases this consensus is achieved only after hard and long negotiations. The most incisive changes of the Basic Law have been the "defence addenda" of 1954/1956 and the "Emergency Constitution" of 1968. The defence addenda regulated the constitutional position of the armed forces which were set up with the accession of the Federal Republic to the Western alliance system. The Emergency Constitution set the framework for wider executive powers in internal or external emergencies which had hitherto rested with the Western allies from the time of the postwar occupation.

But some provisions of the Basic Law cannot be changed at all, not even with a two-thirds majority. These are the federative structure, the division of powers, the principles of democracy, of state power based on law, of social welfare and the commitment to the dignity of man and a system of inviolable basic rights. These provisions are, indeed, so fundamental that their elimination would bring down the entire structure of the Basic Law.

After almost four decades the ideas of the Basic Law have by and large become social reality. Like no former German constitution it has taken root in the minds of the citizens. It has brought forth a state which has been spared constitutional crises. This stability contributes substantially to the society's political credibility and to the wellbeing of its citizens.

The constitutional bodies

The exercise of state power has been assigned by the Basic Law to legislative bodies, the executive and the judiciary. Together they embody the democratic, federalistic, law-abiding state order the Basic Law prescribes.

The Federal President. The head of state of the Federal Republic of Germany is the Federal President (Bundespräsident). He is elected by the Federal Convention (Bundesversammlung), a constitutional body which convenes only for this purpose. It consists of the Bundestag deputies (including those from Berlin [West]) and an equal number of members elected by the assemblies of the Länder. The term of office is five years. Re-election is permitted for only one consecutive term. The Federal President represents the Federal Republic in terms of international law. He concludes agreements with foreign states in its name. He accredits and receives ambassadors, appoints and dismisses federal judges, federal civil servants, officers and non-commissioned officers of the armed forces. The Federal President can pardon convicted criminals. He checks whether laws have come about by the proper constitutional procedure and publishes them in the Federal Law Gazette (Bundesgesetzblatt). He proposes to the Bundestag a candidate for the officie of Federal Chancellor and on the suggestion of the Chancellor appoints and dismisses cabinet ministers.

If a motion of no-confidence in the Federal Chancellor is carried by the Bundestag, the Federal President may, upon the proposal of the Federal Chancellor, dissolve the Bundestag. Premature elections were brought about in this way in 1972 and again in 1983.

The tasks of the Federal President are mainly of a representational nature. He can advise, warn and encourage — this last includes the awarding of decorations.

By and large the Federal Presidency has been given merely titular powers because of the experiences of the Weimar period. The constitutionally strong position of the Reich President in the final phase of the Weimar Republic contributed to the collapse of parliamentary democracy. The office of Federal President demands of its incumbent special political sensitivity and the ability

Theodor Heuss

Heinrich Lübke

Gustav Heinemann

Walter Scheel

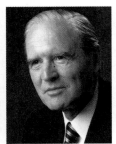
Karl Carstens

Richard von Weizsäcker

The Federal Presidents

Theodor Heuss (FDP)	1st term	1949-1954
	2nd term	1954-1959
Heinrich Lübke (CDU)	1st term	1959-1964
	2nd term	1964-1969
Gustav Heinemann (SPD)		1969-1974
Walter Scheel (FDP)		1974-1979
Karl Carstens (CDU)		1979-1984
Richard von Weizsäcker (CDU)		1984-

Konrad Adenauer

Ludwig Erhard

Kurt Georg Kiesinger

Willy Brandt

Helmut Schmidt

Helmut Kohl

The Federal Chancellors

Konrad Adenauer (CDU)	1st cabinet	1949-1953
	2nd cabinet	1953-1957
	3rd cabinet	1957-1961
	4th cabinet	1961-1963
Ludwig Erhard (CDU)	1st cabinet	1963-1965
	2nd cabinet	1965-1966
Kurt Georg Kiesinger (CDU)		1966-1969
Willy Brandt (SPD)	1st cabinet	1969-1972
	2nd cabinet	1972-1974
Helmut Schmidt (SPD)	1st cabinet	1974-1976
	2nd cabinet	1976-1980
	3rd cabinet	1980-1982
Helmut Kohl (CDU)	1st cabinet	1982-1983
	2nd cabinet	1983-

to mediate. Almost all presidents to date, due to their personalities, have also exercised no small measure of political influence.

The Bundestag. The Deutscher Bundestag (House of Representatives) is the popularly elected federal chamber of parliament of the Federal Republic of Germany. It is elected for four years in general, direct, free, equal and secret elections by a system of "personalised proportional representation" (see p. 120/121). Its main tasks are legislation, the election of the Federal Chancellor and control of the government. In Bundestag plenary session the big issues of home and foreign policy are debated. Television coverage of proceedings improves public awareness. Whether it contributes to the objectivity of parliamentary debates is in dispute.

The extensive preparatory work in legislation takes place not in plenary session but in committees. This is due to the great number of detailed issues usually involved. The plenary assembly would simply be overtaxed in time and expertise if it had to cope with so much detail. The Bundestag committees correspond to the various government departments. The parliament's budget sovereignty lends corresponding prestige and importance to the

Bundestag (House of Representatives) in session

budget committee. Any citizen can turn with requests and complaints to a petition committee.

Bills can be introduced by any Bundestag deputy (MP), by the Bundesrat (Federal Council) or — most frequently — the Federal Government. They go through three Bundestag readings and as a rule are referred to the relevant committee once. The final vote is taken after the third reading. A bill (providing it does not change the constitution) is passed if it gets a majority of the votes cast. (In some cases, however, it still requires the approval of the Bundesrat, i. e. a majority of Federal States, to become law.)

The deputies are not bound by orders and instructions but subject only to their conscience. In line with their party allegiances they form parliamentary groups (Fraktionen). Freedom of conscience and solidarity with party colleagues can on occasion collide. If a deputy feels he can no longer identify with the policies of his party and leaves it he does not lose his Bundestag seat. It is on this point that the deputy's independence becomes most evident.

The relative strengths of the party groups in the house determine the allocation of seats on the various committees. The President (Speaker) of the Bundestag is elected, according to old German constitutional custom, from the ranks of the strongest parliamentary party. The two allied Christian CDU and CSU parties have since 1949 formed one joint parliamentary group in the Bundestag which was mostly the strongest party grouping.

The Bundestag deputies are paid a "compensation" (Entschädigung) corresponding to the highest civil service category salaries. Anyone who has been a member of parliament for at least six years is paid a pension upon reaching retirement age. The federal deputies are entitled to travel free of charge on the Federal Railways and on domestic flights of Lufthansa Airlines.

The Bundesrat. The Bundesrat (Federal Council) also participates in legislation. It is not elected but consists of members of the Länder governments or their delegates. Each Land has at least three votes. Länder with larger populations have four or five votes. A Land's votes can be cast only as a block.

Laws require the express approval of the Bundesrat if they touch on Länder interests. This is the case in more than half of all laws, above all those which intervene in the financial or administrative sovereignty of the Länder. In the remaining cases — that is those for which Bundesrat approval is not mandatory — the Bundesrat has the right of objection, though this can be overruled by the Bundestag. If Bundesrat and Bundestag cannot reach agree-

State structure of the Federal Republic of Germany

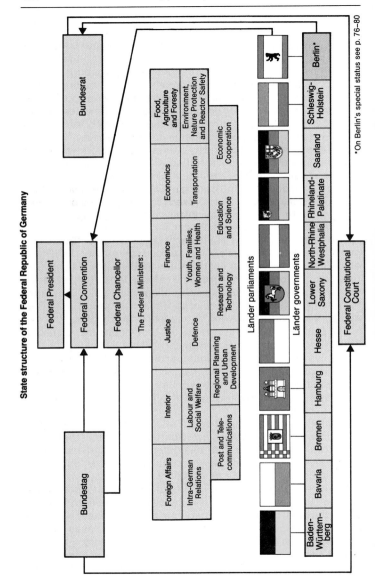

Bundestag

Bundesrat

Federal President

Federal Convention

Federal Chancellor

The Federal Ministers:

Foreign Affairs

Intra-German Relations

Interior

Labour and Social Welfare

Post and Telecommunications

Justice

Defence

Regional Planning and Urban Development

Finance

Youth, Families, Women and Health

Research and Technology

Economics

Transportation

Education and Science

Food, Agriculture and Forestry

Environment, Nature Protection and Reactor Safety

Economic Cooperation

Länder parliaments

Länder governments

Baden-Württemberg

Bavaria

Bremen

Hamburg

Hesse

Lower Saxony

North-Rhine Westphalia

Rhineland-Palatinate

Saarland

Schleswig-Holstein

Berlin*

Federal Constitutional Court

*On Berlin's special status see p. 76–80

ment, a mediation committee composed of members of both chambers must be convened and this, in most cases, is able to work out a compromise. From 1980 to 1984 the mediation committee was called to intervene on 21 bills.

The various Länder having varying interests, voting majorities often change in the Bundesrat. Bundesrat members are not, however, only ministers of their respective Länder but at the same time also members of political parties, so that party-political interests do play a role apart from Länder interests. This is why Bundesrat votes often split along party lines. For the federal government this can spell trouble if the party which is in opposition in the Bundestag commands the majority in the Bundesrat.

According to a fixed rota the Bundesrat elects from among the Länder prime ministers (Ministerpräsidenten) its President for a year. The Bundesrat President exercises the powers of the Federal President if the latter is prevented from so doing.

The Federal Government. The federal government (Bundesregierung) in Bonn, often referred to simply as the cabinet, consists of the Federal Chancellor and the Federal Ministers. The Federal Chancellor is nominated by the Federal President and elected by the Bundestag. In making his proposal, the Federal President takes into account the voting strengths in the Bundestag. He will nominate only a candidate who has prospects of being elected. The Federal Ministers are nominated by the Chancellor and formally appointed by the Federal President.

The Federal Chancellor has a strong position. This is why the Federal Republic's system of government is often referred to as a "chancellor democracy". The chancellor is the only member of government elected by parliament and he alone is responsible to it. He determines the guidelines of government policy. The ministers direct their departments within these guidelines, independently and under their own responsibility.

Mindful of the Weimar Republic experiences, the Basic Law introduced the "constructive vote of no-confidence". It is to prevent opposition groups who agree only on the rejection of government policy but not on any alternative programme of their own from being able to overthrow the government. If a Bundestag majority wants to pass a vote of no-confidence in the chancellor they must, under this provision, at the same time elect his successor in a majority vote.

Of the two attempts to bring down a chancellor with the aid of a constructive no-confidence vote, only one has succeeded. A no-

Federal cabinet in session

confidence motion in 1982 removed Helmut Schmidt from office and Chancellor Helmut Kohl was elected to succeed him. There is no Basic Law provision for no-confidence motions against individual federal ministers.

The Federal Constitutional Court. An institution for which there was no counterpart in German constitutional life before the foundation of the Federal Republic is the Federal Constitutional Court (Bundesverfassungsgericht). It is the guardian of the Basic Law. The Federal Constitutional Court rules, for example, in disputes between the Federation and the States, or between individual federal bodies. Only this court has the power to declare that a party is trying to undo the free, democratic order of the Federal Republic and is thus acting anti-constitutionally, in which case it orders its dissolution. It examines federal and Länder legislation as to its conformity with the Basic Law. If it rules a law unconstitutional it can no longer be applied. The court acts in these and many other matters only if called upon by certain bodies, such as the federal government, Länder governments, parliament, lower courts, etc..

Every citizen also has the right to turn to the Federal Constitutional Court with a constitutional complaint if he feels his basic rights violated by the state. Before doing so he must as a rule

Election of Federal Constitutional Court judges

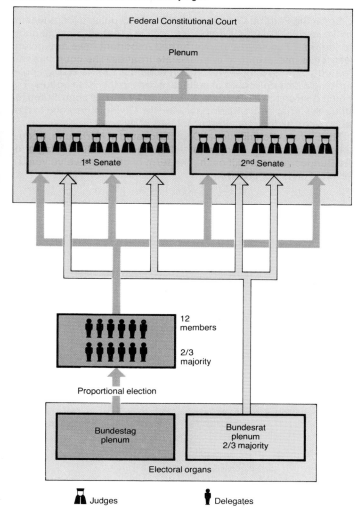

have been unsuccessful in the responsible lower courts, however.

So far the Federal Constitutional Court has passed judgment in well over 50,000 cases. Some attracted the greatest possible public interest. The court has overturned important laws and given restrictive interpretation to inter-state treaties. The court has repeatedly stressed, however, that it does not see its task as prescribing a certain course of political action to the state bodies. To a high degree the Federal Constitutional Court has contributed to filling the letter of the Basic Law with life. Giving substance to the basic rights is the most important part of its work.

The Federal Constitutional Court is located at Karlsruhe. It consists of two senates, each with eight judges. The Bundestag and the Bundesrat elect half each. The term of office is twelve years. Re-election is not possible.

The legal system

The Federal Republic's law is predominantly written law, most of it federal. It comprises more than 4,000 laws and ordinances having the force of law. There are also Länder laws, which apply mainly to cultural affairs, i. e. education. Other sources are customary and case law.

Precedence also plays a part in legal practice. In most cases it appears meaningless to begin proceedings if higher courts have dismissed similar suits in a constant line of decisions. But fundamentally no judge is bound by any superior court's ruling on a similar case, with the exception of some by the Federal Constitutional Court, which are binding on all other courts.

The free, law-governed state. Historically Federal German law goes back partly to Roman law and partly to numerous regional German sources of law. In the liberal state governed by the rule of law, as it developed gradually in Germany in the 19th century, a centralised private law for the entire German Reich was created for the first time. The Civil and Commercial Codes to this day preserve the liberal tradition. They are dominated by the principle of freedom of contract.

The traditional rule of law becomes most clear in criminal law and criminal procedure. Here the tenet applies that no offence (act or omission) may be punished unless its punishability had been laid down before it was committed (nulla poena sine lege). This means that a criminal court judge is banned from ordering punishment on the basis of legal provisions having an analogous relationship. The administration of justice is entrusted to judges who, as a rule, cannot be dismissed or transferred against their will and who are subject only to the law.

Almost all these fundamental principles were already laid down by the 19th century judiciary laws: a Judicature Act (regulating structure and organisation of courts), the Code of Civil Procedure and the Code of Criminal Procedure. It has gone largely unnoticed abroad that both the Civil Code which went into force on January 1, 1900 and the Civil and Criminal Procedure Codes (both dating from 1877) were wrested by liberals from the imperial government towards the end of the last century in long drawn-out parliamentary reform struggles.

Some German codified laws have found their way into foreign legal systems. For example, the Civil Code largely influenced its Japanese and Greek counterparts.

The citizen and public administration. While the principles applicable in a state governed by the rule of law had already been implemented in criminal and civil procedures, in the relationship of the citizen to public administration the authoritarian state thinking continued to dominate for a long time to come. It took more than 100 years of development in legal policy to overcome it.

"Administrative Courts" were established in several German Länder in the 19th century to control the public administration in the interests of the legal protection of the individual citizen. These courts were set up in Hesse in 1832, Baden in 1863, Württemberg in 1876, Bavaria in 1879 and in Prussia only in 1883. But even then, only certain, legally listed types of administrative acts could be contested before these courts by those they concerned. It took until 1949 for the Basic Law to give everyone throughout the Federal Republic recourse to contesting in court any administrative act concerning them if they felt it was unlawful or had come about through the abuse of power, thereby violating basic civic rights. This applies to all types of administrative acts, be they tax assessment notices or the decision whether or not to promote a school pupil to the next grade, be it withdrawal of a driving licence or the refusal of a building permit. The condition is that the plaintiff himself must be affected by the administrative act; it is not possible for anyone else to sue, unless they themselves are affected.

The order achieved by the constitutional state is crowned and guarded by the Basic Law and the jurisdiction of the Federal Constitutional Court respectively. The Basic Law guarantees to all Germans (and in parts also to resident foreigners) a catalogue of basic rights going far beyond the classic human rights. It also guarantees the principles of the modern, law-governed state such as the ban on retroactive punishment and the death sentence.

Anyone can turn to the Federal Constitutional Court with a complaint of unconstitutionality provided he has exhausted all other legal instances or if the progression through all the instances offered no effective legal protection. The Federal Constitutional Court can respond to such a complaint by ruling a law invalid if it does not conform to the Basic Law.

Justice in the social welfare state. In the 20th century it became ever more necessary to take into account social welfare require-

Civil courts

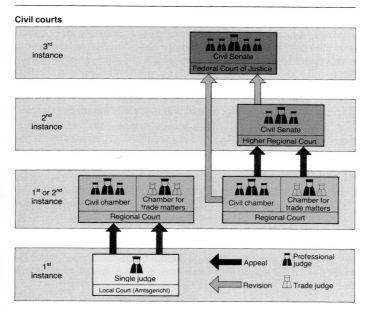

ments when legislating. In Articles 20 and 28 the Basic Law commands that the democratic and social order be expanded. In this spirit a great deal of labour and social welfare legislation has been enacted since the formation of the Federal Republic which assures the individual financial support in situations over which he has no control, such as illness, accident, old age invalidity and unemployment. It also helps those who are partially or wholly to blame for their own predicament to make a new start.

A very impressive example of the legal fulfilment of the social welfare state principle is labour law. Originally it was set out in only 20 paragraphs of the Civil Code under the term "service contract". Now federal German labour law comprises a great number of laws and collective agreements. Of particular importance are the Labour Courts Act, the Collective Agreements Act, the Works Constitution Act and the Worker Participation (codetermination) Act.

Organisation of the legal system. The Federal German courts system is marked by the completeness of legal protection (no lacunae) and far-reaching specialisation. It consists of five branches:

1. The so-called "ordinary courts" are responsible for criminal and civil proceedings (except labour law). There are four types: Local Court (Amtsgericht), Regional Court (Landgericht), Higher Regional Court (Oberlandesgericht), Federal Court of Justice (Bundesgerichtshof). A case can be heard for the first time in any of the first three named courts, depending on the type of action, and can be taken to either one or two more for appeal or revision.

2. The labour courts. These are of three types: Local Labour Court (Arbeitsgericht), Regional Labour Court (Landesarbeitsgericht) and Federal Labour Court (Bundesarbeitsgericht). They are responsible for employer/employee disputes, disputes between trade unions and employers and matters concerning the works constitution and worker participation (co-determination).

3. The administrative courts — Local Administrative Court (Verwaltungsgericht), Higher Administrative Court (Verwaltungsgerichtshof or Oberverwaltungsgericht) and Federal Administrative Court (Bundesverwaltungsgericht) — handle all administrative law proceedings except those falling under the jurisdiction of the social and fiscal courts and disputes of constitutional law.

4. The social courts — Local Social Court (Sozialgericht), Higher Social Court (Landessozialgericht) and Federal Social Court (Bundessozialgericht) — rule on disputes in the entire field of social insurance.

5. The fiscal courts — Finance Court (Finanzgericht) and Federal Finance Court (Bundesfinanzhof) — deal with taxation and allied matters.

Separate from these five branches is the Federal Constitutional Court which is not only the highest court in the land but also a constitutional body.

Thus the system of legal remedies is complex and provides for numerous possibilities for review. In principle, there are two appeal courts. Appeals provide for both effective and legal control which means that new evidence can be introduced at the appeal hearing. On the other hand, usually the revision, second resort, leads only to a review of points of law and formalities of procedure. People are increasingly resorting to the courts and appeal possibilities. The result is that courts are over-burdened and cases are taking ever longer to resolve. This is why it is now being considered to shorten and simplify proceedings at all court levels.

Criminal courts

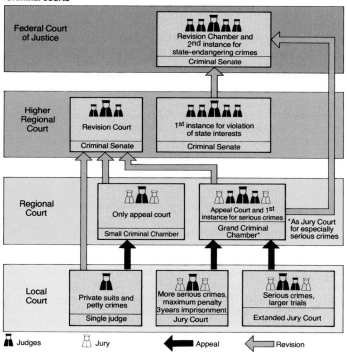

The administration of justice is carried out in the Federal Republic by more than 17,000 professional judges, more than three quarters of whom are assigned to the ordinary courts. Judges are appointed for life, are independent and subject only to the law. In a number of courts they sit together with lay judges. Although in legal questions too much is often demanded of the jury, as people who know life and by virtue of their non-legal backgrounds they help the courts to make realistic decisions. Over and above that they embody part of the citizen's direct responsibility for the state.

The public prosecutors (state attorneys), of whom there are about 3,600, are public servants who, in contrast to the judges, are subject to the orders of their superiors. Professionally independent are the 40,000 or so attorneys-at-law in the Federal Republic. They, too, are "organs of the administration of justice" and are therefore subject to special duties and the jurisdiction of special courts of honour. More recent legislation has clarified these duties.

Professional judges, public prosecutors and attorneys-at-law must be "qualified to be a judge". That means they must have graduated in law from a university, either coupled with, or followed by, practical legal training and they must have passed final state examinations.

Legal reforms. The years since 1970 have been marked by legal reforms. A comprehensive reform of criminal law was completed with the coming into force in 1975 of the revised Criminal Code which liberalised many offences. Major later revisions were the 1976 provisions on the treatment of abortion in criminal law and new laws in 1976 and 1980 on environmental protection and economic crime.

The new Prison Act of 1976 can be mentioned in the same category. This law is based on the notion that social rehabilitation of offenders is the best way to prevent them committing new crimes. The objective is to enable released prisoners to live and work among their fellow citizens without breaking the law again. Hitherto the rate of recidivism was still higher than 70 % and about 60 % of prisoners had no vocational training at the start of their period of sentence. The new Prison Act aims at remedying this. If possible, prisoners are to receive vocational training in detention and their remuneration is to be gradually improved. Since 1977 working prisoners are included, like the general public, in the unemployment insurance scheme.

Protection of young working people was strengthened by the completely rewritten Youth Labour Protection Act of 1975. Worker participation in management decision-taking in large enterprises was strengthened almost to full parity. The new matrimonial and divorce law of 1977 attempts to bring about the full equality of women. In cases of divorce the court no longer pronounces on guilt but merely declares the "breakdown of marriage". The burdens of the divorce are shared out as equitably and justly as possible. Adoption has been made considerably easier since 1977 in order to give the security of a proper family life to as many orphans and children from completely broken homes as possible.

The legal relationship between parents and children was newly regulated in 1979 in the right of parental care. No particular model of upbringing is to be prescribed to the intact family, while on the other hand the aim is to bring speedier state aid to neglected or endangered children, even if their parents are not to blame for the problem.

In civil contractual law consumer protection has been considerably strengthened (see pages 177 − 179). The completely reformed food law, in force since 1975, and reforms in the fields of environmental protection serve the preservation and restoration of human health. The same purpose is pursued by the new Medical Drugs Act of 1978. A new Narcotics Act which went into force in 1981, in respect of the drug addict proceeds from the principle of therapy rather than punishment; in respect of the professional narcotics trafficker the state retains its right to punish.

The citizen's legal security was strengthened by a revision of Poor-Law (in forma pauperis, Legal Proceedings Cost Aid Act of 1980) and out-of-court legal counselling. The federal and state legislation enacted since 1977 on data protection belongs in the same context (see pages 154/155).

The basic aim of these reform laws is to strenghten rights of liberty and through the further development of social welfare to encourage the citizen to make use of them.

Political parties and elections

In any democracy political parties are among the most important political institutions. The Federal Republic's Basic Law takes due account of this in devoting to them an article of their own (Art. 21), in contrast to former German constitutions which made almost no mention of them. The Basic Law defines their task as participating "in the forming of the political will of the people". The parties must be democratically structured and render public account of the sources and expenditure of their funds and their assets. Details are laid down by the Parties Act of 1984.

The parties. There are at present five parties in the Bundestag, the House of Representatives in Bonn. They are the Social Democratic Party of Germany (SPD), the Christian Democratic Union of Germany (CDU), the Christian Social Union (CSU) in Bayern (Bavaria), the Free Democratic Party (FDP) and The Greens (Die Grünen). The CDU has no membership in Bavaria, leaving the field there to its sister party, the CSU, which in turn operates only in Bayern. At national level, in the Bundestag, the two sister parties form one joint parliamentary CDU/CSU block.

Christian Democrat (CDU) chairman and Federal Chancellor, Helmut Kohl, after winning the 1983 federal election

*Christian Social Union (CSU) chairman, Franz Josef Strauss,
campaigning in Augsburg*

The four parties came into being from 1945 to 1947. The SPD
was a re-creation of the former mainly labour-oriented party of
the same name which the Hitler regime outlawed in 1933. The
other parties saw themselves as completely new formations,
building only in part on the traditions of the Weimar Republic be-

*Electoral party of the Free Democrats (FDP). Foreign minister,
Hans-Dietrich Genscher, party chairman from 1974 to 1985*

Johannes Rau, Social Democrat candidate for federal chancellor in the January 1987 national election, at a delegates' congress of his party

tween the world wars. In contrast to the Catholic Centre Party (Zentrumspartei) of the Weimar period the CDU and CSU sought their electoral support among both of Germany's two major Christian creeds, Roman Catholicism and Protestantism. The

The State (Länder) parliaments

Land	Election year	Total number of deputies	CDU*	SPD	FPD	Greens**	Others
Baden-Württemberg	1984	126	68	41	8	9	—
Bayern	1986	204	128	61	—	15	—
Bremen	1983	100	37	58	—	5	—
Hamburg	1986	120	54	53	—	13	—
Hessen	1983	110	44	51	8	7	—
Niedersachsen	1986	155	69	66	9	11	—
Nordrhein-Westfalen	1985	227	88	125	14	—	—
Rheinland-Pfalz	1983	100	57	43	—	—	—
Saarland	1985	51	20	26	5	—	—
Schleswig-Holstein	1983	74	39	34	—	—	1***
Berlin (West)****	1985	144	69	48	12	15	—

* In Bayern CSU
** Other names used in some states, e. g. "Alternatives"
*** One deputy of the Danish minority South Schleswig Voters Association (SSW)
**** On the special status of Berlin see pages 76 – 80

FDP laid claim to the heritage of German Liberalism which was shared by quite a number of parties before 1933.

In the more than three decades since their establishment all the parties have undergone significant changes. Nowadays all perceive themselves as "popular" parties representing all classes of people.

The SPD, CDU and FDP all have very distinct right and left wings. This is not only due to their histories but also because in a modern parliamentary democracy with only few big parties all kinds of views and positions seek integration in these "popular" groupings which appeal to a broad spectrum of voters.

In 1983 "The Greens" (Die Grünen) won seats in the Bundestag for the first time, after they had been in six state parliaments previously. "The Greens" developed into a political party out of a radical environmental protection movement, uniting opponents of nuclear power and other protest groups and representing pacifist tendencies. The new party's organisation and programme are not yet very firm. It finds most of its support in the young generation. The Greens have had a federal organisation only since 1979.

The emergence of The Greens has brought some changes in the political landscape. For more than 20 years there had been practically a three-party system in the Bundestag (where the CDU and CSU have always formed one group), and each of the parties has been the coalition partner of the other two on one or more occasions. The Greens are a fourth grouping in the house. Initially

Party congress of The Greens in Hanover, 1986

none of the other three parties would coalesce with it. The first coalition with The Greens was established by the SPD at state level in Hesse in 1985. It remains to be seen whether The Greens can play a lasting role in Federal Republic politics.

Small parties and the five per cent barrier. There has always been a fluctuating number of smaller parties which have also tried to get into the parliaments. In the first Bundestag election in 1949, these smaller parties together polled 27.9% of the votes, compared with a mere 0.4% in the 10th Bundestag poll in 1983. This decline is mainly the result of a "five per cent debarring clause" now contained in all state and federal electoral laws. This clause stipulates that only parties gaining at least 5% of the votes in the given election area can send deputies into parliament. The Federal Constitutional Court has expressly ruled that this provision conforms to the Basic Law.

Extreme right or left-wing parties have rarely overcome this five per cent hurdle. The Communist Party of Germany (Kommunistische Partei Deutschlands, KPD) was only once represented in the Bundestag, with 15 deputies, from 1949 to 1953. The communist groupings which exist today have so far failed to move into any state or federal parliament, although they are represented on a number of municipal councils. Of the more extreme right wing parties, only the German Reich Party (Deutsche Reichspartei) has had a small Bundestag representation — five deputies in the 1949–1953 parliament. The ultra-right-wing National Democratic Party (Nationaldemokratische Partei, NPD) was represented in a number of state assemblies (Landtage) from 1966 to 1972 but lost all its seats in subsequent elections.

The five per cent clause is waived for the representations of ethnic minorities. This is why the Southern Schleswig Voters Association (Südschleswigscher Wählerverband), representing the Danish minority, is in the Landtag of the northernmost state of Schleswig-Holstein although it accounts for less than five per cent of the votes.

The results of local government elections sometimes differ greatly from the federal and state elections. At community level so-called "town hall parties" often play a major role. These are small groups of voters, on the whole concerned purely with local affairs, and independent of the main political parties.

Party bans. "Parties which, by reason of their aims or the behaviour of their adherents, seek to impair or abolish the free democratic principle or to endanger the existence of the Federal Republic of Germany" (Art. 21 of the Basic Law) can be ruled unconstitutional by the Federal Constitutional Court upon application and thereupon disbanded. According to this provision the Socialist Reich Party (Sozialistische Reichspartei), probably the most extreme postwar right-wing party, was outlawed in 1952. In 1956 the Communist Party of Germany (Kommunistische Partei Deutschlands, KPD) was also ruled to be unconstitutional.

The German Communist Party (Deutsche Kommunistische Partei, DKP) has taken over its political heritage without, however, attaining the importance of the former KPD. Neither the Federal Government nor the Bundestag or Bundesrat have so far made use of their right to seek the outlawing of the DKP or the other communist parties which have formed meanwhile, through the Federal Constitutional Court.

Bundestag elections performance

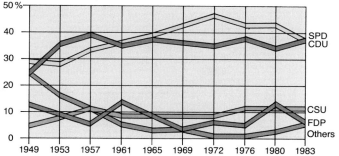

Bundestag seats held*

	SPD	CDU	CSU	FDP	Others		
1949	136	118	24	53	79		
1953	162	197		52	53	45	
1957	181	222		55	43	18	
1961	203	201		50	67		
1965	217	202		49	50		
1969	237	201		49	31		
1972	242	186		48	42		
1976	224	201		53	40		
1980	228	185		52	54		
1983	202	202		53	35	28	

* at the start of the legislative term in each case; including the deputies from Berlin (West)

Membership and finances. In 1984 the parties represented in the Bundestag had the following memberships: the SPD 916,400, the CDU 730,300, the CSU 183,900, the FDP about 71,000, The Greens about 35,000. Of the other national parties the only ones with notable memberships were the DKP with 50,400 and NPD with 5,000.

All parties ask their members to pay subscriptions, but these cover only a small part of their financial requirements. Nor do grants they receive from political sympathisers suffice. Moreover, grants pose the danger of the donor's trying to sway the party to his will or expecting something in return. This is why the Parties Act stipulates that donations in excess of DM 20,000 a year have to be publically declared. The problems of donations to political parties is presently under lively public discussion, triggered by court proceedings and inquiries of the Bundestag. Over and above their own revenues, the parties receive state subsidies for their election campaigning costs. All parties which win at least 0.5% of the votes — and that includes many small ones — receive DM 5 per vote from public revenue.

1983 Bundestag election

Party	Party list votes	%	Deputies (Berlin deputies bracketed)
SPD	14,865,807	38.2	193* (9)
CDU	14,857,680	38.2	191 (11)
CSU**	4,140,865	10.6	53 —
FDP	2,706,942	7.0	34 (1)
The Greens	2,167,431	5.6	27 (1)
Others	201,962	0.4	— —
Total	38,940,687	100.0	498 (22)

* Including one "overhang" mandate each in Hamburg and Bremen (see p. 121)
** CSU exists only in Bayern

The electoral system. Elections for all legislative bodies are general, direct, free, equal and secret. Every German who has attained the age of 18 is eligible to vote and to stand as a candidate. There are no run-up primary elections. Candidates are chosen only by the members of the parties.

The electoral system for the Bundestag is complicated. It is a so-called "personalised proportional representation" system, that is to say a mixture of first-past-the-post constituency voting and national representation by party lists. Half the Bundestag members (not counting those of Berlin [West], who do not have full voting powers), 248 in all, are elected according to the simple majority system in the constituency, the remaining 248 from lists nominated by the Land groupings of the parties. Every voter has two votes, one for a local candidate, the other for a party. Distribution of all votes cast is done in such a way, however, that the Bundestag is constituted almost in proportion to the votes cast (barring the votes for the below-5% parties). If a party wins more direct mandates in the constituencies (i. e. has more "first-past-the-post" winners) than it would be entitled to by its Land list share, it keeps these so-called "overhang" mandates. In that event the Bundestag consists of more than the usual 496 members with full voting rights. The Bundestag deputies of the Land of Berlin are elected from the members of the Berlin Chamber of Deputies.

The Federal Republic's citizens show keen political interest in all elections. Participation in the 1983 Bundestag poll was 89.1 %. Even local government elections attract up to 80 % turnout.

The parties in the Bundestag:

Sozialdemokratische Partei Deutschlands
Ollenhauerstr. 1
5300 Bonn 1

Christlich-Demokratische Union Deutschlands
Friedrich-Ebert-Allee 73–75
5300 Bonn 1

Christlich-Soziale Union in Bayern
Nymphenburger Str. 64–66
8000 München 19

Freie Demokratische Partei
Baunscheidtstr. 15
5300 Bonn 1

Die Grünen
Colmantstr. 36
5300 Bonn 1

Federal, regional and local government

The name "Federal Republic of Germany" already expresses the federative structure of the West German state. The Federal Republic consists of the "Länder" (federal states, see pages 24 − 44).

The Länder were partly reconstituted, partly newly created after 1945. They are no mere provinces but states in their own right with their own sovereign powers. Each Land has its own constitution (Landesverfassung) which must conform to the principles of the republican, democratic, social welfare, law-abiding state as laid down in the national constitution, the Basic Law (Grundgesetz). Apart from that the Länder are free to shape their constitutions as they wish.

German traditions. The federative structure is an old German constitutional tradition, interrupted only by the Hitler regime up to 1945. German federalism has historic roots and in the past was often lamented as an expression of national fragmentation or even as a national misfortune. Today the federal structure is proving a great advantage. It makes it possible to a great extent to do justice to regional peculiarities, wishes and special problems.

In several countries the concentration of administration, industry, commerce and cultural facilities in the capital city, or in few large centres, has proved to be a disadvantage. All over the world the call for regionalisation is becoming stronger. The traditional German federalism has contributed to the Federal Republic's being spared such difficulties.

There has been barely any manifestation in the Federal Republic of Germany of the centrifugal tendencies often cited as drawbacks of federalism. Small in area in any case, it is well served by all means of transport and its population is more unitary than those of many other countries. The once very marked tribal differences have been blurred somewhat by the great postwar population movements and the great mobility modern economic life entails.

Why federalism? Paradoxical as it may appear, the sense of federalism must today be seen more from the point of view of the state as a whole. Democracy becomes more lively if the citizen can take part in the democratic process through elections and referendums at the more readily understandable regional level. Administration works closer to the people within the framework of a federal state or region. To the citizen it is nearer and more familiar than the administration in the federal capital. The regional government for its part is better able to act on its knowledge of regional requirements and conditions. It can contribute, for example, to the preservation of cultural characteristics and regional ethnic peculiarities. A regional government is also able, in certain fields such as education, to test new systems which may later serve as national models.

Parties which are in opposition at national level are often at the same time in government in several states. Thus all parties have the chance democratically to carry responsibility and prove their ability to govern.

But above all, the federal states, especially by their participation in national legislation through their assembly, the Federal Council (Bundesrat) can contribute to the balance of power. This role is seen as so fundamental that both the federal structure and the states' participation in national legislation are laid down as irremovable by the Basic Law.

The powers of the Federal States. The powers of the federation in legislation and administration according to the original 1949 text of the Basic Law appear very restricted in comparison to the states. However, the Federal Republic's economic and social development has been such that the Basic Law has allotted to the federation's legislations ever more spheres, owing to their supra-regional importance.

The states have nevertheless retained important lawmaking fields. These include local government law, parts of environmental protection (a competency currently very much in dispute) and the major part of the police system. Police law is, however, to be standardised in all the states to improve crime prevention and detection across inter-state boundaries.

The Länder's principal field of lawmaking is in cultural affairs. Elementary, secondary and special schools (e. g. for the handicapped) are under state jurisdiction, as is the increasingly important field of adult education. Major aspects of vocational and university education are also regulated by Länder laws. For these two last, however, as well as for further vocational training, federal lawmakers also have some jurisdiction. Overall, however, the autonomy of the states is most strongly felt in cultural life (see also page 330).

The major activity of the states is administration. Apart from the few federal authorities with regional branches (for example the customs and armed forces administrations) the states are solely responsible for applying federal laws. This is also German tradition.

By and large, independently and free of detailed directives from the federal authorities, the states implement federal legislation. The federal government merely ensures that the application of federal law conforms to valid law. Only a few administrative tasks, expressly listed in the Basic Law, are carried out by the states on instruction from the federation. In these matters the states are also subject to federal directives in regard to the execution of the law.

Local self-government. Local government, as an expression of civic freedom, has a long and great tradition in Germany. It may be traced back to the privileges of the free towns in the Middle Ages, when civic rights freed people from the bonds of feudalistic serfdom. ("Stadtluft macht frei — town air makes free", a German saying of the time went.) In modern times local government is primarily linked, however, to the great reforms of the Prussian minister Freiherr vom Stein, in particular the Municipal Order of 1808.

This tradition of civic liberty is manifested in the self-government of towns, communes and counties expressly guaranteed by the Basic Law and all state constitutions. The Basic Law stipulates two things: the states must guarantee to local governments the rights to regulate their own communal affairs — within the framework of the law; all towns, communities and counties must be democratically organised. For historical reasons the municipal constitutions vary greatly from state to state. But local administrative practice is by and large the same everywhere.

Every community governs itself in all local affairs. This includes, above all, short-distance public transport, local road-building, electricity, water and gas supplies, housing construction, building and maintenance of elementary and secondary schools, theatres and museums, hospitals, sports facilities and public baths, adult education and youth welfare. In these fields of self-government local authorities are subject only to legal control by the Land. That is to say that the Land is only allowed to ensure that the law is abided by; the purpose of its actions is determined by each community itself.

Many of the tasks named overtax the financial and organisational resources of small municipalities but these affairs can be taken over by the next higher level of local government, the county, or "Kreis". The "Kreistag", the "parliament" of the county, is directly elected by the local population, as are the representations of the towns and communes.

Municipalities and counties also put into practice many federal and state laws. In this they are subject not only to legal control by the Land but in some cases are given detailed directives to work to.

Topical problems of self-government. Local self-government and communal autonomy must wither if local authorities lack the money they need to fulfil their tasks. This is why the question of adequate funding of the communities is at the centre of many discussions.

The major communal revenues are taxes. The communities have a constitutional claim to income from certain taxes. The major ones are business tax and land tax as well as a number of minor taxes such as dog tax and beverage tax. On top of that the communities receive shares of other tax revenues from the federation and the states, e. g. wages and income tax. In return, they must transfer part of their income from business tax to the federation and the states.

Various legislative measures of the federation to ease taxes have greatly reduced income from business tax, the major source of communal revenue, in recent years. That is why most towns and communes no longer take in enough taxes to be able to meet their tasks. All too often, even in typical local government fields, they depend on state subsidies. As a rule this brings with it state control and local administrations fear that they will become rubber stamp organs of the states.

That is why local governments are demanding a far-reaching reform of the system of communal taxes. In response the federal states have set up a working group to devise a new system.

There is agreement that municipal self-government must be preserved and strengthened. It gives the citizen scope for an almost day-by-day codetermination and control, whether it be through conversation with the local councillors, through access to rezoning and building plans or through insight into communal finances. Thus towns and local governments in a sense are the state's smallest political cells, whose independent and democratic functioning is a prerequisite of freedom and justice in state and society.

Town hall in Schwalenberg, Weserbergland

New city hall in Mainz

Regional planning and rezoning

Working and living conditions are not the same all over the Federal Republic. Life in a densely inhabited industrial area is unavoidably different from that in a thinly populated rural one. Every inhabitant should nonetheless be able to live in an environment in which elementary needs of life can be satisfied. That means adequate provision must be made for the various spheres of human life — housing, employment, care, recreation, education, transport, communication. Society, the economy and the environment must be in optimal balance.

Tasks of regional planning. Such a balance does not come about of its own accord. The state must contribute to the best possible distribution of housing, jobs and recreational areas, cultural and social facilities and their linkage by transportation and communication systems. This is the broad field covered by regional planning.

The general principles and aims of regional planning are set out in the Federal Regional Planning Act (Bundesraumordnungsgesetz) of 1965. All three levels of government — federal, state and local — are charged with its implementation. Every four years the federal government publishes a regional planning report in which it accounts for what has been done in the field. Guideline of regional planning policy are the Federal Regional Planning Programme of 1975 and the "Programmatical Priorities of Regional Planning" whose implementation is the task of the Länder which are responsible for the concrete realisation of regional planning and settlement policy, with local government taking part in it.

The areas of emphasis in regional planning policy lie in the overburdened conurbations, the economically retarded areas and the frontier zone abutting the German Democratic Republic (GDR) and Czechoslovakia.

With the expansion of built-up areas and the constantly growing pollution of the air, soil and water, environmental and nature protection are becoming increasingly important. The major ground water reserves and raw material deposits must be secured. Even fringe areas are being increasingly affected by pollution emanating from the industrial centres through the natural exchange of air and water over large areas.

The total settled area of the federation is only about 12 % but the density varies considerably by regions. Great problems are posed by the expansion of already densely settled regions since the recuperation areas and green zones that still exist near them are indispensable. Hence one of the major tasks of regional planning is to protect these areas. Thus necessary measures should be implemented in such a way that as few as possible of these green zones are lost and as many new ones as possible are created.

In less densely settled areas the differences between centres and villages are even more apparent. The population of rural regions continues to decline as young people move to the conurbations.

In the retarded areas living and working conditions overall are worse than the federal average. This is particularly so in areas solely dependent on agriculture for their livelihood. Here there are too few non-agricultural employment opportunities and social and cultural facilities. Priority measures for improving living and working conditions in these regions are the attraction of industrial and service enterprises, the construction of universities and hospitals and the improvement of transportation facilities.

But the areas with one-sided industrial structures, including parts of the Ruhr region and the Saarland as well as the coastal cities of Hamburg and Bremen, have been showing structural problems for a number of years. High environmental strains from heavy industry, low residential quality and lack of green areas for recreation combine. Moreover, the rate of unemployment there is as high as in structurally weak rural regions. New industries are to be attracted to restore a broader, viable economic basis. As well as the employment problems there are also integration difficulties, mainly in large cities. In the conurbations the German population is declining because of urban exodus and low birth rates while the number of foreigners is growing.

Preference is given to the so-called "Zonal Fringe Region" (Zonenrandgebiet), a 30 to 50 km belt abutting the GDR and Czechoslovakia. Here regional planning faces particular difficulties because the enforced drawing of the boundary has arbitrarily cut apart formerly viable transportation, economic and cultural units. Many towns have lost their former hinterlands which now lie over the border in the GDR. The extensive zonal promotion programme has brought some improvement in living and economic

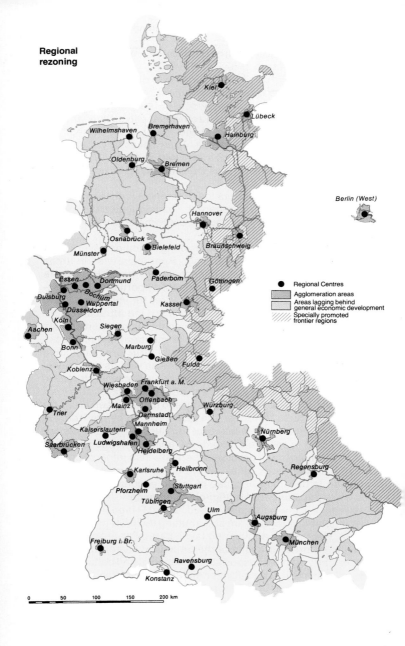

Regional rezoning

Kiel

Lübeck

Wilhelmshaven
Bremerhaven
Hamburg

Oldenburg
Bremen

Berlin (West)

Hannover

Osnabrück
Bielefeld
Braunschweig

Münster
Paderborn

Essen
Dortmund
Göttingen

Duisburg
Bochum
Wuppertal
Düsseldorf
Kassel

Köln
Siegen

Aachen

Bonn
Marburg

Gießen
Fulda

Koblenz

Wiesbaden
Frankfurt a. M.

Mainz
Offenbach
Würzburg

Darmstadt

Trier
Mannheim

Kaiserslautern
Nürnberg

Saarbrücken
Ludwigshafen
Heidelberg

Karlsruhe
Heilbronn
Regensburg

Pforzheim
Stuttgart

Tübingen
Ulm
Augsburg

München

Freiburg i. Br.
Ravensburg

Konstanz

● Regional Centres

Agglomeration areas

Areas lagging behind
general economic development

Specially promoted
frontier regions

0   50   100   150   200 km

conditions in this region. Special attention is also given to promoting Berlin (West). Because the city has been deprived of its natural hinterland special efforts are needed to preserve and enhance its attractiveness. One priority in this is stronger economic and transportation linkage to the federal area.

Difficulties. But ever since regional planning has been pursued in the Federal Republic, society and the economy have proved only slightly influenceable. The prosperity gap between the conurbations and rural and retarded regions, including the frontier belt, has only narrowed insignificantly despite scores of billions of marks spent by the federal government alone. The exodus to overcrowed, economically more attractive conurbations continues. The countryside away from the big towns threatens to depopulate further. As long as the fundamental problem cannot be solved, namely to encourage the prosperous regions to forego further industrialisation and to attract investors to less developed areas even during economic recessions, the imbalance regional planning is intended to eliminate will remain.

Local government rezoning. Planning and development can be sensibly approached only if there is the greatest possible identity of administrative, economic and habitation areas. Most of the historically grown structures of administrative regions dated from pre-industrial times. To adapt them to the needs of present-day society sweeping administrative rezoning began in 1968 in all Länder except Hamburg, Bremen and Berlin (West) which ultimately reduced the number of autonomous local authorities (Gemeinden) in the Federal Republic by almost two thirds. Before the reform there had been 24,000, after its conclusion in 1978 there were about 8,500. The number of independent towns and cities (kreisfreie Städte) fell from 139 to 91, that of counties from 425 to 237. By mergers of smaller communities, often with nearby conurbations, the number of cities with more than 100,000 inhabitants rose from 57 to 65.

One of the major aims of the reform, reducing the number of planning authorities and creating efficient administrative units, has by and large been achieved. But the gain in efficiency has often been at the expense of "nearness to the citizen". Geographically and emotionally the administration has moved further away from him. People feel less inclined than before to become directly involved in their local affairs. The intended personnel and costs savings could not be proved so far. On the contrary, in some cases costs have increased. Some optimal territorial structures could not be created because local politicians prevented it. And so the local government rezoning has also generated quite a deal of annoyance and dissatisfaction. On the whole, however, rezoning has strengthened local government. For example, it brought full-time professional administration to rural areas and improved local facilities for the citizens.

The Federal Republic of Germany in the world

The Federal Republic of Germany lies in the heart of Europe, at the line dividing East and West. Its eastern neighbour is the other German state, the GDR. The dividing line between them separates not only Germany but also marks the frontier of two opposing systems of society. Nowhere is the difference between East and West clearer than in this divided country.

The Federal Republic of Germany is one of the major industrial and trading states with worldwide economic interlacements. It depends on a stable and functioning world economic system and hence is directly affected by all conflicts between North and South, between industrial and developing countries.

Because of its geopolitical location and economic interests, but also because of the Germans' national cause and the experiences of recent history, German policies today must first and foremost be peace policies.

The basis of this foreign policy is and will remain the Federal Republic of Germany's permanent place in the ranks of the free democracies, its membership of the European Community and the Atlantic alliance. This poses four fundamental foreign policy objectives: continuation of the work of European unification, maintenance and strengthening of the Atlantic alliance, the further development of the policy of détente with the East and consolidation of cooperation with Third World countries.

The Federal Republic of Germany at present has diplomatic relations with 160 states. It has 201 missions abroad, 127 of which are embassies.

European unification. Since its foundation in 1949 the Federal Republic has pursued the objective of European unification. In 1957, together with Belgium, France, Italy, Luxembourg and the Netherlands, it was one of the founders of the European Community (EC). The Community has meanwhile been joined by Denmark, Great Britain, Ireland, Greece, Spain and Portugal. By the foreign policy cooperation of the member countries which has grown organically and now covers all fields the Community has gained a new dimension. In the European Council of heads of state or government and Foreign Ministers the Community has been given a

European Community summit in Stuttgart, 1983

leadership body which has considerably strengthened its ability to take political action. The European Parliament which the citizens of the member countries of the community elected directly for the second time in 1984 is giving additional impetus to the process of unification.

Almost all tariff and trade barriers between the member countries have been abolished. This has created a common market for more than 320 million European people in which goods are freely exchanged.

Towards non-members the European Community pursues a common, worldwide trade policy which aims at a world economic order on market economy lines and resists all protectionist tendencies. Its economic and trade relations with outside countries are shaped on the basis of a close network of trade, cooperation and association agreements.

Indicative of the objectives of partnerlike cooperation with the developing countries is the Lomé Convention entered into with sixty-six African, Caribbean and Pacific states, the so-called ACP countries.

The European Act signed in Luxembourg in 1986 has ushered in a new phase on the way into the European future. After the building up phase and the three expansions the community's main tasks are:

☐ international development on the basis of the Luxembourg Act;

☐ formulation of new policies with respect to environment, social security, transportation, justice and culture;

☐ realisation of the internal market, needed inter alia to pool the community's great technological potential;

☐ precise definition of European foreign policy and security interests.

The European Community helps strengthen freedom and democracy in Europe. It is based on the solidarity of its member countries. As the economically most powerful member the Federal Republic of Germany makes considerably larger contributions to the community's expansion and consolidation than any other partner. It will continue to do all in its power to promote further community development and integration. European policy stems from the knowledge that the community is vital to each of its member states and that the Federal Republic itself owes its security, stability, prosperity and economic strength to the community. Therefore its financial contributions to the community also serve its own interests. The Federal Republic today does half its foreign trade with community partners.

Further, this policy is the basis for the freedom of movement of people in Western Europe and strengthens communication among the people of Europe. It aims at the elimination of barriers and boundaries, the continuing improvement of social conditions in Europe and thereby also at more freedom and security for the individual.

The Atlantic alliance and the alliance partners. The Atlantic alliance, NATO, is the indispensable foundation for the security of the free, democratic states of Western Europe. Under its protection, they were reconstructed after the war. Only under its protection can they develop further.

To secure the freedom and independence of the country and its citizens from military and political pressure the Federal Republic joined NATO in 1955. From the outset it placed its armed forces completely under the NATO supreme command. Only the balance of military forces between NATO and the Warsaw Pact can, in the long term, guarantee peace and ensure the continuance of free democracies. To maintain this balance the presence of American and Canadian armed forces in Europe is indispensable.

Close and trusting relations, of vital importance to its security, link the Federal Republic with the United States of America. They have grown in more than three decades into a friendship based on shared values and long-term identity of interests. This rapport

Paris Treaties, 1954.
From left: Mendès-France, Adenauer, Eden, Dulles

determines the close cooperation in the alliance, in security policy and in all questions concerning Berlin, as well as in foreign,
world economic and monetary policies and also at international
conferences involving the two countries.

The reconciliation with France, begun by the first postwar chancellor, Konrad Adenauer, and the treaty of friendship signed by
him and President Charles de Gaulle in 1963, have grown into a
trustful partnership. The network of regular mutual consultations
provided for by the treaty has been continually knitted more
closely. The semi-annual summit meetings of the heads of state
and government in which a number of other specialised ministers
also take part are of particular importance. The policies of both
countries are being ever more closely coordinated in an increasing number of fields, including security; this is also in the interest
of cooperation within the European Community and the Atlantic
alliance.

The Federal Republic of Germany also maintains friendly relationships with other Western states. In particular the cooperation
with Great Britain has been consistently expanded and deepen-
ed. The two countries' heads of government also meet every half
year. Similarly the Federal Republic is closely linked with its
other Western neighbours and allies by a tightly woven fabric of
agreements, consultations and mutual visits.

Securing the peace and détente. The relationship of the Federal Republic to the East European states was initally governed by the confrontation between the Western and Eastern blocs. In 1955 Bonn took up diplomatic relations with the Soviet Union. With the beginning of the worldwide détente efforts a chance developed to complement the policy of permanent integration of the Federal Republic in the Western alliance system with a policy aimed at normalisation and good-neighbourly relations with the East. One of the first steps in this direction was the establishment of diplomatic relations with Romania in 1967.

In 1970 a treaty was signed in Moscow between the Federal Republic of Germany and the Union of Socialist Soviet Republics in which the two sides renounced the threat or use of force and undertook to settle their disputes only by peaceful means. Borders as they presently exist in Europe were declared inviolable. In a "Letter on German Unity", handed over in connection with the signing of the agreement, the Federal Government declared "that this treaty does not conflict with the political objective of the Federal Republic of Germany to work for a state of peace in Europe in which the German nation will recover its unity in free self-determination".

Also in 1970 a treaty was signed in Warsaw between the Federal Republic of Germany and the People's Republic of Poland which laid down that the existing boundary line along the Oder and western Neisse rivers constitutes the western state frontier of Poland (see page 67). This treaty laid the foundations for normalisation and development of relations between the two countries. A treaty on mutual relations was entered into with Czechoslovakia in 1973. It established that both sides treat as null and void in their relations the Munich Agreement of 1938. The assumption of diplomatic relations with Bulgaria and Hungary was also agreed.

In a joint declaration of 17 May 1972 the Bundestag emphasised that the treaties of Moscow and Warsaw do not pre-empt a peace treaty for Germany and create no legal basis for the present borders. The Bundestag declared that the inalienable right to self-determination is not diminished by the treaties and that the Federal Republic of Germany makes no territorial claims or claims to change boundaries. In a ruling on both treaties the Federal Constitutional Court emphasised that by them the Federal Republic of Germany has not disposed of the territorial status of Germany nor of the rights to assets of former inhabitants of these areas.

Signing the Moscow Treaty, 1970

The treaties of Moscow and Warsaw smoothed the way to the 1971 Four Power Agreement on Berlin (see page 78) and the 1972 Treaty on the Basis of Relations between the Federal Republic of Germany and the German Democratic Republic (see p. 74/75). Relations between the two German states are not part of foreign policy because in the Federal Republic's view the German Democratic Republic is not a foreign country, but they cannot be shaped independently of foreign policy as they are an integral part of the overall development of relations between East and West.

The Federal Republic of Germany and the German Democratic Republic are members of different alliance systems. The frontier between them is at the same time the dividing line between the two alliances and between contrasting systems of society. Following two decades in which there were no relations between the two parts of Germany, the Basic Treaty, as it is called for short, provides the foundation for a regulated co-existence, human relief and more contacts between their inhabitants. With this the Federal Republic pursues the aim of keeping alive the feeling of all Germans that they belong together and of ameliorating the effects of the division.

The Federal Republic pursues to a policy vis-à-vis the East which rests on two principles: maintaining the security of the West by adequate defence capability and simultaneous readiness for dialogue and cooperation with the countries of central and Eastern Europe. This policy is designed for the long term and time and again suffers setbacks. But the Federal Republic perseveres with it steadfastly. The goal is lasting détente between East and West based on a realistic assessment.

With its policy the Federal Republic of Germany also smoothed the way to the convening of the Conference on Security and Co-operation in Europe (CSCE). In the final Helsinki document (1975) all European states (except Albania), the USA and Canada agreed on a code of conduct for improving their relations and con-tinuing the CSCE process. The Federal Republic's priorities in this are respect for human rights, development of trust between nations, expansion of economic and scientific cooperation, re-union of separated families and the easing of contacts between people. The Madrid follow-up conference brought progress in all these fields and convened the conference on Confidence and Security Building Measures and Disarmament in Europe. Also agreed was another follow-up conference in Vienna, thus se-curing continuation of the CSCE process.

Precondition to viable détente is a reduction of military con-frontation. The Federal Republic of Germany has already made concrete contributions to securing peace, disarmament and arms control in the past, in particular by eschewing ABC weapons, signing the nuclear test ban treaty, joining the nuclear non-prolif-eration treaty and eschewing the export of arms to areas of ten-sion. But it also supports all further-reaching efforts aimed at re-ducing the danger of military confrontation and achieving a bal-ance of forces between East and West on as low as possible a lev-el. This applies to the US-Soviet negotiations in Geneva about preventing an arms race in space and ending it on earth, the limi-tation and reduction of nuclear weapons and the firming of strate-gic stability.

It applies also to the negotiations in Stockholm about confi-dence and security building measures and disarmament in Europe, to the Vienna negotiations about mutual and balanced re-duction of forces in Europe (MBFR), to the negotiations of the Geneva Conference on Disarmament (CD) on a worldwide and reliably verifiable ban of all chemical weapons and to the efforts of the United Nations for disarmament and arms control on a glo-bal scale.

Policy vis-à-vis the Third World. Cooperation with the countries in the Near and Middle East, Africa, Latin America and Asia has become an ever more important element of German foreign poli-cy. This turning towards the Third World reflects the increased responsibility of the Federal Republic in the world, its global economic involvement and its vital interest in a worldwide peace order.

Respect for the self-determination and equal rights of nations was an essential foundation of the policy of the Federal Republic of Germany from the beginning. It maintains relations with the states of Africa, Asia and Latin America on a basis of balanced and egalitarian partnership. It fully backs their claim to independent and sovereign development. It strives for no spheres of influence and wants to export no ideologies; the Federal Republic works towards a world in which all nations determine their political, economic and cultural affairs themselves and in which they cooperate as partners.

To achieve this objective the prosperity gap between industrial and developing countries in North and South must be narrowed. The Federal Republic faces up to co-responsibility for solving these most important international tasks of our time, especially vis-à-vis the least developed countries. Together with its EC partners it makes constructive contributions to the dialogue between industrial and developing countries, helping in the struggle against hunger and misery, for improved living conditions and for more transfer of resources to the developing countries.

The efficiency of the cooperation and increased help is promoted by a well functioning world economy, especially by the freest possible exchange of goods. All states and groups of states are therefore called upon to participate with substantial contributions to the ongoing dialogue and balancing of interests between North and South, regardless of their economic and social orders. A few decades ago, after the devastation of World War II, the German people urgently needed outside help to rebuild their country and they got it. It is therefore self-evident that now the Federal Republic of Germany supports countries which need help to develop. Since its existence it has spent continuously rising amounts on development aid. By 1984 the official and private aid to developing countries had totalled more than DM 240,000 millions. More increases are planned in official aid for the years immediately ahead (see also pages 217 − 221).

Membership of the United Nations. The Federal Republic of Germany has been a member of the United Nations since 1973 but long before that had cooperated with its sub and specialised agencies. It takes an active part in the multilateral international cooperation in the world organisation. In line with the Charter of the United Nations it supports worldwide efforts to secure peace,

Western economic summit in Bonn 1985

economic and social progress and the implementation of human rights and the right of self-determination of nations. It condemns in the sharpest possible terms all kinds of racism and colonialism and resists with determination the creation of new spheres of power and influence.

Foreign cultural policy. Cultural policy is state promotion of cultural exchange. It has the twin task of

☐ presenting Germany in the world at large as a nation of culture and

☐ disseminating knowledge of other cultures in Germany.

Culture in this sense encompasses all the facets of life and thought of peoples, including their civilisatory and societal problems. Regardless of different scientific and technical development, cultural exchange presupposes the same dignity of all cultures.

The aim of German cultural policy abroad is to break down prejudices and to strengthen mutual respect between peoples so as also to create a viable basis for economic and political cooperation. Responsibility for cultural policy abroad rests with the foreign office of the federal government which cooperates closely in this field with the governments of the Länder.

The Federal Republic of Germany has cultural agreements with 49 countries. Such an agreement is not, however, a prerequisite to close cultural exchange. Most of the exchange activities are carried out by specialised agencies, of which four are of particular importance:

☐ The Goethe Institute which has 135 branches in 66 countries concentrates on teaching the German language and providing comprehensive information about Germany.

☐ The German Academic Exchange Service (Deutscher Akademischer Austauschdienst, DAAD) is responsible for the exchange of postgraduates and students.

☐ Inter Nationes looks after foreign guests in Germany and produces and disseminates all manner of films, tape recordings and printed matter.

☐ The Institute for Foreign Relations (Institut für Auslandsbeziehungen) specialises in organising German exhibitions abroad and foreign exhibitions in Germany.

Public finance

In many states, more and more tasks which used to have a private character are now being taken care of by the state. Consequently, the importance of public finance has grown. This also applies in the Federal Republic of Germany.

The Federal Republic's total public budget comprises not only the federal budget but also the budgets of the Bundesländer (federal states) and about 9,000 communes (local governments) and local government associations as well as a number of special accounts. One must always keep this in mind when making comparisons. For example, the military expenditure of the Federal Republic is easy to ascertain because defence is a federal matter and spending on it appears as a self-contained block in the federal budget. By contrast, it is not easy to tot up the total spending on cultural amenities – education, science, arts, etc. – because it is spread among the budgets of the federal government, the Länder, the communes and many non-state institutions.

The distribution of tasks. The lowest administrative level on which public services are rendered is the commune (Gemeinde). It deals with all local affairs. These comprise manifold basic needs of the public such as water, gas and electricity supplies, garbage

Federal, State and local government spending (1983)
Total DM 848,900 millions
Categories in percent

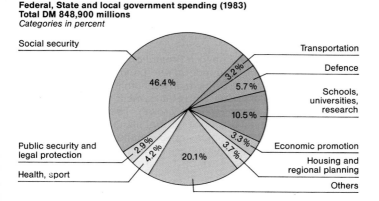

Social security — 46.4 %

Transportation — 3.2 %

Defence — 5.7 %

Schools, universities, research — 10.5 %

Economic promotion — 3.3 %

Housing and regional planning — 3.7 %

Others — 20.1 %

Health, sport — 4.2 %

Public security and legal protection — 2.9 %

disposal, maintenance of communal roads and, together with the Länder, the schools system and other cultural amenities.

The tasks of the Länder lie mainly in the field of culture, primarily the schools and other education facilities. They are also responsible for the police forces and public health services.

The greatest load of public tasks is carried by the federal government. Two large fields predominate: social security and — as already mentioned — defence. In addition the federal government has important tasks in many other fields: transport and communications (Federal Railways, posts, road construction), education and vocational training, science and research, energy and economic promotion, agriculture, housing and urban works, public health, internal security and development aid.

Apart from this there are tasks addressed jointly by the federal government and the Länder. These include the expansion and new construction of universities, improvement of regional economic structures, agricultural structure and coastal protection, as well as cooperation in education planning and scientific promotion.

Financing the public budgets has become more and more difficult since the mid-1970's. Especially the spending on social security but also the Federal Republic of Germany's payments to the European Community have risen enormously since then. All levels of government are also finding it increasingly difficult to bear the growing administrative costs, especially for personnel, and the cost of debt servicing. The increasing burden on the state has consistently narrowed its scope for action and more and more reduced the public funds available for investment. That is why consolidation of the public budgets is a high priority task for federal and state governments and will remain so in the years to come despite the headway already made.

Finance planning. A 1967 Law on Promotion of Stability and Economic Growth requires the federal and Länder governments to orientate their budgeting to the main economic policy objectives. These are stability of prices, high employment, balanced foreign trade and steady, commensurate growth. The federal government and Länder must draw up financial plans for their areas of responsibility in which incomes and expenditures are listed for a period of five years. The main purpose of this finance planning for several years ahead is, above all, to harmonise public incomes and expenditures with national economic resources and requirements. Public expenditure is to be brought into line, in order of

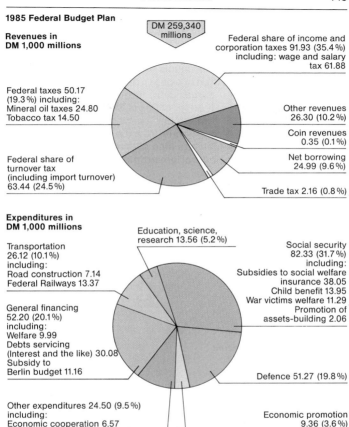

1985 Federal Budget Plan

Revenues in DM 1,000 millions

DM 259,340 millions

Federal share of income and corporation taxes 91.93 (35.4%) including: wage and salary tax 61.88

Federal taxes 50.17 (19.3%) including: Mineral oil taxes 24.80 Tobacco tax 14.50

Other revenues 26.30 (10.2%)

Coin revenues 0.35 (0.1%)

Net borrowing 24.99 (9.6%)

Federal share of turnover tax (including import turnover) 63.44 (24.5%)

Trade tax 2.16 (0.8%)

Expenditures in DM 1,000 millions

Education, science, research 13.56 (5.2%)

Transportation 26.12 (10.1%) including: Road construction 7.14 Federal Railways 13.37

Social security 82.33 (31.7%) including: Subsidies to social welfare insurance 38.05 Child benefit 13.95 War victims welfare 11.29 Promotion of assets-building 2.06

General financing 52.20 (20.1%) including: Welfare 9.99 Debts servicing (Interest and the like) 30.08 Subsidy to Berlin budget 11.16

Defence 51.27 (19.8%)

Other expenditures 24.50 (9.5%) including: Economic cooperation 6.57 Housing, regional planning 3.27

Economic promotion 9.36 (3.6%) (including agriculture)

priority, with the total economically justifiable financial possibilities. The local government regulations of the states stipulate that communal governments must also draw up mid-term finance plans.

The great importance of the public budgets requires close coordination through all administrative levels. The most important body of this voluntary cooperation is the Financial Planning Council, set up in 1968, in which federal government, Länder, communes and the Federal Bank (Deutsche Bundesbank) participate. The Business Cycle Council of the Public Authorities also has a coordinating function (see page 166).

Distribution of revenues. The major source of the revenue the federal, Länder and local governments need to carry out their tasks is taxes. There are more than two dozen different types. But five of these alone — income, corporation, turnover, mineral oil and trade taxes — raise more than four fifths of the entire tax revenue. Before 1914 the Reich, Länder and communes each received about a third of the total tax revenue. With the reweighting of tasks the share of revenue intake has also shifted in favour of central government. Today the federal government controls about half the entire tax revenue.

The distribution of tax revenues among the three levels of government is complicated. Income, corporation and turnover taxes

Tax revenues in the Federal area *(in millions of DM)*

Tax type	1970	1980	1984
Shared taxes	99,949	267,300	305,104
Wage	35,086	111,559	136,350
Income	16,001	36,796	26,368
Capital gains	2,021	4,175	5,591
Corporation	8,716	21,322	26,312
Turnover, import turnover	38,125	93,448	102,181
Federal taxes inc. EC shares	27,396	46,053	54,059
Customs, excise	2,871	4,603	5,332
Tobacco, coffee, sugar	7,718	12,906	16,137
Brandy monopoly	2,228	3,885	4,238
Mineral oil	11,512	21,351	24,033
Other consumer	451	244	245
Surcharge	948	39	17
Other	1,667	3,026	3,379
Länder taxes	9,531	16,072	18,581
Assets	2,877	4,664	4,492
Motor vehicles	3,830	6,585	7,284
Beer	1,175	1,262	1,255
Other	1,650	3,560	5,550
Local government taxes	15,679	35,736	36,951
Real estate	2,683	5,804	6,771
Trading (profits and capital)	10,728	27,091	28,320
Other	2,267	2,597	1,528
Total	152,555	364,918	414,695

are "joint taxes". They are shared between the federal government and Länder according to a fixed, in the case of sales tax a periodically renegotiated format. The local authorities also receive a part of the income tax revenue. In exchange they have to surrender to the federal government and Länder part of the trading tax they raise, which used to be a purely local government tax. Another part of the sales tax goes to the EC.

Other taxes go to only one level of government. Federal government sources are the customs and excise duties (after deduction of the EC share), the incomes from finance monopolies (e. g. brandy monopoly) and various consumer and traffic taxes (e. g. mineral oil, tobacco and capital transfer taxes). The Länder receive the motor vehicles, assets, inheritance and beer taxes as well as a number of smaller taxes. The communes receive the revenues from real estate and local consumption and expenditure taxes.

The highest revenues are brought in by income tax. This is the one which most strongly affects the average person. Dependently employed, i. e. wage-earning or salaried workers and public servants, have it deducted from wages or salary by the employer who remits it to the tax office (the "pay-as-you-earn" principle). The rate of taxation rises with income. After allowance of certain non-taxable sums it comprises at least 22 % and at most 56 %.

Apart from tax revenues a major source of public finance is state borrowing. The Federal Republic's public budgets in 1984 were DM 702,000 millions in debt which broke down to about DM 11,400 per inhabitant. This was a high level of public debt. In recent years new borrowing at the three national budget levels was able to be cut by a consistent savings policy. This consolidation course is to be continued in principle to cut the debt burden further.

Financial offsetting. The tax-raising capability of the Länder varies considerably because their natural conditions and economic structures are also very different. For example Nordrhein-Westfalen (North-Rhine Westphalia), Baden-Württemberg and Hessen are comparatively wealthy in terms of tax revenue while other, less industrialised states, are relatively poor. In addition, some have special public tasks to carry out, e. g. maintenance of sea ports which are heavy financial burdens. These differences in tax raising potential are by and large balanced out by a "horizontal financial offsetting". This is achieved in part by a differential sharing of the Länder's turnover tax income partly by offset payments of the stronger tax revenue Länder to the weaker. In addition the federation supports the financially weak Länder to reduce the finance gap further.

A "vertical financial offsetting" takes place between Länder and local governments. The tax and other revenues of the communes are inadequate for their tasks. The municipal governments therefore depend on subsidies from the Länder. Some of these are tied to specific purposes but others are freely disposable. This municipal finance offsetting aims at ameliorating the differences between communes with high tax revenues and those with low tax revenues.

Public service

For the average citizen the state as such is an abstract concept. It takes on flesh and blood only in the person of its servants. In the Federal Republic some 4.5 million people are in public employment, 3.8 million fulltime, for federal, state and local governments, the public law agencies, institutions and other authorities. Only some of them carry out administrative work in the strictest sense. Public servants include various groups, e. g. ministerial officials and dustmen, swimming baths supervisors and professors, judges and nurses, teachers and locomotive drivers but also the soldiers of the Federal Armed Forces.

Professional civil servants. About 40 % of the public servants comprise what are called "Beamte" in German, meaning permanent civil servants. The permanent civil service is a specifically German characteristic which in the Federal Republic continues, under different political conditions but legally almost unchanged, the tradition of the German Reich. The Basic Law expressly rules that "the law of the public service shall be regulated with due regard to the traditional principles of the professional civil service". A professional civil service is to ensure that public tasks are carried out reliably and free of extraneous influences at all times.

The Basic Law entrusts the civil servant with "the exercise of state authority". This authority is exercised by an official, for example, when he orders a dangerously delapidated house torn down, regulates traffic, issues a fine or chases a robber with a pistol. The public servant's "status, service and loyalty are governed by public law".

The "Beamte" has a special obligation of loyalty to his employer. He is dutybound at all times to defend the free democratic order as laid down by the Basic Law. All his actions must be aimed at the common good and conform to administrative law. Even where he has scope for decision he may never take action as he thinks fit but only in line with duty-abiding discretion. His superior can demand obedience from him, yet he remains responsible himself for the legality of his actions. Even in his basic rights the Beamte is subject to certain limitations. Although Beamte, like all citizens, have the right to become politically active they are obliged to exercise moderation and restraint. They also have the "coalition right", that is the right to form professional groups, but are not allowed to strike.

As against these special obligations, Beamte also have special privileges. They are usually appointed for life. The state has to take care of its permanent civil servants and their families in many fields. In case of sickness they continue to draw their salaries. If they become incapacitated or when they reach retirement age, Beamte receive a pension from their employers.

Status and pay in the civil service are hierarchically structured. Every Beamte belongs to one of four "career levels": sub-clerical, clerical, executive or administrative service. Which of these categories he is grouped in is determined by educational standards achieved and professional qualification. Generally, the highest grouping, for example, demands university graduation. Moving from a lower to a higher category is difficult, although it has in recent years been eased. Within the various categories there are several differently remunerated grades.

Wage and salary earners in the public service. About 60 % of public employees are non-Beamte status wage and salary earners. In many respects they have the same rights and status as their colleagues in private enterprise. Therefore they have to pay contributions into the social insurance schemes and are not from the outset employed for life. They become indismissable only after 15 years and after the age of 40. Over the years their status has, however, been more and more adapted to that of the permanent civil servants. Yet significant differences remain in their legal position although sometimes non-Beamte public employees do the same, or similar, jobs as their Beamte colleagues.

The problem of extremists. The public service, above all its permanent civil servants, put the constitution and legislation into practice. In this they implement overall the order of the state. For this reason most states put their civil servants under higher than normal obligations of loyality. They demand that they be always ready to defend and promote the constitutional order.

However, the procedures according to which civil servants are appointed vary. Many countries have chosen very pragmatic ways. For the Federal Republic, the Federal Constitutional Court has laid down that an applicant's loyalty to the constitution must be tested as one prerequisite for his employment, but that a rejection must be justified with facts which can be reviewed by an independent court.

The Beamte appointment practice was, and is, not uniform everywhere. A decision by the heads of the federal and state governments in 1972, the so-called "radicals decree" (Radikalenerlass), brought no clarification at the time. Depending on the political standpoint, individual cases of rejection were used as arguments in the occasionally vehement debate over an appointment procedure which did justice to all the requirements of a state ruled by law.

Meanwhile highest court rulings have pointed the way to a procedure conforming to the principles of a state governed by the rule of law. Accordingly, the federal government in 1979 adopted new "Principles for Testing Loyalty to the Constitution" ("Grundsätze für die Prüfung der Verfassungstreue") for the federal administration.

Internal security

Maintenance of public security and order is one of the state's most important tasks. In the Federal Republic it is carried out by federal and state (Land) authorities.

The police of the Länder. Principally the police forces are under the jurisdiction of individual federal states. The federal states having legislative power in this field, there are eleven different Land police laws which are nevertheless similar in many major points. Close cooperation between the state police forces is assured by regular conferences of the Land interior ministers which the federal interior (home affairs) minister also attends. Until 1977 the police forces of the Länder still had different uniforms. These, too, are now the same throughout the Federal Republic.

Police tasks are varied. The police body with whom the citizen has most contact is the traffic police. All federal states also have general police forces (Schutzpolizei, Bereitschaftspolizei and Wasserschutzpolizei) as well as criminal police, the only plain-clothes part of the forces. For police training and for manpower support of the regular forces, the states also keep uniformly trained Alert Forces (Bereitschaftspolizei) numbering about 26,000 men. The Alert Forces are uniformly equipped and supervised by the federation.

The Federal Border Police. The Federal Border Police (Bundesgrenzschutz, BGS) is a federal police force responsible to the federal interior minister. Its overall strength is about 21,500 men. The main task of the BGS is controlling the Federal Republic's external borders. It checks incoming and outgoing traffic. In the frontier region it has to ward off threats and remove disturbances.

The Federal Border Police also keeps watch on federal installations (e. g. the official residence of the Federal President and the federal chancellery) and threatened foreign missions, and it is used for security work during state visits and similar events. A special border police unit operative since 1973, the "Grenzschutzgruppe 9", won worldwide recognition when in October 1977 it freed 86 hostages held by terrorists in a Lufthansa airliner at Mogadishu, Somalia.

In internal emergency the Federal Border Police can be assigned special tasks. In particular, they can be brought in to avert a threat to the existence of the free democratic order of the federation or a federal state. In an external emergency, i. e. an armed attack on federal territory from outside, the Bonn government can, if necessary, deploy the BGS in the entire federal area.

The Federal Criminal Investigation Agency. The Federal Criminal Investigation Agency (Bundeskriminalamt, BKA) which is based at Wiesbaden and has a major branch office near Bonn is the centre for cooperation between federal and state law enforcement agencies. It collects information and documentation for crime-fighting by the police and evaluates them. The BKA has technical and identification facilities and functions as the national centre for INTERPOL, the international criminal police organisation.

The BKA handles serious crimes itself, e. g. drug trafficking or when it is asked to do so by a Land. A BKA security group based in Bonn protects the federal constitutional organs and their guests. BKA personnel strength has been almost quadrupled since 1969 to 3,500. This was an important contribution to strengthening internal security in the Federal Republic of Germany, especially to fighting violent crime by terrorist groups and serious crime in general.

Agency for Protection of the Constitution. One of the instruments to protect the constitutional order in the Federal Republic of Germany is the Agency for Protection of the Constitution, provided for by the Basic Law. Protection of the constitution is a joint task of the federation and the states and involves the collection and evaluation of information about extremist and security-threatening movements.

Another important field of activity in protecting the constitution is counter-espionage, that is fighting the secret service activities of foreign powers on the territory of the Federal Republic of Germany.

The constitution-protection agency of the federation and central collecting point for documents relating to this work is the Federal Agency for Protection of the Constitution (Bundesamt für Verfassungsschutz, BfV) in Köln (Cologne). The BfV is accountable to the interior ministry. It cooperates with the corresponding agencies of the federal states. The agency is a pure information gathering service. It has no executive police powers.

Police attending to a traffic accident

The federal and state constitution-protection authorities are subject to several levels of control. It is exercised by the responsible ministers, the parliaments and the data protection ombudsmen. The agencies are also subject to control by the courts, public opinion and the media.

Data protection. The protection of the individual citizen has the same rank in the law-governed state as the security of the state. To keep both interests in harmony is the constant task of legislation and jurisdiction. Electronic data processing has given rise to completely new problems in this area.

Computers are used in almost all fields in the modern industrial society. Be it in accounts handling in banks, seat reservations with an airline, the issuance of tax statements by the tax office or the collection of data on lawbreakers by the police – electronic data processing has become indispensable everywhere. It enables gigantic amounts of data to be so stored as to be retrievable at any time. This modern technology has greatly eased and speeded up the work of many firms and authorities. For example the statutory German pensions insurance can now process pension applications much faster than before and the police have achieved great successes in apprehending criminals with the aid of computers. At the same time it has become clear, however, that modern data technology also poses dangers. The stored data could be illicitly used and fall into the wrong hands. Anyone who has possession of enough data gains insights into the people's private sphere which must remain inviolable.

To avert these dangers data protection in the Federal Republic began to be regulated by federal and state legislation in 1977. These laws stipulate what personal data authorities and business enterprises may store. In all other cases the storing of such data is forbidden. Personnel of agencies processing data are bound to secrecy. The citizen has a legal entitlement to obtain from every data processing agency information on the data it holds on him. He can demand the correction of wrong data, the blockade of disputed ones and the removal of any that have been improperly obtained. To control public data processing the Federal President, on the recommendation of the federal government, appoints a Federal Ombudsman for Data Protection who exercises the office independently of other authorities. Any citizen who feels that his data interests have been violated by public agencies can turn to him with a complaint. The data ombudsman reports annually to the Bundestag. The federal states also have data protection ombudsmen. Business enterprises using data are also obliged to name a data protection ombudsman. These are subject to supervision by the relevant authorities in the various Länder which monitor adherence to data protection regulations.

The data protection legislation of the Federal Republic is among the most modern and comprehensive in the world. It has helped sharpen public awareness of the need for data protection. To remain responsive to technical developments which will continue to be subject to rapid change it must remain open to adaptation like hardly any other legislation.

Defence

The external security of the Federal Republic of Germany is assured only within the Atlantic alliance. Since 1955 the country has been a member of the North Atlantic Treaty Organisation (NATO). Even in peace time all major units of the army field forces are assigned to NATO and in cases of tension or defence emergency they come under NATO operational command. The air defence and air surveillance forces are under NATO command even in peace time.

In a defence emergency the task of the Federal German armed forces and allied troops is to repel the aggressors as close to the borders as possible ("forward defence") and to retake lost terrain. In case of overwhelming superiority of the aggressor his attack must be contained until the political leadership are able to end the military conflict by political means or NATO decides to respond in one of the ways provided for by the agreed alliance strategy.

The Bundeswehr. All men in the Federal Republic are liable to general conscription. Basic military service lasts 15 months; it will be extended to 18 months from July 1, 1989. The Bundeswehr (Federal Armed Forces, the official collective name of the armed services) cannot, however, be regarded as a pure conscript force.

Armed forces manpower

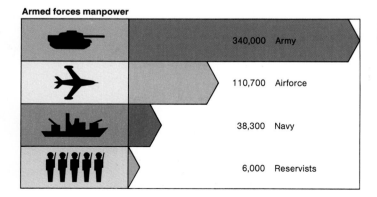

340,000	Army
110,700	Airforce
38,300	Navy
6,000	Reservists

Forces comparison central Europe (forces present without France and Spain)

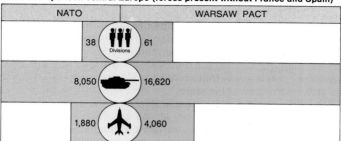

NATO		WARSAW PACT
38 Divisions		61
8,050		16,620
1,880		4,060

* Tactical fighter planes

For its advanced technology equipment the Bundeswehr needs to have soldiers at its disposal longer. At present about 490,000 enlisted men, non-commissioned officers and officers are serving. About half are conscripts, the remainder are regulars or extended service volunteers for terms ranging from two to 15 years. The Bundeswehr consists of army, airforce and navy. It is indisputably one of the well equipped forces in the Atlantic alliance. Combat effectiveness and capabilities of all three services have been improved and strengthened by introduction of new and improvement of existing weapons systems and equipment. Improvements will continue. Deterrence is credible only if armament and equipment are continually adapted to the recognised threat.

The growth in combat effectiveness poses no threat to other nations. The Bundeswehr has a purely defensive character. It has neither strategic offensive weapons nor nuclear, chemical or biological warheads or agents. Neither in terms of personnel, materials and logistics nor its command and control system is it equipped for a strategic offensive.

In peace time the defence minister has supreme command of the Bundeswehr. If the Bundestag declares a state of defence (Article 115 of the Basic Law), power of command over the armed forces passes to the Federal Chancellor.

The Bundeswehr sponsors soldiers' vocational training and further education. Longer-serving ones can attend a variety of courses and take examinations which will benefit them in their later working lives. Since 1973 the Bundeswehr has had universities of its own where officer candidates can take fully valid tertiary degrees. An Armed Forces Command and Staff College trains officers for higher command duties.

The soldier in society. Army and democracy were for a long time irreconcilable concepts in Germany. The Bundeswehr has succeeded to a great degree in harmonising the requirements of military life with democratic principles. The soldier is a "citizen in uniform", that is to say that while he is serving he does not cease to be a free citizen of his state.

The primacy of political leadership over the armed forces is particularly evident in the very strong constitutional position of parliament. Their numerical strength and the basic principles of their organisation are determined by the Bundestag in its defence budget allocation. Parliamentary control is centred on the defence committee of the Bundestag which stays in office even between legislative periods and has powers of a commission of inquiry.

Another instrument of parliamentary control over defence and for safeguarding basic rights is the Parliamentary Commissioner for the Armed Forces (Wehrbeauftragter des Deutschen Bundestages). He watches over the constitutional rights of the citizen in military service. The commissioner is elected by the Bundestag

NATO manœuvre

every five years. Every soldier has the right directly to turn to him with complaints without going through channels. He is not allowed to be exposed to discrimination in his military service or subjected to disciplinary action because of this. Every year some 6,000 such complaints reach the commissioner. He is empowered to inspect the records of all military agencies and organisations and visit any Bundeswehr installation without notice.

In accordance with the Basic Law "no one may be compelled against his conscience to render military service involving the use of arms". The state is dutybound already in peace time to exempt him from military service. The conscientious objectors "may be required to render a substitute service" (Art. 12a) in civilian institutions, e. g. hospitals, care of the aged and handicapped and so on.

In Germany, for understandable reasons, there cannot be as unchallenged an acceptance of military traditions as in other countries. This was why the buildup of the Bundeswehr involved many psychological difficulties. In the more than three decades they have existed, however, the Federal Armed Forces have developed a tradition of their own and are integrated in the democratic society.

Civil defence. Civil defence involves preparation and execution of all defence measures in the non-military sector. It lies exclusively in the jurisdiction of civilian authorities. Its main tasks are maintenance of national administration and government functions, protection of life and health of the population from the effects of war, provision of supplies vital to survival of the population and defence efforts and support of the armed forces.

The main task of civil defence is protection of the population. The central authority for this is the Federal Civilian Defence Agency (Bundesamt für Zivilschutz). Among other things it is responsible for warning and alerting services, air rescue, shelter construction in residential buildings, schools and hospitals. The job of the Federal Self-Protection Association (Bundesverband für den Selbstschutz) is to instruct the population about the effects of attack and strike weapons and protection possibilities. So far more than 5.5 million people have taken part in its courses.

Economics

The economic system

The Federal Republic of Germany is one of the major industrial countries. By overall economic performance it comes fourth in the world; in world trade it even takes second place. Its Gross National Product — i. e. the value of all goods and services produced for the market — has more than doubled in the past two decades, from 1960 to 1984. (Expressed in 1976 prices it has risen from DM 613,400 millions to DM 1,300,000 millions. In terms of market prices it rose from DM 303,000 millions to DM 1,750,000 millions.) Since in this period the number of gainfully employed and the average working time have diminished, the growth of the social product is due to a mighty rise in productivity. The Federal Republic was also hit by the worldwide recession which began in 1974. The slowing of economic growth and the persisting unemployment have been its most pressing problems for a decade.

Social market economy. The Federal Republic's economic system has developed since the war into a socially responsible market economy coupled with macroeconomic management. This system rejects equally the old style laissez-faire and government interventionism. It combines the free initiative of the individual with the principles of social progress. The Basic Law which guarantees freedom of private enterprise and private property stipulates that these basic rights be exercised to the public good. Under the tenet of "as little state as possible, as much state as necessary" the state has a mainly regulatory function in the market economy. It sets the general framework of conditions within which market processes take place. The question as to which and how many goods are produced and who gets how much of what is decided above all in the marketplace. In the Federal Republic there is almost no state intervention in price and wage fixing.

Market economy. The prerequisite for the functioning of the market mechanism is competition. Without it there can be no market economy. But competition demands effort. And so it is understandable that entrepreneurs time and time again try to neutralise competition, be it by agreements between competitors or by mergers of firms. To prevent such attempts is the objective of a Law Against Restraints of Competition (Cartel Act), first enacted

in 1957 and substantially improved meanwhile. It forbids concerted practices and agreements which influence market conditions
by restricting competition. Enforcement of the law is the function
of the Federal Cartels Office (Bundeskartellamt) in Berlin (West)
and the cartels offices of the Länder. In exceptional cases cartels
can be permitted insofar as they do not impair competition.

The driving force of the market economy is the striving for profit. This is why it is bound to fail wherever no profits are, or can be
made. For this reason a number of sectors of the German economy were never completely subject to the market economy system, for example agriculture, transportation and in recent years
the steel industry. Above all for social reasons agriculture cannot
be completeley exposed to free market competition. Moreover, it
is subject to the regulations governing the common market organisations of the EC in agriculture. The German Federal Railways (Deutsche Bundesbahn) and the German Federal Post Office (Deutsche Bundespost) are publicly owned. They cannot
orientate their activities purely to profit but have to serve the

Gross Domestic Product of important industrial states 1984

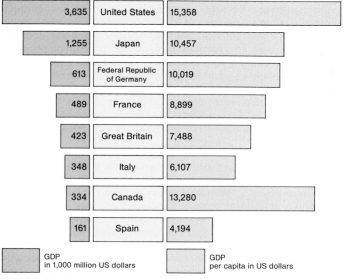

GDP (1,000 million US dollars)	Country	GDP per capita (US dollars)
3,635	United States	15,358
1,255	Japan	10,457
613	Federal Republic of Germany	10,019
489	France	8,899
423	Great Britain	7,488
348	Italy	6,107
334	Canada	13,280
161	Spain	4,194

GDP in 1,000 million US dollars

GDP per capita in US dollars

Source: OECD, Main Economic Indicators, February 1986

Generation of gross domestic product 1984 (DM 1,745,000 millions)

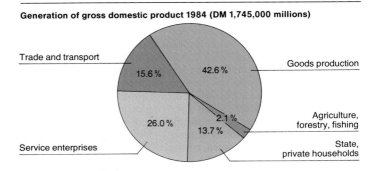

Trade and transport — 15.6 %

Goods production — 42.6 %

Agriculture, forestry, fishing — 2.1 %

State, private households — 13.7 %

Service enterprises — 26.0 %

general public. The railways must, for example, offer socially acceptable fares and the post office cannot exclude remote villages from its services.

The shortage of housing resulting from the war initially led to the housing market being state-controlled. In the meantime it has by and large become free again. The state does, however, watch that competition on it does not result in socially intolerable conditions. The most important measures to this end are laws protecting tenancy, the payment of rent supplements to low-income households, the promotion of building projects and the modernisation of housing. In a number of vocations, in which on principle there is free competition, lawmakers have made entry into the market dependent on certain prerequisites. Thus craftsmen and retail traders must prove they have the necessary professional qualifications before they can set up in business. For other vocations the state demands a special training and a minimum age, for example in the fields of health, law practice, accountancy and taxation consultancy.

Industrial relations. In the labour market, too, the free play of forces applies. There is free collective bargaining. That is to say that labour-employer agreements on pay, working hours, duration of vacation and general working conditions are freely negotiated. The organisations of the two parties to the agreements, the trade unions and the employer associations — called "social partners" in Germany — thus play an important role in economic life. Granted, their main task is to represent their members' interests with determination and, on occasions, with hardness. However, at the same time they bear a large measure of responsibility for the

Use of Gross National Product 1984 (DM 1,750,000 millions)

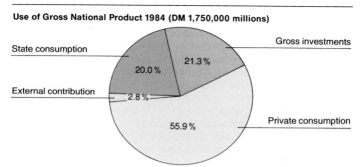

State consumption — Gross investments — 21.3% — 20.0% — External contribution — 2.8% — 55.9% — Private consumption

economy as a whole. The way they conduct their bargaining can greatly influence the functioning of the economic system.

Labour and employers in the Federal Republic have been aware of this responsibility. To a large degree the stability of the economic system is due to them. The realistic policies of the trade unions have in recent years contributed to limiting the effects of the world economic crisis on the Federal Republic's workers. Here the specific form of trade unionism which has grown in West Germany since the war shows its worth. The trade unions of the Federal Republic of Germany are "unitary trade unions" in a double sense: each represents all the workers in an entire branch of industry (i. e. not only the members of a certain craft or skill) and they are party-politically and denominationally neutral (i. e. not split into various allegiances). This structure gives them their strength, spares them rivalries and makes them pillars of social stability.

Distribution of national income 1984 (DM 1,340,700 millions)

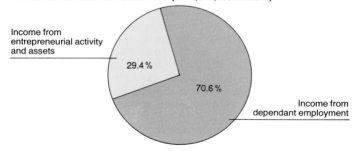

Income from entrepreneurial activity and assets — 29.4% — 70.6% — Income from dependant employment

Social welfare. One major reason why hitherto it has been possible to preserve the social peace in the Federal Republic better than in other countries is that its inhabitants are protected by a close social security network. Social protection is considerable, especially for employees. Whether an employee is old or sick, injured by accident or jobless, affected by the bankruptcy of his employer or taking retraining in a more promising occupation – most of the financial problems are solved by the welfare system.

This support is not charity. It is based on a system of solidarity. Those in employment pay contributions to the various branches of the social insurances and are thus assured of getting what they need when they need it.

However, the social system extends far beyond the employees' contributions. It includes allowances for every child, rent supplements, social benefits for the needy and compensation of war victims. The entire public and private expenditure on social security amounts to about a third of the national product.

Macroeconomic management. Even in the market economy undesirable developments can jeopardise stability. The state cannot simply stand by and let them take their course. A 1967 Stability and Growth Act commits the federal and Länder governments to management of the economy over the business cycle. It demands that stability of prices, a high level of employment and external economic balance under conditions of steady and adequate growth be secured. However, it is not only the state which is called upon to implement these hard-to-reconcile aims. The independent German Federal Bank (Deutsche Bundesbank) als well as the trade unions and employer associations also bear decisive responsibility for the way the economy fares. The following bodies participate in the coordination of economic and fiscal policy:

The Business Cycle Council consists of the federal ministers of economics and finance, one member from each Land government and representatives of the communes and communal associations. The Federal Bank can also take part in the consultations which take place twice a year. The council tries to achieve as unitary an approach to cyclical policy as possible by all concerned. The similarly composed Financial Planning Council (Finanzplanungsrat) has the task of coordinating the finance planning of the federation, Länder and communes, i. e. the central, regional and local authorities.

The federation and Länder are committed to drawing up finance plans for several years ahead so that public revenues and

**Gross National Product of the Federal Republic of Germany
in actual annual prices and prices compared with 1976**

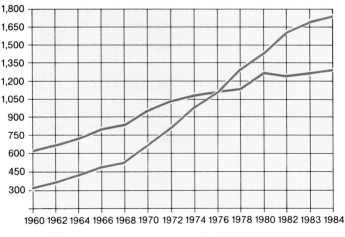

1960 1962 1964 1966 1968 1970 1972 1974 1976 1978 1980 1982 1983 1984

━━━━━ GNP in actual annual prices
(DM 1,000 mill.)

━━━━━ GNP in 1976 prices (DM 1,000 mill.)

expenditures can be harmonised with the needs and capacity of the national economy.

In 1963 the Council of Experts for Evaluation of Overall Economic Developments (Sachverständigenrat zur Begutachtung der gesamtwirtschaftlichen Entwicklung) was set up. This panel of five independent economic experts (popularly known as the "five wise men") draws up an evaluation of overall economic developments every autumn which is to help all concerned in economic decision-taking.

Every January the federal government presents to the Bundestag and Bundesrat the annual economic report which contains a response to the annual assessment of the Council of Experts, an outline of the economic and finance policy objectives pursued by the federal government in the current year and the planned economic policy.

Current objectives. Although prices rose moderately in recent years economic growth has increased and the number of people in work is also rising again; nevertheless the persistent high unemployment remains a serious problem. In this situation the federal government put its greatest effort into reinvigorating market forces and stimulating investment. Both are important prerequisites to reducing unemployment. The same aim is pursued by retraining and further-training programmes to keep workers fit for constantly changing demands on them. The federal government's policy on small and medium-sized businesses is designed to help them improve their efficiency which also contributes to the protection and creation of jobs.

The Federal Republic of Germany favours free world trade and rejects all forms of protectionism. Because it exports around 30 % of its GNP it depends on open markets. For the economy of the Federal Republic it is vital for the European internal market to be expanded and outside the European Community for old markets to be held and new ones developed.

Employment

In the first decades of the Federal Republic's existence the greatest influence on its labour market was the influx of expellees from the eastern territories and refugees from the GDR. Despite of great economic difficulties it was possible to integrate these millions of people into the work process. Indeed, they contributed greatly to the Federal Republic's economic advancement.

The labour force (including self-employed) rose from 20.4 millions in 1950 to 27.2 millions in 1965. From about 1960 onwards the increase of the workforce was due mainly to ever larger numbers of foreign workers streaming into the Federal Republic. In 1965 the number of "guest workers" (Gastarbeiter), as they are popularly called, had risen above a million and in 1973, at the peak of foreign worker employment, it was more than 2.6 million. Since then, recruitment of foreign workers has been cut, with the exception of those from European Community member countries. In 1984 there were 1.6 million foreign workers in the Federal Republic. The biggest contingent are the Turks, followed by Yugoslavs, Italians, Greeks and Spaniards.

For a decade and a half, from the late 1950's to the early 1970's, the Federal Republic enjoyed full employment; there was, in fact,

Gainfully employed by vocational status

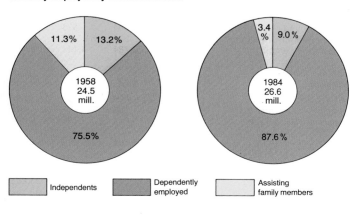

| Independents | Dependently employed | Assisting family members |

a labour shortage. With an annual average of around 150,000 the number of jobless fell to its lowest level. At the same time there were almost 800,000 job vacancies. Thereafter the labour force diminished gradually and the number of unemployed has been rising since 1974. It rose over a million in 1975 and since 1982 there have been more than two million jobless. Almost every 10th person capable of working was without a job.

There are various reasons for the high unemployment. A major one was certainly the international economic crisis of the 1970's. The inflationary development which appeared in all Western industrial countries was exacerbated by the explosion of petroleum and other raw material prices. But there are also causes for weak

Gainful employment
by economic sectors *(in 1,000's; annual averages)*

Sector	1960	1970	1980	1984
Agriculture, forestry, *stock raising, fishing*	3,623	2,262	1,436	1,376
Self-employed	1,159	767	513	502
Assisting family members	1,931	1,200	680	611
Dependently employed	533	295	243	263
Industrial production	12,518	13,024	11,633	11,130
Self-employed	808	653	565	553
Assisting family members	248	145	83	96
Dependently employed	11,462	12,226	10,985	10,481
Commerce and *transportation*	4,515	4,655	4,841	4,480
Self-employed	766	664	623	588
Assisting family members	˙272	207	96	88
Dependently employed	3,467	3,784	4,122	4,164
Other sectors *(services)*	5,591	6,727	8,392	9,262
Self-employed	541	606	660	787
Assisting family members	181	180	96	101
Dependently employed	4,869	5,941	7,636	8,374
Total	26,247	26,668	26,302	26,608
Self-employed	3,284	2,690	2,361	2,430
Assisting family members	2,632	1,732	955	896
Dependently employed	20,331	22,246	22,986	23,282

Unemployed and job vacancies *(in millions, annual average)*

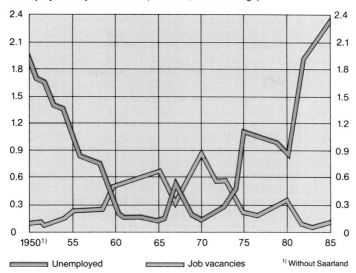

Unemployed ▬▬▬ Job vacancies ▭▭▭ [1] Without Saarland

growth and unemployment at home. The consumption proportion of GNP rose consistently until 1982. This took place at the expense of investments and hence growth and employment. This development was exacerbated by a high state debt and ever more bureaucratic hindrances to industry. And finally, the population also played a part. While the overall population is declining, the number of people able to work is rising. Moreover, many more women than before are now in the work process or seeking work and automation and microelectronics in industry and services have destroyed many hundreds of thousands of jobs.

It must not be forgotten that there are a number of groups hit especially hard by unemployment: the young, the under-qualified, the long-term unemployed, women and foreigners. Great efforts must be made by the state and industry to help them. If their problems cannot be solved, this could have serious repercussions on the Federal Republic's social and political stability.

For the time being there is nothing to indicate such repercussions. This is mainly because the social security system continues to function even though some supports have had to be cut as public funds got scarcer.

Unemployment insurance. Since 1927 there has been a statutory unemployment insurance scheme in Germany. It is covered today by a Labour Promotion Act (Arbeitsförderungsgesetz) of 1969. The authority administering the scheme is the Federal Employment Institute (Bundesanstalt für Arbeit) in Nürnberg (Nuremberg). Responsible to it are about 150 local labour exchanges (Arbeitsämter) with many sub-branches. All employees (except public servants), are subject to obligatory insurance (i. e. payment of dues into the scheme), regardless of how much they earn. Funds for the insurance are provided by both the employee and the employer. Any unemployed person whose previous employment was subject to insurance contribution and who is ready to accept "tolerable" employment offered by the labour exchange is entitled to draw unemployment benefits. The "unemployment benefit" (Arbeitslosengeld) is up to 68 % of the last net pay. As a rule it is paid at most for one year, in the case of unemployed people older than 49 at most for a year and a half. Thereafter anyone who is still unemployed can apply for "unemployment support" (Arbeitslosenhilfe) which can be up to 58 % of the net wage or salary, whereby other sources of income, including those of other family members, are taken into account.

Labour promotion. The Employment Institute has many other tasks, e. g. job placement and vocational guidance. A particularly important function is the promotion of vocational training. The agency gives juveniles and adults subsidies and loans for vocational training if they cannot raise the funds themselves. It also promotes vocational further-training and re-training in other skills. If further or re-training is necessary, e. g. to end unemploy-

Foreign workers in the Federal Republic of Germany

Country of origin	1973	1976	1979	1984
Total	2,595,000	1,921,000	1,934,000	1,593,000
From:				
Greece	250,000	173,000	140,000	98,000
Italy	450,000	279,000	300,000	214,000
Portugal	85,000	62,000	59,000	40,000
Spain	190,000	108,000	90,000	67,000
Turkey	605,000	521,000	540,000	500,000
Yugoslavia	535,000	387,000	367,000	289,000
Other countries	480,000	391,000	438,000	385,000

Foreign workers in a Ruhr coal mine

ment or to acquire a lacking vocational qualification, the agency covers the costs arising from participation under certain conditions and pays a sustenance benefit. Over and beyond this the agency also promotes vocational advancement by granting sustenance loans or covering costs during training. These benefits from the agency help especially the unemployed to adapt their skills to the rapidly changing demands on the labour market.

Labour market and vocational research is another of the Institute's functions. It continuously observes the type and extent of employment and development of the labour market, the vocations and vocational training opportunities. The research findings are submitted to the Federal Minister for Labour and Social Welfare as an aid to decision-taking.

Incomes and prices

Incomes. West Germans' incomes come from a wide range of sources. The major one by far is dependent employment, i. e. wages and salaries. In addition there are shareholders' dividends, property and assets and state transfer payments such as child allowances, unemployment benefits and pensions of various kinds. If from the sum of these incomes one subtracts the public levies, such as taxes and social insurance contributions, one arrives at the disposable income of private households.

In the Federal Republic of Germany this has risen from DM 207,000 millions in 1960 to DM 1,047,000 millions in 1983. This quintupling does not, however, mean that private households were able to buy more than five times as many goods and services in 1983 because one has to allow for price increases. Of the 1960 disposable income 83 % was used for private consumption and 17 % saved. Of the DM 1,047,000 millions in 1983, DM 100,000 millions, i. e. 9.6 %, was saved.

The increases enabled the people of the Federal Republic to spend an increasing share of their incomes for higher-valued goods and services, the so-called "consumer durables", i. e. things making life easier and more pleasant, such as motor cars,

Average employee monthly gross earnings in industry *(in DM)*

Branch	1970	1984	1970	1984
	Male wage earners		Male salary earners	
Industry overall	1,123	2,870	1,522	4,340
Energy production	1,161	3,209	1,468	4,165
Mining	1,133	3,107	1,505	4,757
Iron and steel	1,194	2,830	1,517	4,246
Petroleum processing	1,253	3,671	1,764	5,397
Chemicals	1,204	3,102	1,677	4,481
Machine construction	1,123	2,856	1,516	4,295
Road vehicle production	1,211	3,143	1,651	4,803
Electrical engineering	1,057	2,695	1,440	4,447
Textiles	977	2,444	1,490	3,769
	Female wage earners		Female salary earners	
Industry overall	777	2,076	1,001	2,886

Time worked for acquisition of necessaries

To be able to buy the goods listed an industrial worker had to work:

		1949		1957		1984	
		Hours	Minutes	Hours	Minutes	Hours	Minutes
Radio receiver		504	32	155	9	5	38
Men's shoes		20	23	12	20	5	46
1 kg coffee		22	37	9	12	1	28
1 kg cutlet		4	35	2	36	0	45
1 kg butter		4	13	3	18	0	40
1 kg sugar		0	58	0	33	0	8

labour-saving household appliances, more comfortable furniture, leisure pursuits, recreation and holidaymaking. In 1964 the statistical average monthly income of a four-person employee household was DM 904. Of this, DM 823 was spent on private consumption; in turn 64 % of this outlay went for food, clothing and housing. In 1984 the same type of household disposed of a monthly income of DM 3,474. It spent DM 2,849 on private consumption, of which only about half was for food, clothing and housing. This means that the ordinary family's financial scope has widened. However, other expenditures have increased substantially, e. g. that on transportation, telephone and postal charges from DM 73 to DM 465.

Prices and consumption. The standard of living depends not only on income but also prices. In the Federal Republic consumer prices development is one of the major issues of domestic politics. Opinion surveys have consistently shown that the main thing people expect of the government is that it keep prices stable. This is mainly because Germans personally experienced what devaluation of money means. They have suffered two enormous inflations this century, each resulting in collapse of the currency and sweeping destruction of financial assets.

Although the Federal Republic has not been able to evade the worldwide tendency of rising prices altogether, its authorities have, however, managed to contain the increases better than other countries.

International cost of living comparison *(1980 = 100)*

Country	1972	1977	1984
Australia	41.7	77.1	139.5
Austria	60.5	87.6	122.9
Belgium	54.1	85.9	134.0
Canada	49.8	76.4	137.6
Denmark	44.1	73.8	139.8
France	44.6	72.9	149.2
Germany, Federal Republic	67.7	88.7	118.4
Great Britain	32.5	69.0	133.4
Israel	3.8	16.1	5,522.3
Italy	30.4	64.1	174.3
Japan	46.9	86.1	112.1
Kenya	42.7	75.9	180.0
Mexico	23.9	57.0	679.2
Netherlands	56.8	86.0	119.6
Switzerland	70.0	91.8	119.3
Uruguay	1.7	25.4	336.5
USA	50.8	73.5	126.1

The price rises varied with the goods and services. The cost of electricity, gas and fuels, motor vehicles and rent have risen more strongly than others. The overall cost of living in the Federal Republic rose by up to 6 % a year since the 1970's. In the interim there were periods with less inflation. In April 1986 the cost of living was lower — by 0.2 % — for the first time in 27 years than in the same month of the previous year. This was due mainly to the drastic fall in the price of petroleum.

Price policy. In the Federal Government's view successful price policy can be pursued only with measures which do not tamper with the market mechanism. Interventionist measures would greatly disturb the system of self-steerage which has proved more effective than others. Apart from a small number of fields in which state intervention does take place (notably transportation and agriculture) prices form freely in the marketplace. State price policy is conducted mainly by means of credit, fiscal and competition policies.

Consumer protection

Supply and demand are the driving forces in the market economy. Suppliers and consumers face each other with equal rights. The entrepreneur is free to produce and offer any goods he chooses and the consumer is free to buy or reject these goods. The consumers have a vast choice when buying. There is an almost unlimited variety of goods. Products made in Germany compete with goods imported from all over the world. But so broad a variety always poses dangers to the consumer, too. Hardly anyone is able properly to assess quality and value for money. Although advertising does provide some information to help people decide its main aim is one-sidedly to influence buyers. On top of that, the odds are usually on the side of the seller. In the everyday situation the consumer mostly faces a well-informed businessman who knows more about what is on offer.

These consumer disadvantages are to be offset by consumer protection. This is done both by information and counselling and by legislation. Thus in 1964 the Federal Government established a goods and services testing foundation in Berlin (West). This "Stiftung Warentest" assesses and tests consumer goods of all kinds from the ballpoint pen to the prefabricated house, according to various quality and value for money criteria. It also examines their compatibility with the environment. The foundation publishes a monthly magazine ("test") with all the interesting results of these tests.

In addition people can get advice and support from state-supported consumer associations. Consumer information is also served by a number of labelling regulations, for example for foodstuffs. Food packages must indicate durability, conservation materials used, manufacturer and contents. The German Society for Product Information organises the cooperation of industry, commerce and consumers in standardising product information for many domestic appliances. This is done on the basis of a voluntary agreement between the groups involved and, as far as possible, within the framework of the European Community.

Over and above this, important legislative measures are taken to protect consumers. Some of the great number of them are to be presented here. Very often consumers got into trouble with the complicated terms of hire purchase contracts. An Instalment Payments Act, first adopted in 1970 and further improved four years later, gives the buyer clarity about the special obligations he enters into with instalment payment schemes. In cases of dispute court action can be initiated only at his place of residence, for only there can he properly defend himself. Very frequently it was the "small man" in particular who was steam-rollered at his front door by instalment payment transactions. But now the law gives him a week to cancel an order, time to think about the long-term commitments often involved — for instance, about a subscription to a publication or instalment purchase of a multi-volume reference work.

Since 1974 there has been a general ban on manufacturers or wholesalers dictating binding prices to retailers. The only exceptions still permitted are certain traditional publishing products such as books, newspapers, periodicals, sheet music and maps.

In 1977 a revision of the law as it affects "General Conditions of Sale" (Allgemeine Geschäftsbedingungen) went into force. This covers standard clauses in the shape of forms, or so-called "general forms of contract", unilaterally fixed by the entrepreneur (seller, owner of a repair workshop, chemical cleaners and so forth) which supplement, and above all are to standardise individual contracts. Frequently entire branches of business have such kinds of "General Conditions of Sale". For decades, the advantage was on the side of the economically stronger partner. The trail-blazing revision of 1977, however, has outlawed most of the abuses which used to occur. Especially important in practice is a provision of the new law according to which the customer is no longer presumed to accept general sales conditions without reference being made to them and without his having the opportunity to read them before engaging in a contract.

The long-standing duty of sellers of goods to mark their prices in display windows or sale rooms was extended to cover services, e. g. those of barbers and hairdressers, in 1973.

A Travel Law protects "package holidaymakers", i. e. those who buy from tour operators all-inclusive arrangements of transportation, accommodation and organisational attendance, from unfair business practices. Serious abuses to the customers' disadvantage, especially in air tourism, have been taking place in this field.

A Correspondence Instruction Law is to protect participants in correspondence courses from false advertising promises, questionable recruitment methods and financial exploitation.

Especially important, too, is consumers' protection from health and safety hazards. Thus cigarette advertising is banned on radio and television since the danger to health from smoking has been proven.

The Pharmaceuticals Law is to provide the necessary safety in the trading of medicines, especially in respect of quality, effectiveness and non-toxicity. In this connection mention must also be made of the Appliance Safety Law. It stipulates that the maker or importer may trade only in appliances which have been certified safe and are so designed that the user is protected against health hazards.

The consumer protection thus comprehensively strenghthened by the state is backed up and supplemented by private consumer protection associations, some of which have existed since the 1950's. The private "Association of Consumers" (Arbeitsgemeinschaft der Verbraucher, AGV), for example, runs more than 150 local advisory centres. They answer, free of charge, all possible consumer questions about the quality and prices of goods. These organisations receive financial support from the state. The mass media are devoting more and more attention to their work. When consumer protection laws are being prepared, the associations have the right to be heard by parliament. Several consumer protection laws give them the power to litigate as collective entities.

All advances notwithstanding, consumer protection is still not comprehensive enough in the Federal Republic. An important task in the coming years will be to deal satisfactorily with this new field of social policy.

Consumer organisation:
Arbeitsgemeinschaft der Verbraucher
Heilsbachstr. 20
5300 Bonn 1

Farming, forestry, fishing

The Federal Republic is not only highly industrialised, it also has an efficient agriculture producing about three quarters of its requirements.

Farming. Since World War II farming in Germany has undergone great change. A great number of farmers left the land to work in industry and service enterprises. Whereas in 1950, 20 out of 100 gainfully employed still worked in farming, it is now five. Over the same period the number of farms with more than a hectare of agricultural area fell from 1.6 million to fewer than 750,000.

Although land consolidation schemes have raised the number of medium-sized and larger farms since 1950, small and medium holdings up to 30 hectares are still in the majority. Almost half the farms are worked only part-time. That means that the main income of the families operating these farms comes from non-farming activites. This form of farming is especially prevalent in the southern part of the Federal Republic. An incomparably greater part in supplying the population is played by the fulltime farms because they work almost 90 % of the agricultural land.

Modern management methods and the replacement of human and animal labour by machines have brought astounding production successes. The increasing mechanisation in German agriculture is reflected, for example, by the number of combine harvesters which has grown from a few hundred in 1950 to about

Farms

Area used for agriculture		1949	1960	1971	1984
1 to less than	2 hectares	305,723	230,368	138,255	91,528
2 to less than	5 hectares	553,061	387,069	225,420	137,292
5 to less than	10 hectares	403,699	343,017	213,417	132,958
10 to less than	15 hectares	171,819	188,172	146,951	91,827
15 to less than	20 hectares	84,436	98,298	105,822	71,503
20 to less than	30 hectares	72,170	79,162	108,214	95,344
30 to less than	50 hectares	40,251	42,853	58,478	76,098
50 to less than 100 hectares		12,621	13,672	17,899	30,943
100 and more hectares		2,971	2,639	3,241	5,017
Total		1,646,751	1,385,250	1,017,697	732,510

Field crops (in 1,000 tonnes)

	1970	1975	1984
Wheat	5,662	7,014	10,223
Rye	2,665	2,125	1,931
Barley	4,754	6,971	10,284
Oats	2,484	3,445	2,507
Maize	507	531	1,026
Potatoes	16,250	10,853	7,272
Sugar beet	13,329	18,203	20,060

Livestock

	1970	1975	1984
Horses	252,500	341,000	370,200
Cattle	14,685,300	14,493,200	16,041,500
Pigs	19,627,200	19,805,100	23,683,700
Sheep	842,500	1,087,000	1,609,000
Fowl	98,600,700	88,705,200	78,708,200
Ducks	1,610,000	892,400	1,087,100

150,000. Particularly the specialised farms, such as for poultry raising or pig and cattle fattening, are today more like mechanised industrial plants than the farms of old. The progress made is illustrated by the fact that one German farmer now produces the food consumed by 60 people, compared with only 10 people in 1950.

The main crops are flour and feed grains, potatoes, sugar beet, vegetables, fruit and wine. Most farmers, especially in Niedersachsen (Lower Saxony), Bayern (Bavaria), Hessen and Schleswig-Holstein, raise production livestock, mostly cattle. The horse population, long declining, is again increasing slowly. Most are used for leisure riding.

The Common Agricultural Market. The Federal Republic of Germany is a member of the European Community. With the creation of the common agricultural market the most important areas of agricultural policy were made the responsibility of the European institutions, especially foreign trading, market and price policies and a large part of structural policy. The aims laid down for the common agricultural policy were raising agricultural productivity and thus farmers' incomes, stabilisation of markets, security of

Farm work against an industrial backdrop

supplies and fair consumer prices. Much was achieved in the two decades of common agricultural policy. But because of the enormous increase in production on the basis of guaranteed prices for many products (e. g. butter, meat, wine) the supply of food now exceeds demand by far. The overproduction is leading to a substantial fall in producer prices and hence farm incomes. The European Community is trying to bring production of these products down to sensible levels.

National agricultural policy. With most of the powers now delegated to the EC, few areas of responsibility remain for national agricultural policy. They include agricultural structural and social security policy. But regional, tax and environmental policy are also important focal areas. The top priority aim is to secure and strengthen family farms. The mixture of full and part-time farming is to be retained. In this way an important contribution can be made to promoting living conditions and development of rural regions and preserving the cultivation and recuperation landscape, reducing environmental burdens and improving protection of the natural foundations of life. Part of this is also to stop the trend towards farming operations on an industrial scale.

The main individual measures of state promotion are village modernisation, land consolidation and investment aids for modernising farms and residential houses. Income aids in deprived areas and subsidies to social security for farmers and their families are other major areas of national agricultural policy.

Forestry. The Länder with the largest forest areas are Bayern (Bavaria), Baden-Württemberg, Hessen and Rheinland-Pfalz (Rhineland-Palatinate). Overall, about a quarter of the Federal Republic's land is forest. The state and local authorities own about four million hectares of it, the other three million are private property.

The law demands that forest must be properly and consistently managed. Land laws oblige forest owners to replant harvested areas or to re-afforest thinned out ones.

Altogether about 30 million cubic metres of timber are harvested in the Federal Republic per year. But to meet domestic re-

Forestry

quirements large quantities of round and sawn timber and lignite have to be imported.

Forests are important not only as sources of timber but also as recreation areas for the inhabitants of industrial conurbations. Furthermore, they have a beneficial influence on soil, air and climate in that they retard water runoff, weaken wind impact, clean the air and provide protection against soil erosion and avalanches. In short, they are very important in protecting the environment.

A "Forest Preservation and Forestry Promotion Act" was enacted in the Federal Republic in 1975. This stipulates that forest can only be cleared for other uses of the land with approval from the relevant Land authority. To preserve or restore the natural appearance of the forests, more and more state forests are being taken out of commercial exploitation. They are planted with a mixture of trees and everything else is left to natural development. Since the early 1980's increasing damage has been found in the forests of the Federal Republic of Germany. The trees lose their needles or leaves, their growth slows down and finally they die. Nearly half the forest area in the Federal Republic is affected. The suspicion has hardened that this dying of the forests is due to a large degree to air pollution by industrial plants, motor exhaust fumes and domestic fuel burning. Part of the pollution is carried in by the wind from neighbouring countries.

The Bonn government is trying to cut air pollution by national and international activities. Many techniques are also being tried to save the forests.

Fishing. The fishing industry has also undergone structural changes in recent decades. Many states have expanded their fishing zones and traditionally important stocks were decimated by over-fishing. The great shrinkage of its fishing areas has reduced the high seas fishing fleet of the Federal Republic of Germany to 16 ships. In 1970 there were still 110.

In 1970 the European Community enacted regulations on the introduction of a joint structural policy for the fishing industry and a common market organisation for fish products. In 1977 the EC member states declared 200 sea-mile fishing zones in the North Atlantic and the North Sea. In these waters all member states are, in principle, permitted to fish as equals. Since 1983 an agreement regulates catch quotas, national coastal reserves and measures to sustain stocks. Despite the vast changes in maritime law and the limits to exploiting potential catches there is a basis for a re-

Herring fishing in the Baltic Sea

duced German high seas fleet and potential for developing smack fishing for certain varieties.

Food policy. The aim of the federal government's nutrition policy is to ensure adequate quantity, quality and variety of food supplies for the population at fair prices. Since there is a close connection between agricultural production and food supplies these two fields of policy are handled by one ministry. The Federal Ministry of Food, Agriculture and Forestry has to present a food report every legislative period in which — based on latest scientific findings — the nourishment situation and problems connected with it are comprehensively outlined to aid the federal and Länder governments in their health and agriculture policymaking. The report also serves as a basis for consumer education about proper nutrition and guides producers and processers in adapting their production to nutritional requirements.

High seas and coastal fish catches *(in tonnes)*

	1970	1976	1984
Total	591,411	425,832	293,170
comprising: Herring	166,285	22,752	25,098
Cod	174,335	106,380	68,282
Sea salmon	60,433	102,060	29,456
Redfish	71,552	54,696	27,831

The federal government supports research and dissemination of scientific findings about proper nutrition as well as information on offers and prices, favourable shopping opportunities and private stockkeeping, brought to consumers' attention in various ways, from the mass media to personal advice.

The average per capita food consumption has changed substantially in the Federal Republic in the past 25 years. There was an appreciable fall in the consumption of potatoes, cereal products, legumes and milk, while that of fruit, vegetables, cheese, eggs and meat, especially pork, rose considerably.

Farmers' association:
Deutscher Bauernverband
Godesberger Allee 142 — 148
5300 Bonn 2

Industry

Industry is concentrated in the Länder of Nordrhein-Westfalen (North-Rhine Westphalia), Bayern (Bavaria), Baden-Württemberg, Niedersachsen (Lower Saxony), Hessen and Saarland. It underwent a rapid upswing after the war. Today industry and the crafts together account for almost half the Gross National Product.

Policy. A major factor in this development was the 1948 changeover from the controlled economy to the social market economy order. One of the pillars of the market economy system is entrepreneurial self-responsibility, that is where the entrepreneur himself must see to his enterprise's growth and adjustment to changing conditions. The state restricts its intervention to furthering social balance and creating favourable economic frame conditions. The Federal Government takes the view that competition between enterprises is the best way to assure the technological

The largest industrial firms in the Federal Republic of Germany *(1984)*

Firm, base	Sector	Turnover (DM millions)	Employees
1. Veba AG, Düsseldorf	Energy, petroleum, chemicals	48,611	76,795
2. Siemens AG, Berlin-München	Electrical engineering	45,819	319,000
3. Volkswagenwerk AG, Wolfsburg	Motor vehicles	45,671	238,353
4. Daimler-Benz AG, Stuttgart	Motor vehicles	43,505	199,872
5. Bayer AG, Leverkusen	Chemicals	43,032	174,755
6. BASF AG, Ludwigshafen	Chemicals	42,596	115,816
7. Hoechst AG, Frankfurt	Chemicals	41,457	177,940
8. Thyssen AG, Duisburg	Iron and steel	32,430	132,954
9. Rheinisch-Westfälisches Elektrizitätswerk AG, Essen	Electricity	26,759	70,359
10. Ruhrkohle AG, Essen	Coal mining	22,415	135,857
11. Deutsche Shell AG, Hamburg	Petroleum	18,679	4,129
12. Bosch GmbH, Stuttgart	Electrical engineering	18,373	134,571

and structural competitiveness of German industry on world markets.

Structure. The number of industrial enterprises in the Federal Republic has been falling for years. In 1966 there were more than 100,000 processing enterprises; in 1983 it was only 45,000. More than half are small, employing fewer than 50 people, 42 % are medium-sized and employ from 50 to 500 and just under 5 % are large, with workforces over 500. Yet far more than half the industrial labour force works in the large enterprises which also account for more than half of the total industrial output. The sizes of enterprises vary from branch to branch. Large ones predominate in coal, steel and petroleum processing and in the chemical and motor vehicle construction industries.

Almost all large enterprises in the Federal Republic have the legal form of Aktiengesellschaft (limited company, stock corporation). In 1984 there were 2,118 such companies with a combined share capital of DM 103,000 millions. Of these, 665 companies with a capital of just under 47,000 millions were in processing.

The following are brief outlines of some of the major industrial branches.

Ironmaking. Until the mid-1970's ironmaking was one of the Federal Republic's major industries. After that it was thrown into a sales crisis by an over-supply on the world market. Especially hard hit by this was the heavy industry of the Ruhr and Saarland. By providing public funds the state has promoted modernisation of the steel industry. It is also promoting the attraction of new industries.

Chemicals. The most important basic materials and production goods branch in the Federal Republic is now the chemical industry. Of its total labour force of 586,000 almost half are employed by three large enterprises which are among the eight largest in the country as a whole. In 1984 the combined turnover of the Federal Republic's chemical industry was DM 170,400 millions.

Machine and vehicle construction. Of particular importance in the Federal Republic are the capital goods industries which include, above all, machine, road vehicle and aircraft manufacture, shipbuilding, electrical engineering and production of office machinery and data processing equipment.

Chemical plant

In 1984 3.5 million passenger cars, 237,000 lorries, 119,000 motor cycles and three million bicycles were produced. After the USA and Japan, the Federal Republic of Germany is the third largest automobile producer.

More than a million people work in machine manufacturing which in 1984 made a turnover of DM 142,000 millions, representing about 10 % of all industrial turnover.

The aerospace industry employs 54,000 people. In 1984 the branch turned over DM 8,700 millions. In relation to industry as a whole, the aerospace industry of the Federal Republic is not very large, but it is of considerable importance in terms of technological standard. It makes the highest technical demands on sub-contractors and co-producers and thus in many fields pioneers modern technologies. The development of civil aircraft has been supported by government credits and subsidies since 1963. The Bonn government's objective is to lead the German aircraft makers via joint projects into lasting links with other European enterprises and thereby to contribute to the urgently needed tightening and rationalisation of the structure of the European aerospace industry.

The traditionally strong position of European shipbuilders on the world market was put in question after World War II by the Japanese who today are the top shipbuilding nation. Together with other European countries the Federal Republic is trying to stay in the international running. The West German shipbuilding industry's 1984 turnover was DM 8,200 millions. Although shipbuilding accounts for not even one per cent of total industrial turnover, the branch is of great economic importance to the northern seaboard states of Hamburg, Bremen and Schleswig-Holstein.

Electrical engineering, office equipment, data processing. With its 1984 turnover of more than DM 155,000 millions, its 11 % share of total industrial output and a workforce of more than a million the electrical engineering industry (without data processing) ranks fifth in overall importance, after the food production, road vehicle production, chemicals and machine construction indus-

Automobile plant

Machine manufacture

tries. It is one of the branches with above-average growth and employs a wide range of new technologies.

The electronic data processing sector has a key function for the capital goods industry and beyond that for economic development as a whole. For this reason the state has long been trying to improve the competitiveness of German electronic data processing manufacturers by selective financial promotion. In 1984 Federal German manufacturers of office and data processing equipment had a turnover of around DM 22,000 millions.

Consumer goods, food, drink and tobacco. Total turnover of the Federal Republic's consumer goods industries in 1984 was DM 181,000 millions. The major branches in this sector are textiles and garments manufacture, together employing more than 558,000 people. The food, tobacco and drink industries had a 1984 turnover of DM 173,000 millions. The largest share of this was the food industry's which includes, for example, dairies and beer breweries.

Federation of industry:
Bundesverband der Deutschen Industrie
Gustav-Heinemann-Ufer 84–88
5000 Köln 51

Raw material and energy supplies

Compared with its international rank as an industrial nation the Federal Republic is notably poor in raw material resources of its own. It depends largely on imports for its raw material and energy needs. This foreign dependence is particularly great in mineral raw materials (e. g. copper, bauxite, manganese, titanium, rock phosphate, wolfram and tin). The Federal Republic has its own modest deposits of iron ore and petroleum. Up to a third of the natural gas consumed can be supplied from local sources. The deposits of hard coal, brown coal and salt are sufficiently rich and economic to warrant extraction for many decades to come.

Raw materials and mining. The major hard coal deposits are in the Ruhr region (Nordrhein-Westfalen [North-Rhine Westphalia]) and Saarland. Economically extractable reserves are estimated at 24,000 million tonnes of hard and about 35,000 million tonnes of brown coal. The brown coal lies mainly in the region of the foothills of the Harz mountains (near Helmstedt) and in the Lower Rhenish Bight (Ville hills, near Köln [Cologne]).

Whereas brown coal has proved relatively crisis-free, hard coal mining has been declining for a considerable time since sales to its major users, steelmakers and electricity producers, have also been falling. Hard coal has had to cede its former predominance as a source of energy to petroleum, natural gas and

Primary energy consumption in the Federal Republic of Germany
(in mill. tons hard coal; shares in %)

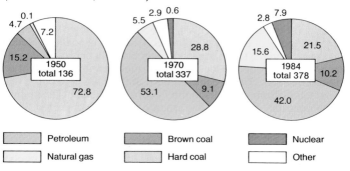

1950 total 136 — 0.1, 4.7, 7.2, 15.2, 72.8

1970 total 337 — 2.9, 0.6, 5.5, 28.8, 9.1, 53.1

1984 total 378 — 2.8, 7.9, 15.6, 21.5, 10.2, 42.0

| Petroleum | Brown coal | Nuclear |
| Natural gas | Hard coal | Other |

Brown coal excavator in open-cut mining

nuclear power. Thus the hard coal share of energy production fell from 73 % in 1950 to 21.5 % in 1984.

But the use of petroleum is also declining. Because of the high prices of oil on the world market and the promotion of other energy sources the oil share fell from 55 % in 1973 to 42 % in 1984. The oil crisis since the mid-1970's in particular has shown how important continuity of energy supplies is. That is why coal production will remain important because coal is the only source of energy for which the Federal Republic of Germany is not dependent on other countries. The processed hard and brown coal comes almost totally from deposits in the Federal Republic of Germany.

By contrast, almost all the crude oil must be imported. Main supplier countries are Great Britain, Libya, Nigeria, Saudi Arabia, Venezuela and the Soviet Union.

The Federal Republic's own oil deposits, estimated at 68 million tonnes, are in the North German Plain, the Upper Rhenish

Lowland and the Alpine Foothills. Local production has been declining for many years. Hopes of discovering oil in the German sector of the North Sea have so far been in vain.

Home production prospects of the next most important energy source, natural gas, look more promising. Following new discoveries in the north-western Emsland region bordering on the Netherlands and in the North Sea, natural gas reserves are estimated at 300,000 to 500,000 million cubic metres. Natural gas accounts for 15 % of energy consumption. Of this, about one third comes from West German fields. Major foreign suppliers are the Netherlands, Norway and the Soviet Union.

There are small deposits of uranium in the Federal Republic. But all the enriched uranium needed for nuclear energy has to be imported.

Energy production. A secure energy supply is one of the prerequisites for the functioning of a modern economy and the satisfaction of people's basic needs. Without adequate energy the necessary growth, and thus jobs, cannot be secured. Reliable, timely and favourably priced energy is crucial to international competitiveness. All forms of energy damage the environment, some more, some less. In view of the burdens already on the environment careful use of all energy sources is a priority task for energy producers and consumers. That is why, in the view of the Federal Government, the energy producers should ensure that the environment is not over-burdened by building clean power stations or fitting filters. In the unanimous view of all great industrial states it would be impossible to keep the world adequately supplied with energy in the coming decades without the use of nuclear generation of electricity. This is particularly so in the Federal Republic, poor as it is in alternative energy raw materials.

Like everywhere else in the world, energy consumption in the

Extraction, import and export of mining products (*in 1,000 tonnes*)

	Domestic production		Imports		Exports	
	1970	1984	1970	1984	1970	1984
Hard coal	111,271	79,426	9,138	8,847	15,906	11,116
Brown coal	107,766	126,739	1,103	2,615	968	860
Petroleum	7,535	4,055	98,786	66,934	134	5
Iron ore (effective)	6,762	977	48,128	42,924	10	3
Potash salts	21,030	29,543	–	–	48	42

Federal Republic has risen continuously. Estimated future growth in electricity consumption demands expansion of generating capacity from the present 82,000 megawatt by about 28,000 megawatt. Construction of nuclear power stations which already produce 36 % of the public electricity supply is indispensable to achieve this. Nineteen nuclear power stations are in operation in the Federal Republic, three of which are research reactors. More are being built.

Construction and operation of the nuclear power stations have long been the subject of public controversy. Although experience gained in the use of nuclear energy shows that nuclear power is a safe source of energy, easy on the environment, many fear that the environment might be damaged and there could be disasters. There is a great number of civic action groups agitating against nuclear electricity production.

The Bonn government is trying to allay these misgivings by effective safety measures and public information drives. Because of the federative structure of the Federal Republic the expansion of nuclear energy depends mainly on the federal states which issue the construction licenses for nuclear power stations. Several times court rulings have stopped construction works already in progress. No satisfactory solution has yet been found for the waste disposal problem. A 1977 updating of the federal energy programme foresees radioactive waste from nuclear power stations being stored deep in a huge salt deposit in northern Germany.

Energy policy. The Federal Government is striving for close international cooperation in energy policy within the European Community, between the industrial states within the International Energy Agency and with the developing countries. Emphases in the Federal Government's energy policy continue to be:

☐ energy saving and sensible use of energy;

☐ cutting the supply share of the riskiest energy source, oil, while raising the shares of coal, gas, nuclear energy and the renewable energy sources; special consideration for the preference for German hard coal in electricity production;

☐ distribution of the imports of all energy sources, especially oil, among as many states as possible;

☐ energy production and consumption sparing on the environment.

The Federal Republic of Germany has made much headway in energy saving since 1973. From 1978 to 1983 alone the consump-

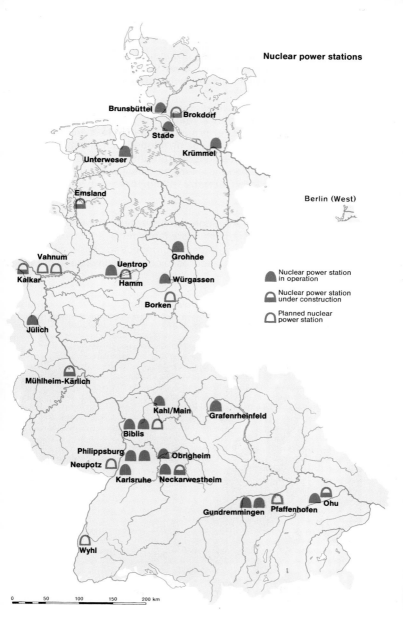

Nuclear power stations

Brunsbüttel
Brokdorf
Stade
Krümmel
Unterweser
Emsland
Vahnum
Grohnde
Kalkar
Uentrop
Hamm
Würgassen
Borken
Jülich
Mühlheim-Kärlich

Berlin (West)

Nuclear power station
in operation

Nuclear power station
under construction

Planned nuclear
power station

Kahl/Main
Grafenrheinfeld
Biblis
Philippsburg
Obrigheim
Neupotz
Karlsruhe
Neckarwestheim
Gundremmingen
Pfaffenhofen
Ohu
Wyhl

0   50   100   150   200 km

tion of heating oil, for example, dropped from 29 to 20 litres per square metre of accomodation. Over the same period fuel consumption of new motor vehicles was cut by almost 17 % (or 1.7 litres per 100 kilometres).

The government subsidies for German hard coal mining amount to DM 5,000 millions a year.

Although the present energy supply situation is favourable, renewable energy sources must be developed. But one must warn against exaggerated expectations from these alternatives such as solar, geothermal or wind energies. Their share in supplying the Federal Republic of Germany will be very small for the foreseeable future.

Raw materials policy. Although the security of the Federal Republic's raw material supplies is presently not in doubt, the overall supply situation necessitates the prospecting of new deposits at home and abroad and measures to counteract wastage of raw materials.

Fuelling a nuclear reactor

Solar heating plant for an outdoor swimming pool

Recycling, the processing and utilisation of residues and wastes and the reintegration of scrap materials into the economic cycle, is growing increasingly important. The same holds for substitution, the replacement of one raw material by another, often synthetic one.

To safeguard continuity of supply against temporary disturbances such as strikes, blockage of transport routes or interruption of imports, the raw material-consuming industries keep reserve stockpiles.

The federal government sees the best precondition for secure raw material supplies in keeping world markets functioning. In its efforts to safeguard free international trade it is supported by the market economy-oriented Western countries.

On the other hand, however, the federal government is also striving for cooperation with the state trading countries in raw material prospecting and extraction because many important materials occur in precisely these countries.

The Federal Republic's cooperation with the raw material-rich but under-industrialised countries rests on the following principles:

☐ maintaining the functionability and growth of the world economy;

☐ stabilisation of commodity export earnings, particularly of the least developed countries, and securing continuity of raw material supplies;

☐ acceleration of industrialisation in the developing countries and easing technology transfer from industrial to developing countries;

☐ opening the markets of the industrial countries to the imports of finished and semi-finished goods from the developing countries;

☐ promotion of a continuous transfer of capital to the developing countries and protection of investors from disappropriation;

☐ increasing transfer of resources in favour of the developing countries by greater help from *all* countries able to provide it.

The crafts

"Handwerk hat goldenen Boden", says an old German adage, "a manual trade has a golden foundation". The saying dates from the Middle Ages when the crafts were in full bloom. Elaborately ornamented guild houses and many mighty cathedrals throughout the country still testify to the accomplishment and cultural importance of medieval German craftsmen.

The trades in the industrial age. The free crafts appeared seriously jeopardised by the advancing 19th century industrial revolution. Many did not survive the fierce competition with the vastly cheaper, mass-produced industrial goods. Others were reduced to repair work — such as the shoe and watch makers. But in many fields — where very specialised needs must be met, where personal accomplishment and above all close personal contact with the customer are important — the independent trades are holding their own. Butchers and bakers are examples.

Moreover, industry itself has created new manual trades, such as those of the electrician and motor mechanic. Introduction of the electric motor and establishment of purchasing and credit cooperatives greatly improved the craftsmen's competitiveness. On the whole the crafts have shown great adaptability, holding their own alongside the other branches of the economy.

Economic importance. The number of craft businesses in the Federal Republic fell from 902,800 in 1949 to 463,600 in 1984. But their combined and individual workforce has grown in the same period, from 3.2 to 3.7 million, making a statistical average of eight employees per business. Accounting for about 9 % of the gross domestic product, the crafts sector is of great economic importance in the Federal Republic, ranking third after industry and commerce.

By size of workforce, the major trade is that of the stone and concrete masons. Then follow the building cleaners, the motor mechanics, the bakers, the butchers, the barbers and hairdressers, the cabinet makers, the painters and the electricians. By turnover, the masons, the road vehicle repairers and the butchers top the list.

A display of a fair cross section of the broad range of craft pro-

Apprentice training

duction is given each year by the International Light Industries and Handicrafts Fair in München (Munich). With more than 1,400 exhibitors and more than 400,000 visitors it is the largest fair of its kind in the world.

State support. The Federal Government supports medium-sized enterprises to strengthen and secure their efficiency and competitiveness and to help them adapt to structural changes ("help towards self-reliance"). This promotion covers tax relief, entrepreneurial consulting and soft loans with long maturing periods.

Organisation. The plying of a trade and the vocational training in it are permitted only to persons listed in the Crafts Register (Handwerksrolle), the roll of independent craftsmen in a Crafts Chamber's (Handwerkskammer) district. The usual qualification is a master tradesman's examination. A master craftsman must

Employment and turnover in the crafts *(1984)*

Trade	Employees	Turnover (in mill. DM)
Total	3,774,000	329,139
Stone and concrete masons	607,000	54,003
Building cleaners	369,000	4,139
Motor vehicle mechanics	245,000	46,275
Bakers	214,000	15,923
Butchers	204,000	30,539
Barbers and hairdressers	202,000	5,667
Cabinet makers	192,000	17,620
Painters and varnishers	181,000	10,751
Electricians	179,000	13,942
Plumbers, gas and water installers	121,000	10,320
Fitters and turners	115,000	11,830
Radio and television technicians	30,000	3,893

be at least 24 years old to employ and train apprentices. The crafts play an important role in training skilled workers in the Federal Republic of Germany. The number of trainees with craft enterprises in 1984, for example, was some 700,000, two fifths of all trainees in the Federal Republic.

At municipal (Stadtkreis) or county (Landkreis) level tradesmen are grouped together in craft guilds for their specific fields. Their main responsibility is vocational training and further qualification. They can also conclude collective agreements and set up health insurance funds for their members.

The self-administration organs of the crafts as a whole are the Chambers of Crafts (Handwerkskammern). Their tasks include

Share of the crafts of important economic data

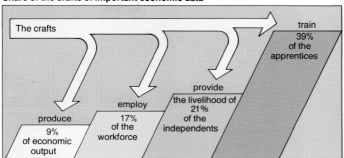

Expanding and shrinking crafts *(by number employed)*

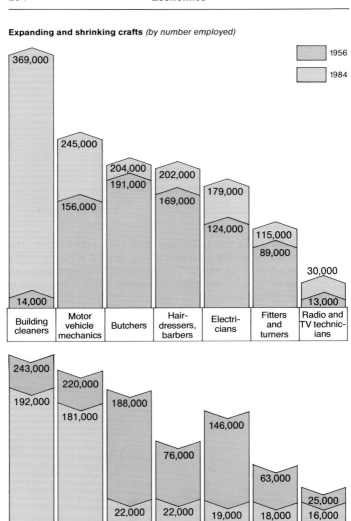

1956

1984

Building cleaners: 369,000 / 14,000

Motor vehicle mechanics: 245,000 / 156,000

Butchers: 204,000 / 191,000

Hair-dressers, barbers: 202,000 / 169,000

Electri-cians: 179,000 / 124,000

Fitters and turners: 115,000 / 89,000

Radio and TV technic-ians: 30,000 / 13,000

Joiners: 243,000 / 192,000

Painters and varnishers: 220,000 / 181,000

Tailors: 188,000 / 22,000

Printers, typesetters: 76,000 / 22,000

Shoe-makers: 146,000 / 19,000

Smiths: 63,000 / 18,000

Watch-makers: 25,000 / 16,000

keeping the Crafts (Handwerksrolle) and Apprentices (Lehrlings-rolle) Registers and supervising vocational training and examinations. All formal apprenticeships in Germany are contracts which have to be listed in the Lehrlingsrolle.

The umbrella organisation of the guilds and craft chambers is the Central Organisation of German Crafts (Zentralverband des Deutschen Handwerks).

Association of craft entrepreneurs:
Zentralverband des Deutschen Handwerks
Johanniterstr. 1
5300 Bonn 1

Commerce

Commerce has developed over the past hundred years into an important sector of the national economy. In fulfilling its distribution functions it facilitated the emergence of a modern economy based on division of labour. In the Federal Republic of Germany about 3.5 million people work in the approximately 550,000 commercial enterprises (wholesale, retail, agents).

Wholesale trade. The wholesale enterprises sell commercial goods to other traders, processors, industrial users and bulk consumers. Wholesalers supply production enterprises with capital goods, raw, support and operating commodities and retailers with frangibles and consumer durables. Wholesale turnover rose from c. DM 50,000 millions in 1949 to DM 810,000 millions in 1984. Competition and costs pressure in this sector have grown in recent years, albeit varying in individual branches. Smaller and less

Modern shopping centre

Index of retail prices *(1976 = 100)*

Trading groups	1980	1984
Total retail trade	116.1	134.5
Food and fine fare	118.8	130.0
Clothing, footwear	120.7	139.4
Hardware, household effects, furnishings	120.2	142.3
Electrical, fine-mechanical and optical products, jewelry, leather, gifts, toys	114.5	123.8
Paper and print products	112.0	133.6
Pharmaceutical and cosmetic products	112.8	131.1
Coal, other solid fuels, petroleum products	154.0	185.4
Vehicles, machinery, office equipment	115.1	134.1
Other goods	114.5	131.0

efficient enterprises dropped out of the market. Rationalisation has strongly reduced the wholesaling labourforce in recent years. It stood at around a million in 1980.

Retail trade. As the last link in the distribution system and in direct contact with the final consumers the retail trade has undergone remarkable development in the past two and a half decades. In the manner of offer and stock ranges as well as in the development of operational forms retail trading underwent revolutionary changes. The advancement of self-service which began in grocery retailing underwent a major simplification of procedures. New types of operation, such as discount or consumer markets, came into being which tried by their own marketing policies to adjust in new ways to the continuously changing consumer needs and demands.

Retail turnover rose from DM 28,000 millions in 1949 to DM 468,000 millions (including value-added tax) in 1984. Sharp competition reduced the number of enterprises from some 445,000 in 1962 to c. 360,000 in 1984. The retailing workforce has also fallen in recent years. It stood at about 2.3 millions in 1984.

The motorisation of a broader section of the populace, the trends towards collective and bulk buying and the advance of problem-free articles favoured the consumer markets and self-service department stores. However, it has been shown that small and medium-sized retailers have their chances vis-à-vis the large enterprises where the customer is looking for items of

Small "corner store"

his own choice, a varied range, qualified advice and personalised service. Membership in cooperative forms has also helped many small and medium businesses to hold or even expand their market positions. Their future will depend crucially on whether these businesses are ready and willing to adapt to changing market conditions.

Retailers' organisation:
Hauptgemeinschaft des Deutschen Einzelhandels
Sachsenring 89
5000 Köln 1

Wholesalers' and foreign traders' organisation:
Bundesverband des Deutschen Gross- und Aussenhandels
Kaiser-Friedrich-Str. 13
5300 Bonn 1

Intra-German trade

Trade between the Federal Republic of Germany and the German Democratic Republic is neither internal nor external trade, since the Federal Republic recognises the GDR as a sovereign but not foreign state. Because of this special relationship there are many peculiarities in intra-German trade.

The formal basis for the trade between the two German states is an agreement concluded in 1951 in Berlin, long before government-level contacts were officially taken up. The agreement also applies to Berlin (West). There are no official exchange rates between the currencies of the two German states. Payments within the framework of this trade are accounted for through the Federal Republic's Deutsche Bundesbank and the GDR's State Bank. A "unit of account" is used which can be equated with DM 1. The GDR has been conceded an interest-free credit line with the Bundesbank known as the "swing" and currently equivalent to 850 million units of account. In 1984 the GDR used 211 million units of account under the "swing" arrangement. Intra-German trade is free of tariffs and adjustment levies to even out price differences.

The Federal Republic buys from the GDR mainly petroleum products, chemical products, agricultural products, textiles and garments. The main GDR purchases from the Federal Republic are chemical products, agricultural products, machinery, vehicles, iron and steel.

Between 1951 and 1982 the value of the purchases of the Federal Republic from the GDR rose from some 120 million to 6,700 million units of account, the value of deliveries to the GDR from 150 million to 6,400 million units of account. After many years of the Federal Republic's delivering more to the GDR than receiving from there, intra-German trade was balanced in 1980. In 1981 and 1982 the Federal Republic again bought more from the GDR than it sold there, the first time since 1965. In 1984 purchases from the GDR totalled 8,240 million units of account, a rise of 9 % on 1983. Sales to the GDR fell 6 % from the 1983 level to 7,250 million units of account.

In economic terms, intra-German trade is much more important for the GDR than for the Federal Republic. Its value is equal to about 2 % of the Federal Republic's foreign trade volume whereas trade with the Federal Republic comprises about 10 %

Intra-German trade *(in 1,000 million Units of Account)*

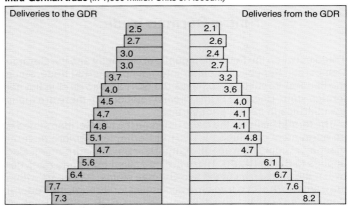

Deliveries to the GDR	Deliveries from the GDR
2.5	2.1
2.7	2.6
3.0	2.4
3.0	2.7
3.7	3.2
4.0	3.6
4.5	4.0
4.7	4.1
4.8	4.1
5.1	4.8
4.7	4.7
5.6	6.1
6.4	6.7
7.7	7.6
7.3	8.2

of the GDR's volume of external trade. Because of the economic advantages it derives from it the GDR accepts the special nature of intra-German trade, although in other fields it strictly rejects any notion of special relations between the two German states. The Federal Republic for its part promotes intra-German trade above all for political reasons. The fact that Berlin (West) has, from the beginning, been included in the Intra-German Trade Agreement is held by Bonn to be particularly important. Beyond this the trade serves as a link between the two German states whose existence contributes to lessening political differences.

Foreign trade

External relations are of major importance to the West German economy. From the outset the Federal Republic opted for integration into the world economy and committed itself to the principle of international division of labour. This stance is in line with a liberal foreign trade policy which has always been directed towards dismantling tariffs and other barriers to trade.

External equilibrium and export dependence. The total value of the Federal Republic's imports and exports rose from DM 19,700 millions in 1950 to DM 922,500 millions 1984. Hence the Federal Republic is second after the United States in world trade. A special feature of German foreign trade is that since 1952 exports have exceeded imports, despite considerable DM revaluations. The exports surplus rose year after year from DM 706 millions in 1952

Exports and imports of the Federal Republic of Germany *(actual values)*

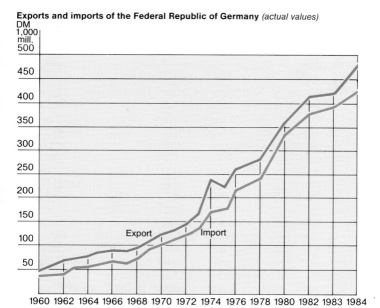

DM
1,000 mill.

1960 1962 1964 1966 1968 1970 1972 1974 1976 1978 1980 1982 1983 1984

Foreign trade of the Federal Republic of Germany 1984

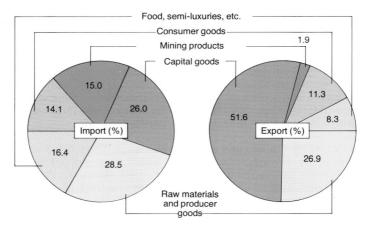

to DM 54,000 millions in 1984. For a number of years the balance was under considerable strain because of the greatly increased cost of imported oil. But since 1982 surpluses have been clearly higher again and the 1984 surplus was the highest since the Federal Republic has existed.

The large export surpluses of the Federal Republic of Germany were sometimes criticised abroad. But they were necessary to offset deficits in other fields. Because of the low export surpluses this offsetting was no longer possible in the period 1979 to 1981. For example, in 1980 DM 13,000 millions more flowed abroad than came in for services; the biggest item here was the high expenditure of German tourists. The remissions of foreign workers in the Federal Republic to their homelands amounted to DM 7,500 millions, and the Federal Republic paid DM 4,100 millions more into the European Community than it received from it. These and other payments far exceeded the export surplus. The current account went into the red, the deficit totalling DM 28,600 millions. The external economic balance was thus sensitively disturbed. Because of relatively low imports and above-average rises in exports a positive current account balance of DM 8,200 millions was again reached in 1982. This positive trend continued in subsequent years; the 1984 surplus was DM 17,700 millions.

Every fourth gainfully active person in the Federal Republic works for export. So large a dependency on foreign trade is due to the fact that the Federal Republic is a densely populated industrial country with few raw material resources of its own. But it has a high standard of technology, a highly skilled workforce and an efficient productive sector. These assets have to be put to use in foreign trade in order to pay for imports of foodstuffs, raw materials and energy sources and also for industrial goods which can be produced better or more cheaply in other countries.

At the top of the list of exports from the Federal Republic are motor vehicles, machinery of all kinds, chemical and electrical engineering products. On the imports side the major items are petroleum and natural gas as well as foods, fine fare and tobacco.

But the close interlinkage between the German economy and that of other countries also entails dependencies. The Federal Republic is vulnerable to all disturbances in world trade — jobs, investments, profits and standard of living depending on how it develops. A stable world economy, free trade and an orderly monetary system are therefore vital to the German national economy.

Container wharves in Hamburg

The Federal Republic of Germany's main trading partners in 1985

DM 1,000 mill.	Import from:	Export to:	DM 1,000 mill.
58.3	Netherlands	France	64.0
49.3	France	USA	55.6
37.2	Great Britain	Netherlands	46.3
37.2	Italy	Great Britain	46.0
32.3	USA	Italy	41.8
29.1	Belgium/Luxembourg	Belgium/Luxembourg	37.0
20.7	Japan	Switzerland	28.9
17.2	Switzerland	Austria	27.4
15.3	Austria	Sweden	14.7
13.6	USSR	Denmark	11.8
11.0	Norway	USSR	10.5
Producer countries	10.9 Sweden	Spain 9.7	Consumer countries

Trading partners. Since the coming into force of the EC treaty in 1958 the member states of the European Community have step by step implemented the objective of the customs union, that is they have freed trade exchange between them of all tariffs and quantity restrictions. As a result the Federal Republic's trade with the other EC states increased on a scale which far exceeds that with other countries. In 1984 about 48 % of the Federal Republic's imports came from EC states while the Federal Republic also sold them 48 % of its exports.

The Federal Republic's two biggest trading partners are France and the Netherlands. On the suppliers list of German importers the Netherlands takes first place, France second. France was the biggest buyer of German exports, followed by the USA. Exports to the USA profited from the economic upswing there and the strong dollar.

The Federal Republic's imports have been a major support in maintaining economic activity in its partner countries. Especially the developing countries which produce no oil benefit from this. Their exports of finished goods to the Federal Republic grew strongly. Oil imports from the OPEC countries have fallen substantially; here the energy savings of recent years are making themselves felt. In the Federal Republic's exchange of goods with the state trading nations the direction of flow has changed in the 1980's. Imports from there grew above average, exports to there below average. This resulted in a negative trade balance following the strong surpluses of the 1970's.

The Federal Republic's exports and imports by groups of countries
(in DM millions)

Group of countries	Imports from 1970	1984	Exports to 1970	1984
Western industrial countries	87,427	337,697	104,715	395,711
thereof:				
EC countries	48,437	208,035	50,259	232,812
Other European	16,634	70,776	28,344	93,853
USA and Canada	13,917	35,154	12,618	51,155
Others	8,439	23,732	13,494	17,891
Developing countries	17,684	69,894	14,904	67,672
thereof:				
Africa	6,688	23,571	3,494	14,454
America	5,343	16,289	5,114	11,972
Asia	5,611	29,206	6,224	41,121
Oceania	43	828	72	125
East Bloc countries	4,394	26,423	5,400	23,325
thereof:				
Europe	4,036	23,597	4,760	20,259
World total	109,606	434,257	125,276	488,223

Foreign investment. Another component of external economic relations is foreign investment, whose importance to the economy of the Federal Republic is growing. Securing and widening export markets is one of the main motives for investing abroad. This is particularly so in the case of machine manufacture and consumer goods production. The basic materials and producer goods industry primarily seeks proximity to raw material deposits. Cost advantages and avoidance of trade barriers also play a large part in deciding whether to invest abroad. Of the 1983 DM 123,000 millions German investments abroad, about 76% were made in Western industrial, and 11% in developing countries (without the OPEC countries).

The Bonn government is trying to overcome the difficulties in the way of German investment in the less industrialised countries — such as lack of sophisticated infrastructure, skilled labour and small popular purchasing power — by various support measures. In particular it gives soft loans and grants for investment by small and medium enterprises. The German Finance Company for Investments in Developing Counties (Deutsche Finanzierungsgesellschaft für Beteiligungen in Entwicklungsländern) also promotes German investments there by intensive counselling, taking on participations and granting of loans. The Bonn government tries to lessen the political risks which can be connected with investments in developing countries by entering into agreements with them.

Foreign direct investment in the Federal Republic is also constantly growing and in 1983 stood at some DM 81,000 millions. Nine tenths of this came from Europe and America.

Wholesale and foreign traders:
Bundesverband des Deutschen Gross- und Aussenhandels
Kaiser-Friedrich-Str. 13
5300 Bonn 1

Cooperation with developing countries

Economic and social conditions in the Third World vary from country to country. But practically all developing countries fit the following description: inadequate food suppply, poor health of the population, inadequate education possibilities, unemployment, low standard of living with often extremely inequitable distribution of the goods and services available. In most developing countries the population is growing especially fast. This leads to population growth and economic growth not keeping in step.

Development aid policy of the Federal Republic of Germany. Development aid policy is part of the global peace policy of the Federal Government. At a time of growing tensions and crises it sees a major development support goal in contributing to political stability by economic and social development in the Third World.

In view of the sickness, hunger and misery in many developing countries, fighting absolute poverty, at state and private levels, is the supreme objective of the aid policy of the Federal Republic of Germany. That is why particularly high priority is given to meeting basic needs, such as the minimum food requirement, housing, clothing, access to vital public services such as clean drinking water, sanitary facilities, public transport, health and education facilities.

Development aid can only ever be help towards self-reliance. It can only complement, not replace, the developing countries' own efforts. Decisive to whether a country develops are the political and economic frame conditions it sets itself. A policy which encourages the creative efforts of the individual instead of smothering them by state regimentation, which aims at social balance and preservation of human rights, an agricultural policy which gives farmers an incentive to produce by sensible prices for their products — these are essential preconditions for development. In constant dialogue with the partner countries in the Third World the Federal Republic works towards frame conditions being created which enable development cooperation to unfold its full potential.

Official development aid. The Federal Republic of Germany cooperates with the developing countries bilaterally and multilaterally. Part of the multilateral cooperation are the contributions to the specialised agencies of the United Nations, to the World Bank and its subsidiaries and to the Development Fund of the European Community. The bilateral cooperation covers all direct disbursements of the Federal Republic of Germany to a specific developing country or to a group of developing countries.

A distinction is made between financial cooperation, i. e. the granting of loans on preferential terms, and technical cooperation, i. e. the assignment of experts and advisers, delivery of capital goods and provision of training free of charge to the developing country. Loans are given mainly for infrastructure and industrialisation projects. Agriculture and rural development are promoted mainly within the technical aid framework, i. e. with grant funds.

A special form of help is debt cancellation. So far the Federal Republic has cancelled the debts on earlier development loans of 24 of the least developed countries. It has written off more than DM 4,000 millions in capital and interest, representing 60 % of the debt cancellations worldwide. All bilateral official aid for the least developed countries is now given as grants.

Private development aid. Many projects to improve the social infrastructure and social welfare, education, health and so on are supported by private or parastatal organisations of the Federal Republic of Germany. These private organisations cooperate with partners in the developing countries which are often better able than state agencies to mobilise self-help among the population. Among the main ones are the churches, trade unions, foundations and voluntary services. The churches are mostly involved in education and health and run many social centres in the developing countries. Their projects are financed partly by public donations, partly by government funds. Several foundations, some with close links to political parties, work in socio-political education. Other organisations involved in private development aid are the German Red Cross, the German Freedom from Hunger Campaign, the German Adult Education Association, Kolpingwerk, Medico International, German Leprosy Relief, Terre des hommes, Andheri-Hilfe and many others.

The German Volunteer Service set up in Bonn in 1963, whose partners are the Federal Republic of Germany and the "Arbeitskreis Lernen und Helfen in Übersee", assigns development helpers who forego financial and vocational privileges to contribute to development of the country concerned. Voluntary helpers are al-

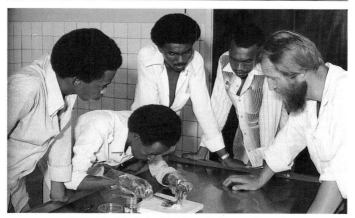

*Staff of the Technical Institute in Burao, Somalia,
with a German adviser*

so sent out by the church organisations, "Arbeitsgemeinschaft für Entwicklungshilfe" and "Dienste in Übersee".

Direct investments by German enterprises and private persons in developing countries are of great importance to the economic development of the countries they flow to. They create jobs in these countries, enable them to earn or save foreign exchange, raise tax revenue and contribute to broadly based transfer of technical knowhow.

The Federal Government promotes investment by private companies in the developing countries in many ways, e. g. by assigning advisers to bring German firms and firms in developing countries together, by federal guarantees for capital investment and by the activities of the federal government-owned German Finance Company for Investment in Developing Countries.

Scale of the aid. Using the internationally agreed computing criteria, the private and official aid disbursements of the Federal Republic of Germany to developing countries reached DM 18,500 millions in 1984. Their proportion of GNP was 1.06 %. The 1 % level set for this by the United Nations was thus exceeded. Total official development aid was DM 7,900 millions, corresponding to 0.45 % of GNP. With this the Federal Republic, as in previous years, lies clearly above the average aid of all Western industrial countries which is 0.36 %.

Disbursements of the Federal Republic of Germany to developing countries *(in DM mill.)*

	1979	1984	1950 — 1984
Official cooperation	6,140	7,916	94,713
Bilateral	3,961	5,315	67,727
Multilateral	2,180	2,601	26,986
Other public disbursements	205	2,831	16,735
Private development aid	714	1,088	9,353
Commercial disbursements	6,301	6,681	120,949
Bilateral	4,560	5,722	101,157
Multilateral	1,701	959	19,792
Total disbursements	13,360	18,516	241,750

Private development aid (disbursements by non-statal organisations such as churches, foundations and associations) reached a record of more than DM 1,000 millions in 1984.

Over and beyond official development aid, however, it is indispensable to improve conditions for greater economic growth through more trade. A major prerequisite to this is the opening of the markets of the industrial countries to imports, especially of finished goods from the developing countries. Deplorably the worldwide economic difficulties of recent years have caused trade barriers to be set up, for example protective tariffs. This is why the Federal Government constantly calls for trade with Third World states to be eased.

Developing countries which depend for their export earnings on a few raw materials are hit particularly hard by price fluctuations on the international commodity markets. This is why the European Community concluded the third Lomé Agreement with 66 African, Pacific and Caribbean states, the so-called ACP countries, in December 1984. It has opened the markets of the European Community to a large number of products and contributes to the Third World countries'export earnings from certain products remaining stable.

Through the European Development Fund the European Community is also an important donor of development aid for the countries linked with it by the Lomé Agreement. The commitment of the Federal Republic of Germany to Europe and to responsibility vis a vis the Third World is also expressed by the fact that with DM 4,400 millions it continues to carry the greatest financial share of the European Development Fund.

Prospects. Development cooperation is an ongoing and difficult learning process for the people in the industrial countries. The great majority of the population of the Federal Republic is in favour of development aid and recognises increasingly how important development in the Third World is also to them. Their readiness to donate and the work of countless groups, especially of young people, is proof of the solidarity with those struggling to live under the harshest conditions.

Many people expected progress in development cooperation to be faster. They overlooked what people in the Third World countries have achieved in the past 20 years. They also tend to forget that economic development in the industrial countries took many generations. Exaggerated hopes and wishful thinking have caused some to capitulate or become cynical. Critics have often taken individual misdevelopments and failures and intolerably generalised them and misused them even in domestic political debate. By this they are doing the people in the developing countries a disservice.

The predominant attitude of people in the Federal Republic to development cooperation is positive. Certainly, critical debate about the effect and success of development aid is also necessary. But failures are not adequate proof against development cooperation. Development cooperation is a task we must continue to face. How we solve it will have a bearing on our own future.

Money and banking

The basic unit of currency in the Federal Republic of Germany, including Berlin (West), is the Deutsche Mark (DM 1 = 100 Pfennigs), introduced in a 1948 currency reform which replaced the Reichsmark. The International Monetary Fund in 1949 first set the parity of the DM at DM 3.33 per US dollar and in the course of devaluation of European currencies in September 1949 at DM 4.20/dollar. The DM has been freely convertible since 1958, that is, it can be exchanged at any time for any other foreign corrency at the going rate. A 1961 Foreign Trade and Payments Act restored free currency trading in the Federal Republic.

The Deutsche Mark and the European Monetary System. In the International Monetary Fund system the US dollar was made the key currency to which all others were oriented. But when the US changed from a creditor to a debtor country it was no longer able to exchange its dollars for gold. Vast amounts of dollars poured into Europe, above all to Germany. Since 1961 the DM had to be revalued vis-à-vis the dollar several times but this was unable substantially to slow down the rise in the DM's external value. In 1973 the Bonn government decided to abandon the fixed exchange rate between the mark and the dollar. Since then the DM's official parity is no longer expressed in dollars but in Special Drawing Rights, the artificial currency of the International Monetary Fund. The dollar dropped to its lowest value, DM 1.71, at the end of 1979. Then began a strengthening of the dollar and a weakening of the mark for complex reasons. Both German current account deficits and the American policy of high interest rates played a part in this. In spring of 1985 the dollar peaked at DM 3.47; since then its value has been falling again.

To fend off excessive inflows of foreign exchange which threatened the domestic stability of the value of money and to avoid revaluation effects which damaged foreign trade the member states of the European Community had created a monetary system in 1972, the so-called currencies snake, which soon fell apart, however. It was replaced on March 13, 1979, by the European Monetary System, to which all EC members except Great Britain belong. Each country has set a firm guiding exchange rate for its currency which is expressed in the new monetary unit, ECU. The ECU is

German bank notes and coins

calculated from a "basket" of the participating currencies. The market exchange rates of every currency can deviate from the bilateral guiding rates by 2.25 % (in the case of the Italian Lira by 6 %) upwards or downwards. If the market rates rise or fall beyond the fixed span, reserve banks intervene to keep the rates within the span by buying or selling currencies. The EMS binds only the participating currencies. In relation to other currencies — including the US dollar — the rates form freely in the currency markets.

Deutsche Bundesbank. The Federal Republic's central bank is the Deutsche Bundesbank in Frankfurt am Main. Its main administration in each of the federal states is called "Landeszentralbank" (Land Central Bank).

Bundesbank bodies are the Central Bank Council and the executive boards of the Land Central Banks. The Central Bank Council, the supreme organ, comprises members of the Bundesbank board and the Land Central Bank presidents and, independent of directives from the Bonn government, determines monetary policy. The executive board implements the Central Bank Council decisions.

Apart from the sole right to issue bank notes the job of the Deutsche Bundesbank is to support the general economic policy of the federal government, to ensure the stability of the DM and to regulate the money supply in circulation. It has various means of doing this. Thus it can inject money into the economy by purchasing securities or withdraw it by selling them (open market policy). The Bundesbank can also influence the amount of money in circulation by setting the volume of minimum reserves which commercial banks must leave with the Bundesbank in relation to their short-term liabilities. Another means is discount policy. Discounting is one of the major forms of lending, and by raising or lowering the discount rate, at which it buys bills, the Bundesbank can influence the demand for credit.

Only since floating was begun in 1973 (which did away with the obligation to buy up dollars in unlimited quantity) has the Bundesbank been able to pursue a deliberate control of money supply. Since 1974 the Central Bank Council announces a money supply target for every year. This figure (note and coin in circulation plus minimum reserves) is intended mainly as an orientation aid for business and public spending.

The currency reserves of the Deutsche Bundesbank, i. e. its entire holdings of gold and claims against foreigners, rose from DM 32,700 millions at the end of 1960 to DM 99,000 millions at the end of 1984. At that time the exchange reserves comprised DM 13,700 millions in gold, DM 38,000 millions in currencies and DM 16,100 millions reserve position and Special Drawing Rights in the International Monetary Fund.

Credit institutions. Public, cooperative and private credit institutions operate in the Federal Republic. At the end of 1984 there were 247 lending banks, 12 giro clearing banks, 591 savings banks, 9 cooperative central banks, 3,707 larger credit cooperatives, 37 mortgage institutions and public mortgage banks, 16 banks with special functions and 82 instalment credit institutions.

Among the private banks are big banks with the legal form of stock company. Giro banks (Land banks) are the central credit institutions of the public savings banks in the various Bundesländer. As the house banks of the federal states they concentrate their activities on regional financing tasks. Most savings banks are operated by local governments or groupings of local authorities. In their legal form they are autonomous public enterprises with unilateral liability, i. e. only the local authority is liable for the savings bank, not vice versa. "Zentralkassen" are the regional central institutions of rural and commercial credit cooperatives. Mortgage banks are private real estate credit institutions which

Counter hall of a savings bank

give mortgages and local authority loans and raise their funds for these by issuing mortgage bonds and local authority bonds. Among the credit institutions with special tasks are inter alia the Reconstruction Loan Corporation (Kreditanstalt für Wiederaufbau), the Equalisation of Burdens Bank (Lastenausgleichsbank für Vertriebene und Geschädigte), the German Settlement and Land Mortgage Bank (Deutsche Siedlungs- und Landesrentenbank) and the Agricultural Mortgage Bank (Landwirtschaftliche Rentenbank). Instalment credit institutions give purchase loans with and without involvement of the selling firm.

The acitivities of all credit institutions in the Federal Republic are supervised by the Federal Banking Supervisory Office (Bundesaufsichtsamt für das Kreditwesen) in Berlin (West) whose main task is to protect savers from losses. If in spite of this control a credit institution has to register bankruptcy, so-called "fire brigade funds" of the banking trade compensate for the losses of savers.

The credit market. The total sum of credits given in the Federal Republic by credit institutions (including the Deutsche Bundesbank) to domestic non-banks (i. e. enterprises, public budgets and private persons) increased continuously in recent years. From DM 543,700 millions at the end of 1970 the level of accumulated lending rose to DM 2,365,000 millions in 1984. Of this, DM 446,800 millions were credits to public budgets.

Private household savings have also risen continuously, from deposits of DM 205,400 millions in 1970 to DM 576,000 millions at the end of 1984. Just under half of these deposits are with public savings banks and giro clearing banks.

The German capital market is characterised by a high absorption of fixed-interest securities. The circulation of bonds of real estate and local authority credit institutions of the Federal Republic at the end of 1984 totalled DM 850,000 millions. Of this, DM 327,000 millions were local government bonds. Their proceeds are used not only to finance loans to local governments but also on a considerable scale for credits to the federation and its special funds, Federal Railways and Federal Post Office as well as the Länder. Direct loan raising by public authorities has also increased in recent years. A substantial part of the funds for housing construction is raised by sale of mortgage bonds. The direct credit taking of industrial enterprises is modest by comparison. The sale of new share issues is considerably smaller in the Federal Republic than that of fixed-interest securities.

Commercial banks:
Bundesverband deutscher Banken
Mohrenstr. 35–41
5000 Köln 1

Public savings banks:
Deutscher Sparkassen- und Giroverband
Simrockstr. 4
5300 Bonn 1

Fairs and exhibitions

Historical development. Trade fairs developed in the early Middle Ages out of individual markets, often in connection with church festivals, as the German word for trade fair, Handelsmesse, "Trade Mass", indicates. Since fairs offered good trading prospects and promoted their region's economy they were under the protection of the princes, who conceded various towns the right to hold them. Thus the fair in Frankfurt am Main was first mentioned in a privilege granted in 1240 by Emperor Frederick II, advancing to experience its heyday from the mid 15th to early 17th centuries. A 1507 privilege of Emperor Maximilian established the Leipzig fair which assumed great economic importance from the 18th century.

A fair is different from an exhibition by being designed primarily for selling, being tied to a certain venue and always taking place at the same time of year. Economic exhibitions give an indication of a national economy's or single industry's potential, advertise a country's or particular industry's products or acquaint visitors with specific economic problems. In the Federal Republic of Germany the former comprehensive fair has been replaced by the fair for one or several economic branches. The broad supply offered by a highly developed national economy makes concentration on certain groups of goods necessary. The worldwide renown of the fairs and exhibitions held in the Federal Republic of Germany is due mainly to this specialisation. Visitors and exhibitors come from all over the world. The broad and differentiated service offered by the German fair companies and their good co-operation with organisations and exhibitors are trade marks of the German fair system.

Fairs and exhibitions in the Federal Republic. The "German Council of Trade Fairs and Exhibitions" (Austellungs- und Messe-Ausschuss der Deutschen Wirtschaft, AUMA) in Köln (Cologne) lists in its calendar about 140 fairs and exhibitions in the Federal Republic of supraregional or international importance. The major fair cities are Berlin (West), Düsseldorf, Essen, Frankfurt am Main, Hamburg, Hanover, Cologne, Munich, Nuremberg and Stuttgart.

Of outstanding importance is the Hanover Fair, founded in

Hanover Fair

1947, which takes place every spring and, with about 750,000 square metres of display are and some 5,700 inland and foreign exhibitors of capital and consumer durables, is the largest fair in the wold. Since 1986 a separate event for office, information and communication technology, "CeBiT", is held in Hanover.

The spring and autumn consumer goods fairs in Frankfurt am Main focus on ceramics, glassware, china, arts and crafts, jewelry, paper and office supplies. In Frankfurt there is also a number of specialised functions such as "interstoff" (Trade Fair for Clothing Textiles), the Fur Trade Fair, International Motor Show, International Trade Fair Sanitation/Heating and Air Conditioning, "HOGA" for the hotel and catering trades. Every autumn publishers and booksellers from around the world meet at the Frankfurt Book Fair.

Many specialised international consumer goods fairs and exhibitions are held in Köln. They include the "ANUGA" (World Food Market), the "photokina" (World Photography Fair), the International Furniture Fair as well as special fairs for household appliances, two-wheelers, hardware and men's and children's wear.

Düsseldorf also hosts many specialised fairs and exhibitions, some in a rota of several years, e. g. "DRUPA" (International Fair Printing and Paper), "GIFA" (International Foundry Trade Fair), "INTERKAMA" (International Congress with Trade Fair for Instrumentaion), "INTERPACK" (International Trade Fair for Packaging Machinery, Packaging Materials and Confectionery Machinery). Twice a year Düsseldorf holds "IGEDO", the International Fashion Trade Fair.

In München (Munich), "BAUMA" (International Construction Machinery Fair) and the International Light Industries and Handicrafts Fair have made big names for themselves. Of growing importance are the fairs which show computers, electronic elements and manufacturing processes in electronics, such as "Systems", the "electronica" and the "PRODUCTRONICA".

Among the major exhibitions in Berlin (West) are the International Green Week (an agricultural and food industry exhibition of worldwide interest), the International Tourism Bourse, the Overseas Import Fair "Partners for Progress" and the International Radio and TV Exhibition. Berlin's new International Congress Centre (ICC) is fully equipped for all types of conferences.

German participation abroad. Since its foundation the Federal Republic of Germany has participated in foreign fairs and exhibitions as a classic instrument of export promotion. It does this in the form of information stands of export industries, displays of representative products, designs and models or joint stands of industrial firms and government departments. At irregular intervals the Federal Republic also organises industrial exhibitions abroad on its own initiative.

Trade fairs council:
Ausstellungs- und Messe-Ausschuss der Deutschen Wirtschaft
Lindenstr. 8
5000 Köln 1

Transportation

Transportation in the Federal Repuclic is one of the major concerns of social and economic policies. It makes people mobile, including abroad, eases their choice of residence and place of work and helps to level out unequal living conditions. Without a functioning transportation system, manufacture and commerce could not perform at peak capacity and flexibility. For a country as greatly dependent on foreign trade as the Federal Republic this is particularly important.

Transportation is also a major economic factor in terms of employment. About 940,000 workers are employed by 81,000 enterprises.

The German Federal Railways. The largest transportation enterprise in Germany are the state-owned Federal Railways (Deutsche Bundesbahn, DB). They currently employ about 285,000 people, with a rail network comprising about 28,000 kilometres, some 11,300 of which are electrified. These routes handle 85 % of the railway services. On the others diesel engines are used, steam locomotives having gone out of use in 1977.

The railways are indispensable above all for bulk and heavy transports and especially long-distance passenger travel. This is why efforts are underway to bring the latest railway technology into use. This includes automation of signalling and switching systems and computerised shunting. High train speeds will accelerate transportation of goods and passengers.

Short-range commuter transportation has become very important. This development began in the 1960's in line with changes in the habitation structure and the growth of new outlying residential areas, giving rise to strong commuter traffic which demanded efficient, fast rail services. This was particularly the case in economic agglomeration regions such as Hamburg, the Rhenish-Westphalian industrial region, Frankfurt am Main, Stuttgart and the fast-growing southern German metropolis of München (Munich).

The average speeds in passenger rail traffic are 80 kms/h (express trains) and 108 kms/h (Intercity trains). The top speed was raised on 440 kms of line in recent years to 200 kms/h. Other sections of line are being prepared for this speed. Two sections of

Intercity express beside the Rhine

line are being built new for speeds of up to 250 kms/h, Hanover-Würzburg (327 kms) and Mannheim-Stuttgart (100 kms). The new DB tracks will be used for mixed operations, i. e. fast passenger and goods trains.

As in other countries, competition from the motor car poses a serious problem to the railways. Despite all efforts, the Federal Railways are deep in the red, with a 1984 deficit of DM 3,100 millions; although the railways that year got federal government support grants of DM 13,400 millions. Of that, DM 9,400 millions went on non-rail tasks, for example pensions.

To improve the economic performance of the railways a number of measures have recently been taken. They include exhausting all rationalisation potentials, modernisation of track and rolling stock, reduction of personnel and closure of uneconomic lines.

Rail transportation can experience an upwsing in the coming years since it uses energy economically and is largely independent of petroleum. But the Federal Railways must exhaust all rationalisation possibilities to increase their efficiency.

Roads. Roads have taken the lead in the competition with rail transport. This is mainly because the efficient network of federal, state and communal roads enables door-to-door goods transportation without reloading. Short and long-distance road goods

Number of motor vehicles, 1950 – 1985

Year	Total motor vehicles	Thereof passenger cars	Passenger cars per 1,000 population
1950	1,949,800	515,600	11
1951	2,493,500	681,600	14
1952	3,274,600	900,400	19
1953	4,053,700	1,126,100	23
1954	4,699,500	1,393,400	28
1955	5,184,200	1,662,900	33
1956	5,672,800	2,029,700	40
1957	6,393,200	2,583,800	48
1958	6,786,700	2,994,400	55
1959	7,193,300	3,684,500	67
1960	8,003,700	4,489,500	81
1961	8,825,400	5,342,900	95
1962	9,714,000	6,335,000	111
1963	10,486,500	7,304,600	127
1964	11,284,500	8,274,200	142
1965	12,167,800	9,267,400	157
1966	13,146,700	10,302,000	173
1967	13,744,600	11,015,900	184
1968	14,391,300	11,682,600	194
1969	15,342,700	12,584,600	207
1970	16,783,200	13,941,200	230
1971	18,027,800	15,115,100	247
1972	19,025,200	16,055,000	260
1973	20,072,000	17,023,100	275
1974	20,424,200	17,341,300	279
1975	21,011,300	17,898,300	289
1976	22,108,100	18,919,700	307
1977	23,308,900	20,020,200	326
1978	24,611,300	21,212,000	346
1979	26,109,100	22,535,500	367
1980	27,116,200	23,191,600	377
1981	27,858,400	23,730,600	385
1982	28,452,000	24,104,500	391
1983	29,122,300	24,508,500	399
1984	29,905,200	25,217,800	412
1985	30,617,600	25,844,500	424

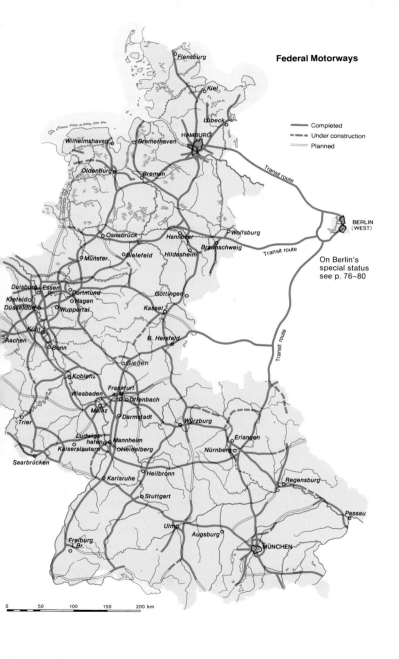

Federal Motorways

Completed
Under construction
Planned

Transit route

BERLIN
(WEST)

On Berlin's
special status
see p. 76–80

Transit route

Transit route

Flensburg

Kiel

Lübeck

HAMBURG

Wilhelmshaven
Bremerhaven

Oldenburg
Bremen

Wolfsburg

Osnabrück
Hannover
Braunschweig

Münster
Bielefeld
Hildesheim

Duisburg Essen
Dortmund
Göttingen

Krefeld
Hagen

Düsseldorf
Wuppertal
Kassel

Köln

Aachen
B. Hersfeld

Bonn

Gießen

Koblenz

Wiesbaden
Frankfurt
a. M.

Mainz
Offenbach

Trier
Darmstadt
Würzburg

Ludwigs-
Erlangen

hafen
Mannheim

Kaiserslautern
Heidelberg
Nürnberg

Saarbrücken

Karlsruhe
Heilbronn

Stuttgart
Regensburg

Passau

Ulm

Freiburg
Augsburg

Br.
MÜNCHEN

0   50   100   150   200 km

transportation today accounts for some 80% of the total and al-most 50% of the transport output in tonne-kilometres. Short-dis-tance haulage alone accounts for more than two thirds of all goods traffic. However, there are many fields where road and rail do not compete, but complement each other. An example is the "pick-a-back" traffic in which loaded or empty trucks are moved on special waggons of the Federal Railways for long distances. In container traffic, too, in which the railways are an important link in the transportation chain, road and rail work together. Both types of combined traffic have greatly grown in recent years.

The rapid development of road traffic is reflected in the number of motor vehicles registered. It rose from 1,9 millions in 1950 to 30,6 millions in 1985, of which 25,8 millions are passenger cars. Just short of four fifths of passenger transportation is by private cars, only one fifth by public facilities. For most people their own car is indispensable for getting to work. In holiday travel it is, with 60%, predominant by far over aeroplanes, ships, trains and bus-es. Motor vehicles will remain the major mode of transport.

The road network has grown from 347,000 kms in 1951 to about 490,000 kms in 1985, when there were 8,196 kms of motorways (autobahns). The length of the net is second to the USA's.

Roadbuilding now is mainly supplementary, with the main em-phases on eliminating bottlenecks and accident hazards, con-necting structurally weak areas to the mainstreams and interna-tional links.

A negative aspect of the growing road traffic are the accidents. Manifold efforts are made to raise road safety. Initial successes have been achieved: whereas the overall number of acidents is continuing to rise slightly, the fatal ones have noticeably declin-ed. In 1970 more than 19,000 people died on the roads; in 1985 it was about 8,400, the lowest figure since 1953.

Shipping. Because it is so export and import-oriented, the Fed-eral Republic needs a strong merchant fleet able to weather any crises and to represent German shipping interests in internation-al maritime trade.

Although most German ships are relatively modern, the indus-try has suffered losses in recent years because of the world rec-ession which brought in its train more protectionism and state controls. With its approximately 1,800 merchant ships, totalling 6.3 million Gross Registered Tons, the merchant fleet of the Fed-eral Republic of Germany has about 1.5% of the world merchant tonnage and holds place 17 among the shipping nations. This is a

At Minden the "Mittellandkanal" crosses over the Weser River

10 % drop in size on 1983. But the use of container ships which are able to carry several times as much as conventional ships has increased competitiveness.

The sea ports — Hamburg, Bremen, Bremerhaven and Lübeck are the largest — although structurally disadvantaged in comparison with foreign ports, have been able to hold their own in international competition. Although foreign North Sea ports such as Antwerp in Belgium and Rotterdam in Holland are closer to the west European industrial centres, the German ports have largely made up for these competitive disadvantages by modernisation investments. The fast-turnaround container terminals are continually being expanded, with the most modern handling equipment and electronic data processing in use. All this has gained German ports the reputation to be fast, able to turn even large vessels around in a matter of hours.

The continous growth in the use of all kinds of containers led in Germany, as elsewhere, to an intermeshing of the various transport systems, with the typical transport "chains".

The expansion of the port facilities in an approach channel to

Wilhelmshaven have made it possible for deep-draught tankers to discharge at the German North Sea coast.

Inland shipping in the Federal Republic has an efficient waterways network at its disposal. The length of the rivers, canals and lakes regularly used by inland ships is some 4,400 kilometres. They include such important international routes as the Rhein, which accounts by itself for two thirds of the inland waterway goods transportation.

The quality of the waterways network is still being improved. Projects begun are being completed. By canalisation of the Saar the Saarland will be linked to the European waterways system. A Rhein-Main-Donau-Kanal (Rhine-Main-Danube-Canal) will link the Rhein with the Donau.

The major inland ports in the Federal Republic are Duisburg, Mannheim, Hamburg, Köln (Cologne), Ludwigshafen, Wesseling, Gelsenkirchen and Karlsruhe.

Bulk goods can be transported especially economically on inland waterways. In 1984 they handled about 236 million tonnes, mainly building materials, oil products, ores and coal. That represented about 25 % of the long-distance goods transportation of the country.

Aviation. Lufthansa is one of the most successful international airlines. In 1984 it carried 15.3 million passengers and 525,000 tonnes of freight. Every year nine million German passengers use Condor, LTU, Hapag Lloyd and a number of smaller charter companies as well as foreign airlines for their holiday flights abroad, especially to the Mediterranean countries. Higher energy costs and greater environmental awareness have accelerated the introduction of more fuel-economic and quieter wide-body aircraft, such as the European-made Airbus. Use of these large-capacity planes has tended to concentrate traffic on the larger German airports, taking business away from the others. In 1984 Berlin-Tegel, Bremen, Düsseldorf, Frankfurt, Hamburg, Hannover, Köln-Bonn (Cologne-Bonn), München (Munich), Nürnberg (Nuremberg), Saarbrücken and Stuttgart handled 51.2 million passengers. International traffic to and from theses airports is shared by about 85 airlines and a growing number of charter companies. Berlin-Tegel, of immense importance to access to the isolated city, is served by Air France, British Airways, Dan Air and PanAm. The airports, which are operated by companies with private legal status, and air traffic control, operated by a government agency, meet international safety requirements to a high degree.

Frankfurt airport

Their safety standards are kept up to date and their capacities are continually adapted to demand.

Future developments. To sustain and improve the quality of transport systems, great efforts must be made. Things have become a lot more difficult. The transportation budget has been stagnant for years, investment is falling, the economic and financial situation of the railways is perilous and public commuter transport is operating at huge losses. Despite this, all levels of government are trying to invest. This applies to rail, road, water and commuter transport. The systems must remain viable and meet safety and environmental demands.

The Post

On every work-day the German Federal Post Office (Deutsche Bundespost) forwards 42 million letters and 812,000 parcels. Almost 17,000 telegrams are delivered and 72 million calls go through the telephone network per day. Nine out of ten households have telephones. The postal giro and savings services make 6.3 million bookings a day. There are nearly 18,000 post offices throughout the federal area. The Bundespost rightly claims to be "the biggest service enterprise in Europe". With almost 88,000 motor vehicles it operates the biggest civilian fleet on the continent.

The Post Office is administered by the federation which has sole legislative power in the postal and telecommunications field. The post office has the sole right to forward letters for payment and it alone is allowed to instal and operate telecommunication facilities for general use. In all other service activities it is in competition with private or other state enterprises.

For example, the post office operates largescale banking services — it is, in fact, the largest financial institution in the Federal Republic. Almost every third inhabitant has a postal savings account, whose great advantage is that deposits and withdrawals can be made at any post office counter. The same holds for the postal giro system, used mainly for non-cash remittances.

The Federal Post Office in figures

	1965	1975	1980	1984
Local telephone calls (billions)	4.5	9.2	14.1	16.5
Long-distance calls (billions)	1.2	4.8	7.8	9.9
Telegrams (millions)	23.1	15.0	7.6	5.9
Letters forwarded (billions)	9.7	10.5	12.2	12.7
Parcels forwarded (millions)	310	264	269	247
Transactions in postal giro service (millions)	1,173	1,396	1,610	1,848
Transactions in postal savings service (millions)	42.5	60.7	61.2	62.7
Personnel	431,199	468,739	476,761	484,070

Reception station at Raisting

Despite increased personnel and material costs the post office since 1975 has been showing a profit after several deficit years. It was produced mainly by the telephone service which is totally self-dialling within the country. In some larger towns it has been possible for some time now to place calls to public telephone boxes. Automatic dialling is possible to almost all countries. Especially strongly expanded was the telephone traffic via satellites, routed through the ground relay stations at Usingen and Raisting. The telex network of the post office with more than 160,000 connections is the second largest national network in the world.

The broadcasting corporations use postal lines for radio and television relaying. The post office also operates the technical transmission facilities of the Second and Third Channel television programmes and Deutschlandfunk and Deutsche Welle radios (see page 325).

Tourism

Is the Federal Republic of Germany a land worth travelling in? It certainly is for the Germans themselves. Almost half the inhabitants who travel in their holidays do so in their own country. Germans comprise the great majority of guests in hotels, boarding houses and private quarters in the Federal Republic. Foreigners account for just under 12 % of overnight stays. (For comparison: In Austria and Spain it is more than two thirds.)

Tourist industry. However, in absolute figures these 12 % are not so little. More than 30 million foreigners stayed overnight in the 1984 season. The foreign guests left about DM 16,000 millions in the country that year. With this income from foreign tourists the Federal Republic comes fifth in Europe after Italy, France, Spain and Great Britain and level with Austria and Switzerland. In other words, seen commercially, it is quite competitive with other countries.

The importance of tourism to the national economy is considerable, about a million and a half jobs directly or indirectly depending on it. It is therefore in the public interest to promote it. But mass tourism also causes problems. The environment of some tourist regions is greatly damaged. Landscape and nature protection measures are quite successfully used to keep the effects of human interference with nature as small as possible. A special role is played in this by regulations aimed at preventing excessive building of holiday houses and hotels in the landscape.

What Germany has to offer. What, then, are the Federal Republic's tourist attractions? Because of the beauty of their scenery, the North and Baltic Seas, Central Uplands (Mittelgebirge) and Alps but also the valleys of the Rhein, Main, Mosel (Moselle), Neckar and Donau (Danube) have the greatest attraction for visitors, and are the preferred holiday resorts. Impressions of a different kind are given by the famous German cultural landscapes. Along the Romantic Road (Romantische Straße), in Rothenburg, Dinkelsbühl, Nördlingen, the Middle Ages come alive for the visitor; in Bayern (Bavaria) there is the lightheartedness of the Baroque, in the north the sternness of Gothic brick architecture. Everywhere — including places not in the tourist guidebook — one

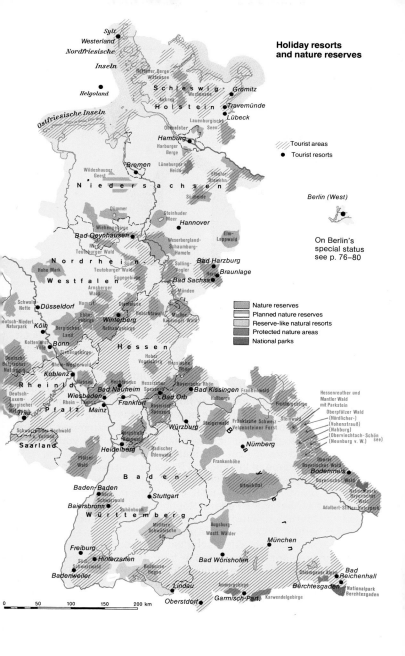

**Holiday resorts
and nature reserves**

////// Tourist areas
● Tourist resorts

Berlin (West)

On Berlin's
special status
see p. 76–80

Nature reserves
Planned nature reserves
Reserve-like natural resorts
Protected nature areas
National parks

Sylt
Westerland
Nordfriesische

Inseln

Helgoland

Ostfriesische Inseln

Hüttener Berge
Wittensee
Ankrug
S c h l e s w i g · *Grömitz*
Westensee
H o l s t e i n *Travemünde*
Lübeck
Oberalster
Lauenburgische
Seen
Hamburg
Harburger
Berge

Wildeshauser
Geest
Bremen
Lüneburger
Heide
Elbufer-
Drawehn

N i e d e r s a c h s e n
Südheide

Dümmer
Steinhuder
Meer
Hannover
Elm-
Lappwald
Wiehengebirge
Bad Oeynhausen
Weserbergland-
Schaumburg-
Hameln
Nord-
Teutoburger Wald
Bad Harzburg

N o r d r h e i n –
Süntel-
Teutoburger Wald
Solling-
Vogler
Harz
Braunlage
W e s t f a l e n
Eggegebirge
Bad Sachsa
Arnsberger
Wald
Münden
Hohe Mark
Homert
Diemelsee
Schwalm-
Nette
Düsseldorf
Habichtswald
Ebbe-
gebirge
Meißner-
Kaufunger Wald
eutsch-Niederl.-
Naturpark
Winterberg
Bergisches
Köln
Land
Rothaargebirge
Kottenforst-
Ville
Bonn
H e s s e n
Siebengebirge
Deutsch-
Belgischer
Naturpark
Rhein-Westerwald
Hoher
Vogelsberg
Hessische
Rhön
Koblenz
Nassau
R h e i n l d –
Heisterberg
Hessischer
Spessart
Bayerische Rhön
Bad Nauheim
Bad Kissingen
Frankenwald
Deutsch-
luxem-
burgischer
Wiesbaden
Rhein-Taunus
Bad Orb
Haßberge
Fichtelgebirge
P f a l z
Frankfurt
Bayerischer
Hessenreuther und
Trier
Mainz
Spessart
Mantler Wald
mit Parkstein
Naturpark
Steigerwald
Fränkische Schweiz
Steinwald
Oberpfälzer Wald
S a a r l a n d
Bergstraße
Veldensteiner Forst
(Nördlicher–)
Odenwald
Würzburg
(Vohenstrauß)
Schwarzw.-Hochwald
Badischer
(Nabburg)
Heidelberg
Ödenwald
Frankenhöhe
(Oberviechtach-Schön-
Pfälzer
(Neunburg v. W.) see)
Wald
Nürnberg
B a d e n –
Oberer
Bayerischer Wald
Altmühltal
Bodenmais
Baden-Baden
Stuttgart
Bayerischer Wald
Murgtal
W ü r t t e m b e r g
Baiersbronn
Schwarzwald
Schönbuch
Adalbert-Stifter-Naturpark
Süd-
Mittlere Schwäbische
Schwarzwald
Alb
Augsburg-
Freiburg
Hinterzarten
Westl. Wälder
München
Baar-
Heuberg
Nationalpark
Badenweiler
Bad Wörishofen
Bayerischer
Wald
Chiemgauer Alpen
Bad
Reichenhall
Lindau
Berchtesgaden
Ammergebirge
Nationalpark
Oberstdorf
Garmisch-Part.
Karwendelgebirge
Berchtesgaden

0   50   100   150   200 km

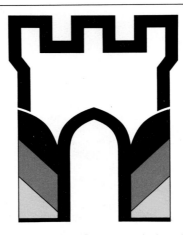

Emblem of the German tourist board

comes unexpectedly across the traces of a history going back many hundreds of years. The cosmopolitan present-day is offered by the modern cities. German Gemütlichkeit — a word difficult to translate — is experienced by the guest at local, costume, wine and many other festivals.

The offering of the catering and accommodation trade is great and varied. It ranges from the farmhouse and cheap private quarters to the international luxury hotel. The accommodation establishments, including private quarters, together have almost more than two million beds for visitors. Almost 2,000 camping sites are located throughout the holidaymaking regions. For young wanderers there are 564 youth hostels.

The landscape of the Federal Republic is traversed by a well-kept and dense network of hiking ways. For the motorised "wanderer" round-routes were built, e. g. in the many nature parks.

The traveller to the Federal Republic can use a widely branched transportation network. There are roads in excellent condition and quantity: motorways (Autobahn) and highways, federal routes and innumerable asphalted side roads. The visitor-frequented regions are traversed by tourist roads, e. g. the German Alpine Road (Deutsche Alpenstraße), the Romantic Road (Romantische Straße), the German Alps-Baltic Sea Holiday Road (Deutsche Ferienstaße Alpen-Ostsee), the Upper Swabian Baroque Road (Oberschwäbische Barockstraße), the Danube Road

(Donaustraße), the German Wine Road and the German Fairy-tales Road (Deutsche Märchenstraße).

The long routes of the German Federal Railways are served by comfortably appointed Trans-Europe, Intercity and express trains, all with dining cars, and most with sleepers as well. The Federal Railways offer cheaper "town tours" throughout the year and other price cuts, e. g. for young people, the elderly and groups. From Belgium, France, Italy, Yugoslavia, the Netherlands, Austria and Switzerland one can also travel by car-train to the Federal Republic.

Most formalities for foreign visitors have been done away with. Citizens of many states can enter the country as tourists for up to three months without a visa. Foreign exchange can be brought in in any amount.

The German National Tourist Board. Apart from the commercial travel operators, the German National Tourist Board (Deutsche Zentale für Tourismus, DZT) carries on promotion abroad for travel to Germany. The foreign offices of the DZT are recognisable by the pictured emblem (see page 242). The Board is a member of international organisations such as the European Travel Commission (ETC). It pusblishes a number of information booklets about Germany in many languages.

Tourist board:
Deutsche Zentrale für Tourismus
Beethovenstr. 69
6000 Frankfurt/Main 1

Society
Welfare
Leisure

Society
Industrial relations
Worker codetermination
Social security
Integration, burden-sharing, compensation
Assets for all
Housing and urban works
Protection of the environment
Women in society
The young
Health
Sport
Leisure and holidays
Religion and churches
Clubs, associations, civic action groups
Mass media and public opinion
The press
Broadcasting

Society

The Federal Republic is a modern industrial society. Of its labour force of about 26.6 millions, 11.1 millions are employed in production (industrial, construction, mining) and 14.1 millions in commerce, transportation and other service industries. In other words, the services, or "tertiary" sector labour force has outgrown the industrial. It is nonetheless still correct to speak of an industrial society because the services sector is strongly shaped by industrial norms; it is, so to speak, "industrialised". Only 1.4 million people, or only 5.2 % of the labourforce, still work in agriculture, stock-raising, forestry and fishing, all of which are also partly heavily mechanised and thus also "industrialised".

By social status the gainfully employed fall into following categories: more than 2.4 millions are self-employed, just over 900,000 assisting family members; 23.3 millions are dependently employed wage or salary earners and public servants. Thus by far the predominant part of the gainfully employed population, about 88 %, are in dependent employment.

The largest number of employees by far are wage or salary earners; each of these two big groups of society numbers more than 10 million people. In legal status the only major differences remaining between them are the shorter periods of notice of dismissal for the wage earners and the different organisation of social insurance schemes (except unemployment insurance). But the amount of benefits and contributions are in principle the same. The number of indismissable public servants (excluding professional soldiers) who have special welfare claims is about 1.8 millions. The public services also employ a number of wage and salary earners, however, so that the total public service payroll is about 4.5 millions.

Similarity of life styles. In their outward style of living and appearance all social groups — leaving aside for a moment the business elite, which comprises about 2 % of the population — have become very much alike. Some experts therefore refer to a "levelled-out middle class society". All the same, it cannot be overlooked that four fifths of the population live completely or predominantly from their capacity to work, whereas a minority are able to live off the profits from their assets.

Disposable monthly net incomes of social groups 1970 and 1982 *(in %)*

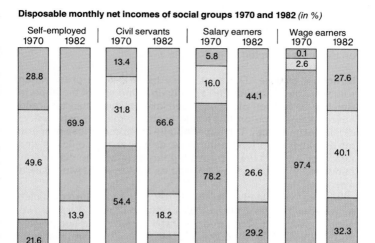

About half of the employee households own their flats or houses. On their own most of them would not have achieved this goal,
however. The grouping together of people wanting to have their
own home in large building societies gave them access to the
necessary long-term, low-interest credit. On top of that came
state home savings supports in the form of bonuses and tax cuts.
The motor car, up to at least 1950 the status symbol of the upper
and upper middle classes, has meanwhile become part of most
worker households. It has increased mobility in vocation and leisure to an unprecedented degree, but at the same time led to an
expenditure on infrastructure (road construction, environmental
protection) so great as to give rise to doubts whether individual
transportation should continue to enjoy priority. High-value consumer goods of medium durability, such as refrigerators, washing machines and television receivers, are to be found in almost
all homes. On top of that almost every employee has a small,
sometimes even medium-sized sum of savings "for a rainy day".

But in many cases this generally high standard of living cannot
be achieved or sustained without both spouses going out to work.

And it is also due in part to the smaller family with one or two children having become the norm. Experts take the view that in the longer term this could be a threat to the viability of old age and invalidity pension schemes which depend for their financial input on the dues collected from those in work.

Structural change. The aristocracy have lost the predominant role they played in German society up to the end of the Imperial Reich in 1918. Their place has been taken by an industrial grand-bourgeoisie which on the whole eschews making ostentatious display of its wealth. The upper middle class comprises primarily top managers in private enterprise, as well as high officials, doctors, well-earning lawyers and big farmers. But the distinctions between the classes have blurred as society underwent fundamental changes.

Whereas one used to be able to depict the structure of society as a pyramid, with a broad lower class, on top of it a narrower middle class and at the peak a small upper class, sociologists nowadays like to use the image of an onion. The lower class has greatly shrunk, with the broadest part now the middle class. This model is borne out, albeit with deviations depending on the yard-

Social strata ("Society-onion")

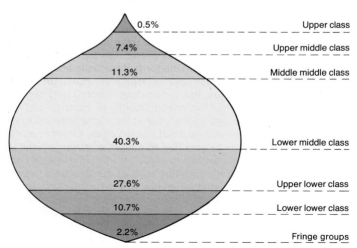

0.5%	Upper class
7.4%	Upper middle class
11.3%	Middle middle class
40.3%	Lower middle class
27.6%	Upper lower class
10.7%	Lower lower class
2.2%	Fringe groups

sticks applied, by all sociological studies made of class structure in the Federal Republic in the past two decades. It made no great difference whether the researchers used income, vocation and education as the criteria or whether they asked people where they thought they belonged. There is an unmistakeable striving towards the middle, however. Many people who by objective criteria belonged in the upper or lower classes see themselves as middle class. The diagram shows a class model based on a study of the mid-1970's.

Social minorities. Special public attention and care is given in the Federal Republic of Germany to so-called social minorities, the "underprivileged" and "fringe groups" which include quite varied strata of the population. Their common denominator is that they cannot handle their problems on their own and need special help. They might be single mothers with children to bring up, large families, the elderly with very small pensions, people out of work for a long time, the physically or mentally handicapped, released convicts.

Sensitivity to the concerns of such social minorities has heightened with critical reporting in the media and through church, trade union and private initiatives. Although they receive a variety of material benefits from the government, it cannot take care of all their needs and above all it cannot replace the practical help of people for each other and self-reliance. Here is a broad field of work for churches, non-denominational groups, welfare organisations, private groups, neighbourhood aid and other non-governmental initiatives. They do extremely valuable social work day in day out and they have achieved much on the way to social integration of minorities. The federal government supports all such voluntary social initiatives and especially encourages other examples of practical help for fellow human beings by recognising and publicly honouring them.

Another integration can be said to have been successful, that of absorbing the approximately 8.5 million expellees from the eastern regions of the former German Reich and the approximately 3.5 million refugees from the communist GDR and Berlin (East). In many respects this successful social fusion may serve as a model for the integration of other minority groups.

Policy towards foreigners. The largest minority in the Federal Republic are the foreign workers and the dependents they have brought with them, altogether about 4.5 million people. Half of them have lived in Germany for 10 years and more and the country has a lot to thank these so-called "guest workers" (Gastarbeiter) for. They contributed greatly to Germany's economic growth. Although most Germans and foreigners try to get along well with each other, living together is not free of friction, especially in some cities where the foreigners comprise more than 20 % of the population. The biggest group, the 1.5 million mainly Moslem Turks, have the greatest difficulties adjusting to the alien lifestyle and culture of their host country. This sometimes generates mistrust and hostility on both sides. Foreigners are harder hit by unemployment than Germans, for example. Things are especially hard for the "second generation" foreigners, that is youngsters who have grown up in Germany. They are very disadvantaged at school and in job prospects compared with their German contemporaries and therefore see a bleak future ahead of them.

No society can absorb limitless numbers of people from completely alien cultures without ultimately putting its identity and stability at risk. This is why the CDU/CSU/FDP federal government has adopted new policies towards foreigners. These are based on three fundamentals:

☐ Integration of workers who have been in the country for a long time is promoted, whereby integration does not mean loss of their identity but coexistence with Germans with as little friction as possible.

☐ No more recruitment of foreigners and restriction of entry of dependents of those already in Germany.

☐ Financial aid for those who wish to return home.

Industrial relations

Of the approximately 26.6 million gainfully active people in the Federal Republic of Germany 23.3 millions are in dependent employment as wage and salary earners, public servants or trainees. They are employees, or Arbeitnehmer, "work-takers", in German. Most of the 2.4 million self-employed also employ other workers, in addition to 900,000 assisting family members. In this sense they are employers, or "work-givers" (Arbeitgeber). Employers are also stock companies, the state, local authorities and other public institutions.

Employers and employees have common interests and depend on cooperation with each other. At the same time they have contrasting interests which sometimes lead to hard confrontation. In the Federal Republic the community of interests is underlined and therefore there is often talk of workers and employers being "social partners". A more neutral definition would be "contract partners", or "Tarifpartner" in German. This indicates the field in which the two sides have most to do with each other: collective bargaining.

Collective bargaining in the Federal Republic is autonomous. That means employers and workers have the right to bargain and enter collective agreements with each other without state interference. The state does set the general conditions by legislation but it does not lay down how much workers should or may be paid. This and many other things — for example the length of vacation — is left to labour and management representatives, the trade unions and employer associations, to negotiate among themselves.

The trade unions. Trade unions are few, but large in the Federal Republic. The biggest labour organisation is the German Trade Union Federation (Deutscher Gewerkschaftsbund, DGB) with nearly 7.7 million members in 17 unions. Characteristic of the DGB unions is the principle of "one union, one industry", that is they enrol workers of an entire industry, regardless of the kind of work each does. Thus a chauffeur and a bookkeeper working in a printing plant would be in the same Printing and Paper Workers' Union (IG Druck und Papier). As a rule, then, the employers of a given branch of industry negotiate with only one labour organisation.

Apart from the DGB there is a number of other trade union organisations. Only the three largest are named here: the German Union of Salaried Employees (Deutsche Angestellten-Gewerkschaft, DAG) with 502,000 members is not an industrial union in the sense outlined, grouping together salaried staff from the most varied branches of industry; the German Civil Servants' Federation (Deutscher Beamtenbund, DBB), with about 800,000 members, is the major organisation of the permanent civil servants. Although because of the peculiarities of Public Servants Law it does not conduct collective bargaining and cannot call a strike, it has all the other characteristics of a trade union. The Christian Trade Union Federation of Germany (Christlicher Gewerkschaftsbund Deutschlands, CGB), with its affiliated unions, numbers some 306,000 members.

The trade unions in the Federal Republic are party-politically

The trade unions of the DGB *(1984)*

	Members in 1,000's	Proportion of women (%)
Bau – Steine – Erden (construction)	517.0	5.1
Bergbau und Energie (mining, energy)	360.3	1.9
Chemie – Papier – Keramik (chemicals, paper, ceramics)	638.1	18.7
Druck und Papier (printing, journalists, writers)	142.3	23.7
Eisenbahner (railways)	364.0	5.0
Erziehung und Wissenschaft (teachers, scientists)	196.7	47.6
Gartenbau, Land- und Forstwirtschaft (horticulture, agriculture, forestry)	42.0	12.9
Handel, Banken und Versicherungen (commerce, banking, insurance)	363.3	57.0
Holz und Kunststoff (wood and synthetics)	147.2	13.3
Kunst (arts)	29.6	37.9
Leder (leather)	49.1	43.8
Metall (metal)	2,498.7	14.4
Nahrung – Genuß – Gaststätten (food and catering)	264.8	32.9
Öffentliche Dienste, Transport und Verkehr (public service and transportation)	1,168.2	29.3
Polizei (police)	165.7	8.3
Post (posts)	455.7	30.3
Textil – Bekleidung (textiles, garments)	260.2	57.8
Deutscher Gewerkschaftsbund (German Trade Union Federation)	7,660.3	21.6

Warning strike to back union demands

and denominationally independent. No-one can be forced to join a trade union. The "closed shop" system prevalent in some countries is unknown in the Federal Republic. The degree of unionisation, i. e. the proportion of workers who are members of unions in certain branches of industries, varies greatly. Amongst railway workers it is almost 100 %, for example, whereas in agriculture and forestry it is only slightly above 10 %.

Average unionisation among all workers in the Federal Republic of Germany for almost 20 years has remained fairly consistently at around 35 %, i. e. only one in three is a trade union member. Two possible reasons for this stagnation are that on the one hand many workers shrink from the not inconsiderable union dues, and that on the other hand they benefit anyway from the improvements fought for by the unions without having to be members.

The unions operate many education facilities for their members. The DGB sponsors the annual Ruhrfestspiele arts festival at Recklinghausen. It awards a highly regarded cultural prize every year. The DGB trade unions are also active in business. For example, they are the main owners of a bank, the "Bank für Gemeinwirtschaft".

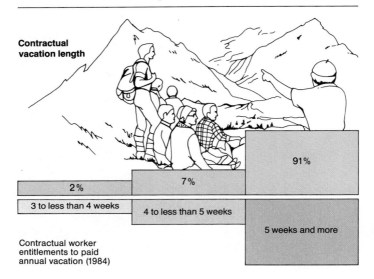

Contractual vacation length

2%

7%

91%

3 to less than 4 weeks

4 to less than 5 weeks

5 weeks and more

Contractual worker
entitlements to paid
annual vacation (1984)

Employer associations. Employers are grouped in several hundred associations, organised both regionally and according to type of industry. Approximately 90 % of employers belong to such associations — far in excess of the percentage of employees in trade unions. There are 13 "Land" employer associations. Their joint umbrella organisation is the Confederation of German Employers Associations (Bundesvereinigung der Deutschen Arbeitgeberverbände, BDA). The BDA itself, like the German Trade Union Federation, does not enter into collective agreements but works as a coordinating organ for fundamental employer interests.

The BDA covers all branches of business — industry, crafts, commerce, banks, insurances, agriculture and transportation. But it represents the entrepreneurs only in their role as employers, i. e. as negotiating partners of the trade unions. All other interests — e. g. taxation or economic policies — are taken care of by other entrepreneurial organisations. Examples are the Federation of German Industries (Bundesverband der Deutschen Industrie. BDI), the Central Accociation of the German Crafts (Zentralverband des Deutschen Handwerks) and the Federation of German Wholesale and Foreign Traders (Bundesverband des Deutschen Gross- und Aussenhandels).

Collective agreements. Some 7,000 collective agreements between unions and employers were concluded in the Federal Republic in 1984. Some covered the entire Federal Republic, most one or several federal states and some individual firms. A collective agreement, called "tariff contract", Tarifvertrag in German, applies in the first instance to the two sides entering it, that is the members of the trade union and employer association involved. But in practice it covers all workers in the industry concerned, whether they are unionised or not, if the firm employing them is a member of the relevant association of employers. Frequently "tariff contracts" are also declared as generally binding by the federal labour minister and then apply to the entire branch of industry concerned.

A distinction is made between two types of collective agreements. The "wages and salaries tariff" regulates pay and in most cases is agreed for a year at a time. The "frame or general tariff" regulates general issues such as working hours, period of dismissal notice, overtime rates, bonuses, etc. and often runs for several years.

The terms of employer/labour agreements are as binding as law on both sides. They must, however, lie within the law which lays down certain minimum requirements. In actual fact, however, most collective agreements go far beyond these. Some examples: Although under the law the highest number of work hours is 48, most German workers have long had a 40-hour week under their agreements and some groups are already down to 38.5 hours a week. Nearly all workers have a contractual paid vacation of five weeks or more while the law demands only three weeks; almost all workers receive additional holiday money or a bonus or both on the basis of collective agreements.

Deviations from a "tariff contract" are admissable only if they are to the advantage of the worker. And such departures are not infrequent: in many cases actual wages, salaries and other payments are considerably above those agreed in the "tariff contract".

Strikes and lockouts. If labour and employer negotiators cannot reach agreement industrial action may occur. There are several safeguards to prevent this happening too easily. Often an impartial arbitrator is brought in to try for a solution But even if arbitration fails a strike is not necessarily immediately inevitable. Within the trade union concerned, several bodies have to approve of the decision to strike. Then a vote has to be taken among the union rank and file. Only if three quarters of the membership vote in favour can a strike take place.

In the Federal Republic the workers' right to strike is countervailed by the employers' right to lock out, i. e. temporarily to close plants in industrial disputes. This lockout right has been expressly confirmed by a Federal Labour Court judgment but it is highly controversial in public opinion. The state remains neutral in labour disputes. This is why neither strikers nor locked out workers receive unemployment money from the state labour exchange for their loss of earnings. Union members are paid some support out of union strike funds. Compared with other countries there are few strikes in the Federal Republic. In 1982 only 15,000 work days were lost through strikes. But in 1984 5.6 million work days were lost by strikes and lockouts. This was due to tough industrial action in the printing and metalworking industries for introduction of the 35-hour week.

Cooperation. Workers and entrepreneurs are not only opponents, they also cooperate in many ways. There is first of all the day-to-day cooperation on the shopfloor. But the representatives of both sides' organisations also meet in many contexts. For example, on the committees which hold the final examinations of vocational trainess there are representatives of labour and management. In the labour courts which rule on employment disputes there are lay judges at all levels from both employer and labour sides. The leaders of various organisations meet frequently when politicians responsible for their field seek their views. These and other forms of cooperation contribute to fostering mutual understanding without blurring the differences in interests.

German Trade Union Federation:
Deutscher Gewerkschaftsbund
Hans-Böckler-Str. 39
4000 Düsseldorf 30

German Union of Salaried Employees:
Deutsche Angestellten-Gewerkschaft
Karl-Muck-Platz 1
2000 Hamburg 36

German Civil Servants' Federation:
Deutscher Beamtenbund
Dreizehnmorgenweg 36
5300 Bonn 2

Christian Trade Union Federation:
Christlicher Gewerkschaftsbund
Deutschlands
Konstantinstr. 11a
5300 Bonn 2

Confederation of
German Employers Associations:
Bundesvereinigung der
Deutschen Arbeitgeberverbände
Gustav-Heinemann-Ufer 72
5000 Köln 51

Worker codetermination

In the 19th century Germany changed from an agricultural into an industrial society. The rapidly growing new class of industrial workers initially lived in abject misery, almost totally without protection or rights. With the help of their organisations the workers were gradually able considerably to improve their material situation and their social security, sometimes only after tenacious struggles.

But the workers continued to be totally dependent on their companies until far into this century. The power of the owners was almost limitless.

Breakthrough to worker participation. Only in recent decades did a process of change and rethinking set in in this field. The undisputed basis of the order of Federal German society is the human being's self-determination. It is, in fact, written into the Basic Law which guarantees a basic right to "free development of personality". This guiding principle of the self-determined human being would be violated if the worker were regarded as no more than a component in a production process determined only by capital interests.

Based on this fundamental premise there is today farreaching agreement that industrial objectives must also take into account the interests of working people and that for industrial decisions affecting the vital interests of workers their democratic participation in decision-taking must be assured. In the Federal Republic there have been attempts to do justice to these demands by giving workers a wide measure of legally secured codetermination (Mitbestimmung) in the firms.

This development began with a 1920 Works Councils Act which for the first time provided for the possibility of setting up elected worker representations in all companies. A big advance towards labour codetermination came in 1951 when in the then two-year-old Federal Republic legislation (Montan-Mitbestimmungsgesetz) was enacted which gave workers in the big mining and steel enterprises important codetermination rights as well as representation in the management.

A Works Constitution Act (Betriebsverfassungsgesetz) adopted the following year by the Bundestag brought workers in almost

Forms of codetermination

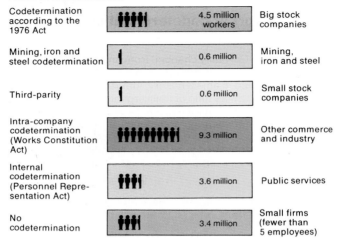

Codetermination according to the 1976 Act	4.5 million workers	Big stock companies
Mining, iron and steel codetermination	0.6 million	Mining, iron and steel
Third-parity	0.6 million	Small stock companies
Intra-company codetermination (Works Constitution Act)	9.3 million	Other commerce and industry
Internal codetermination (Personnel Representation Act)	3.6 million	Public services
No codetermination	3.4 million	Small firms (fewer than 5 employees)

all firms codetermination rights in social welfare and personnel matters and the right to be heard in business policy decisions. Substantial improvements for the worker representations came 20 years later with a new Works Constitution Act, passed in 1972. Another major reform advance was the general Codetermination Act of 1976.

With all this legislation the notion of the "constitutional factory" is becoming reality in the Federal Republic which a few decades ago had still seemed utopian.

The social welfare state principle laid down by the Basic Law is being filled with life in an important field.

The Works Council. The most important organ of representation of worker interests at shopfloor level is the Works Council (Betriebsrat). It is elected by all workers from the age of 18. Foreigners are also entitled to vote and to hold office. Anyone can stand for election, regardless of whether he belongs to a trade union or not. In practice, however, especially in large plants or administrations, the trade unions have great influence on the composition of candidates' lists.

The number of members in a works council depends on the size of the firm. Its period of office is three years. Since an employer could be tempted to dismiss an "irksome" works council member,

Election of a works council

members are under special protection from dismissal during their period of office and for one year after it.

As a rule, works council members exercise their office aside from their normal work duties. But in larger firms one member or — depending on the size of the workforce — several must be released from working.

The civil servants (Beamten), salaried employees and wage earners in the public services also have an organ to represent their interests, the Personnel Council; its tasks and powers are similar to those of the Works Council.

Works council rights. The works council has manifold rights, especially in social welfare and personnel maters. In some it must be consulted, in others it can participate in decision-taking and in some it has a genuine codetermination right, that is the employer cannot decide without approval of the works council. If the two sides cannot agree an arbitration panel on which labour and management are equally represented and which is presided over by an impartial chairman decides the issue.

Without works council approval the management cannot order overtime or short-time working, for example, nor introduce check clocks or other control techniques, piecework payment or bonus schemes, nor evict worker tenants from works-owned housing. The works council can insist that jobs becoming vacant or being

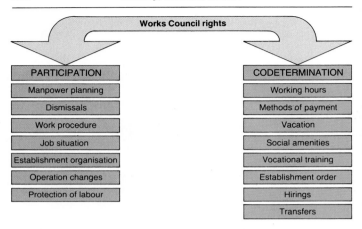

newly created must first be advertised for applicants from within the company.

The council cannot prevent an employee's dismissal but it must be consulted before each one and has a limited contradiction right. If it does disapprove of the dismissal and the employee concerned files suit with a labour court he must be kept on in his job until the court has passed judgment. If the employer plans dismissal of a larger number of workers the works council has to be informed in good time. It then has the right to demand that a "social welfare plan" be drawn up which ameliorates the disadvantages for those concerned, in the form of severance payments or coverage of home removal costs, for example.

Even where the works council has only the right to be consulted, very often it is able by skilful negotiating to achieve improvements for the employees. In practice the works council and the employer are only seldom in irreconcilable confrontation, but mostly work together — as the law expressly demands — and try for sensible compromise.

The individul employee apart from his right to elect the works council has rights which one might call "basic rights within the works". One of the main ones is to be informed about the type of work done and its place in the overall production process. The worker can demand information on how pay is calculated, is entitled to read his personal file and to complain if he feels hard done by or unjustly treated. In most matters the employee can have a works council member support him.

Codetermination in large enterprises. The works council has no influence on the business policy of the enterprise. Only in firms with more than 100 employees is there an obligation to inform the council about it to a certain extent.

But in almost all larger enterprises there are various forms of management codetermination. In the Federal Republic more than half of the large enterprises are stock companies. The German stock company, the Aktiengesellschaft, has two bodies of control: the Aufsichtsrat (Supervisory Council) as control organ, and the Vorstand (Executive Board) which is responsible for day-to-day management. Already by 1952 one third of the Aufsichtsrat members of every stock company had to be elected labour representatives. This provision still applies to small and medium-sized stock companies (up to 2,000 employees) and for other enterprises with 500 to 2,000 employees.

For large enterprises there are two special codetermination systems. In the large mining and steel companies with more than 1,000 employees the "Montanmitbestimmungsgesetz" has applied since 1951. According to this law, owner and labour each have half the seats on the Aufsichtsrat and have to agree on a further, neutral member. On the executive board there has to be a Labour Director with fully equal rights who cannot be appointed against the will of the labour representatives in the Aufsichtsrat.

For other large industrial enterprises employing more than 2,000 a general Codetermination Act, adopted in 1976, is applied. In this law which covers some 500 enterprises of all branches except mining and steelmaking and the press the provisions are somewhat more complicated. On a numerical basis there is full labour/owner parity in the Aufsichtsrat. But in tied votes, the deciding vote is that of the chairman who cannot be elected against the will of the owners. Moreover, the labour side must include at least one representative of the "leading personnel", i. e a staff member with managerial functions.

The trade unions would have preferred the mining and steel companies' codetermination system which has proved successful over a quarter of a century simply to have been applied to other large companies as well. But legislators who saw in this too great a curtailment of the constitutional right to property won the day. The employer organisations took the view that even in this form the law curtailed property rights too much and filed suit against it with the Federal Constitutional Court. The court rejected the suit, ruling that the Codetermination Act is compatible with the Basic Law.

Codetermination in large enterprises

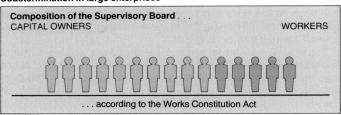

Composition of the Supervisory Board . . .
CAPITAL OWNERS — WORKERS
. . . according to the Works Constitution Act

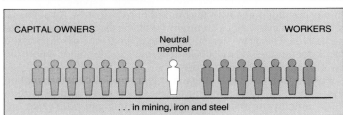

CAPITAL OWNERS — Neutral member — WORKERS
. . . in mining, iron and steel

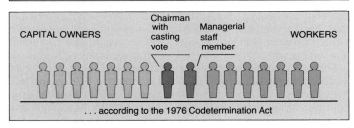

CAPITAL OWNERS — Chairman with casting vote — Managerial staff member — WORKERS
. . . according to the 1976 Codetermination Act

Worker codetermination has proved a stabilising element for the economic and social order of the Federal Republic. This order rests not least on the readiness of all concerned to cooperate fairly. The scope for active participation raises the work motivation of employees and thereby strengthens German industry's efficiency.

Social security

"The Federal Republic of Germany is a democratic and social federal state" — so stipulates its Basic Law. The state is duty-bound to protect each of its inhabitants from social insecurity and to work towards the realisation of social justice. To achieve these aims — thus demands the Social Code of the Federal Republic — it must in good time and on an adequate scale provide the necessary social services and facilities and make social welfare disbursements. These obligations are met by a wide framework of social welfare legislation ranging from sickness, accident and old age to child support, rent subsidy and the promotion of work and vocational training.

Development of social insurance. The Social Insurance (Sozialversicherung) is a combination of self-help and communal help, resting on the one side on the principle of insurance and raising the funds to cover claims from membership dues, while on the other side supporting needy insurants from communal funds.

Social insurance in Germany dates from the Middle Ages when miners first set up common funds to support needy colleagues after work accidents. But it was not until the end of the 19th century that Reich chancellor Bismarck found himself compelled by circumstances to set up a comprehensive social insurance scheme. The trigger was Germany's rapid industrial development. It had brought an extraordinary rise in the number of industrial workers who were hardly or not at all able to accumulate assets or to save for emergencies. Bismarck's prime consideration in introducing the progressive social welfare legislation was to take the wind out of the sails of a strengthening worker movement. It is nevertheless recognised nowadays that this legislation became the foundation for social welfare insurance schemes exemplary for Germany and other countries.

Laws enacted in 1883, 1884 and 1889 established three branches of insurance still covered by German Social Insurance: health, accident and invalidity. In 1911 these three schemes were merged in the Reich Insurance Order (Reichsversicherungsordnung) still valid today, which in addition introduced pensions for widows and orphans.

Whereas only wage earners and low-income salaried staff

were covered by the 1889 Invalidity Act (Invalidengesetz), invalidity insurance was extended to all salary earners in 1911. A 1924 Salaried Employees' Insurance Act (Angestelltenversicherungsgesetz) separated the pensions insurance of salary earners from that of the wage earners and built it up as an insurance scheme in its own right. The social welfare insurance of the miners was standardised in 1923. Statutory unemployment insurance (Arbeitslosenversicherung) came into being as a further branch of social insurance in 1927.

A 1938 Craftsmen's Pensions Act (Gesetz über die Altersversorgung für das Handwerk) also brought craftsmen into the social insurance insofar as they did not themselves wish to provide for old age by taking out life assurance policies.

The development of the social insurance system in the Federal Republic of Germany after World War II was marked above all by the improvement in insurance disbursements. The pensions insurance was substantially revised in 1957 and 1972. A 1957 Farmers' Pensions Act (Gesetz über die Altershilfe für Landwirte) set up a new branch of social insurance. After years of expansion of the social security system, the changed economic situation de-

Major social welfare disbursements *(in DM millions)*

Type of disbursement	1975	1984
Pensions insurance	115,733	180,730
Health insurance	63,416	108,967
Accident insurance	7,040	11,528
Employment promotion	18,416	38,262
Child benefits	14,693	14,967
Family benefits and supports in the public service	10,730	14,831
Pension subsidy to salaried public service employees	3,204	8,155
Continued payment of wages and salaries in sickness	17,500	24,900
Contractual and voluntary employer disbursements (e. g. superannuation)	7,800	14,430
War victims benefits (social compensation)	11,081	13,822
Burden-sharing, restitution	4,247	3,494
Social support	8,880	20,396
Youth aid	4,100	7,088
Training promotion	2,930	698
Housing benefit	1,775	2,654
Public health service	1,350	1,990
Asset-building subsidies	13,326	10,700

mands a standstill in welfare policy. The main needs are now to secure the financial foundations of the social safety net and to curb possibilities of its being misused. It has also proved unavoidable to cut some benefits, delay their being increased and to expand beneficiaries' own participation. Especially in health insurance the rise in costs has to be dampened further and pensions insurance has to be reformed to take changed demographic and economic conditions into account.

Health insurance. Almost all inhabitants of the Federal Republic are insured against the financial disadvantages of illness, be it as obligatory members of statutory health insurance schemes or as voluntary members of private health insurance schemes. In statutory health insurance there is obligatory membership for all wage earners, regardless of income, as well as for salaried staff, the self-employed and a number of other vocational groups up to a certain income. Also insured against illness are all pensioners, unemployed, vocational trainees and students. Those not obliged to insure themselves can continue to do so voluntarily in the statutory schemes.

There are local, vocational and entrepreneurial health insurances as well as specialised ones for miners and seafarers. There are also socalled "Ersatzkassen" (alternative insurances) of particular importance for salaried employees. The insured employee and his or her employer each pay half the member's dues. These average 11.8 % of gross earnings.

The statutory health insurance schemes pay out for sickness, maternity support, death support, family support and measures for early recognition of illnesses. The disbursements for illness cover medical and dental treatment, medication, spectacles, etc. and in the case of incapacity to work sickness money, hospital costs and recuperation expenses.

The accounting procedure is very simple for the insurance member. The patient simply hands a treatment chit in to the doctor. The doctor accounts directly with the insurance. This saves the patient having to advance the money as well as the effort of accounting. In only very few cases does the patient have to bear part of the cost, e. g. in the prescription of medicaments or dental prostheses.

Every employee has a claim to continued payment by the employer of wage or salary for six weeks of illness. After that the health insurance pays sickness benefit money for up to 78 weeks which is 80 % of regular wage or salary. Maternity support covers maternity allowance, midwifery support, a contribution towards the cost of the baby's delivery and the costs of the mother in her home. Family support comprises the benefits disbursed by the health insurance in case of illness, childbearing or death of a member of the insurant's family.

Pensions insurance. The statutory pensions insurance is one of the central pillars of social security in the Federal Republic of Germany. It ensures that workers will not suffer financial need and are able to maintain an adequate standard of living in retirement.

In 1957 wage and salary earners' insurance was revised with the aim of securing social pensions against monetary devaluation and of giving pensioners a share in future productivity growth. The pensions were "index-linked", or "dynamised", i. e. when the average earnings of all workers increase, pensions are raised accordingly.

All wage and salary earners are required by law to be in the pensions insurance scheme. Also to be insured in future are mothers or fathers bringing up a child under one year of age. The self-employed, family members assisting in firms and housewives can join the scheme voluntarily. After the death of an insurant the family dependants retain a certain proportion of the pension.

Contributions to the pensions insurance (currently 19.2 % of gross earnings) are levied up to a certain income level. The worker and the employer each contribute half the sum. When a person is no longer obliged to be in the pensions insurance, voluntary continued membership is possible under certain circumstances.

The wage and salary earners' pensions insurance pays old-age pensions and pensions due to vocational or earning incapacity. The prerequisite for the allocation of a pension is fulfilment of a "waiting period", i. e. a minimum duration of membership in the insurance. The waiting period for the pension for vocational or earning incapacity and for the old age pension from the age of 65 is 60 months. So-called substitute periods, such as military service and the like, count as insured periods.

As a rule the old age pension is paid from the age of 65. On application it is granted from the age of 63 under a so-called "flexible retirement age" provision. The pension can be drawn from the age of 60 if the insurant is seriously disabled, unable to work in his/her vocation, unable to make a living in some other way, was previously unemployed for one year or if she is a woman who has been in predominantly insurance-liable employment for the previous 20 years.

The amount of the pension depends on the duration of insurance and the size of income from employment. In addition, the index-linked pensions principle ensures that the pensioner participates in general income growth.

Payment of pensions is not the only task of the pensions insurance. It also supports the maintenance, improvement and restoration of the insurants' capacity to earn a living. Thus it covers costs of treatment at spas and supports them if for health reasons they have to learn a new vocation.

Company pensions. Many companies give their employees additional old-age benefits. These company pensions are a valuable supplement to the statutory ones. They rest on voluntary agreements, e. g. on individual employment contracts or company awards. Since 1974 a law has been in force which brought those entitled to such company pensions substantial improvements. In contrast to former arrangements they now retain the right to a company pension even if they leave the company before reaching retirement age, provided they have belonged to it for a certain number of years. If the employer becomes insolvent the works pension is still not lost, being then paid out of a fund established for this purpose.

Accident insurance. Protection and support after accidents at work and in the case of diseases arising from a particular vocation is provided by the statutory accident insurance. In the Federal Republic of Germany all employees and farmers are insured by law against accident. Other self-employed workers can join the insurance scheme voluntarily. Since 1971 students, school pupils and kindergarten children have also been covered.

The main carriers of the accident insurance are employers' liability insurance associations (Berufsgenossenschaften), each of which covers a vocation in a certain area. The funds are raised by dues paid only by employers. A claim to payment arises from bodily injury or death resulting from a work accident or illness or death resulting from a disease incurred by the insurant because of the vocation. Acccidents which occur on the way to and from the place of work count as work accidents.

If an insurant suffers damage the accident insurance bears the full cost of treatment. If the worker is incapable of work, injury money is paid. If the insurant becomes incapable of earning a liv-

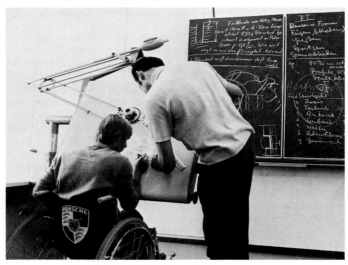

Vocational rehabilitation of a disabled person

ing or dies as a result of an accident or vocational illness the insurance pays a pension or death grant and pension for dependants, as the case may be. Like the other pensions, these are increased in line with general rises in incomes.

The vocational support within the framework of the accident insurance scheme covers vocational training for regaining the capacity to earn a living and periods of re-integration into employment.

The employers' liability insurances are also required to issue regulations on prevention of accidents and combating vocational diseases as well as enforcing their application in the various enterprises.

Unemployment Insurance. All wage and salary earners are insured against unemployment. A jobless worker as a rule is paid unemployment money for at most one year which comprises about two thirds of the last earnings (for more on this see the chapter "Employment", p. 172).

Children Benefit. The upbringing and education of several children is a great financial burden on every family. To ease it, a Federal Children Benefit Act was adopted. It provides for every guardian to be paid child benefit for every child up to the age of 16, in case of school or vocational training up to the age of 27. The benefit is DM 50 for the first child, at least DM 70 for the second and at least DM 140 for each additional one. Parents with low incomes receive higher benefits, at most DM 100 for the second child, DM 220 for the third and DM 240 for every additional one. Apart from children benefit there are tax cuts for parents which are to be expanded. The more children a family has, the less tax it is to pay in comparison with childless couples with equal incomes.

War victims benefits (Social Compensation). The task of the war victims' aid scheme is at least financially to compensate war victims, soldiers' widows and orphans. They are paid pensions, the size of which is adapted according to economic developments. In addition they receive therapy and support in starting work and a career. Soldiers of the Bundeswehr or people doing substitute civilain service whose health has been impaired, and their dependents, are taken care of in the same way.

Social Support. No one who falls into material distress in the Federal Republic of Germany need despair. A Social Support Act provides a net which catches even those unable to help themselves or unable to obtain the help they need elsewhere, for example from family members or from the various branches of the social insurance schemes.

Every inhabitant of the Federal Republic — native or alien — is entitled to social support in such crisis situations: to maintenance grants or grants to help cope with particular circumstances such as disability, illness or old age.

Integration, burden-sharing, compensation

At the end of the Second World War Germany was little more than a vast pile of rubble. Millions of people had perished in the war and under Hitler's regime of violence. It was too late to help them. Millions had saved little more than their bare lives. Germans expelled from the eastern territories had lost their homes and possessions. The inhabitants of the rest of Germany had suffered vast material losses, above all through the bombings. Nor could one forget those whom the Hitler dictatorship had persecuted, humbled, incarcerated or driven out of the country. All these people needed help. That they got it and were fully reintegrated into the economy in spite of the difficult beginning is one of the great political and social achievements of the Federal Republic.

Integration. In 1950 there were about 8.5 million expellees in the Federal Republic. They had initially been encouraged to settle in thinly populated rural regions where they could more readily find a roof over their heads and subsistence than in the destroyed towns. But there was not enough work in these areas. And so from 1949 to 1961 a resettlement programme was carried out in the course of which about a million expellees changed their places of residence.

From the outset the expellees were given rights equal to those of the native population. The objective was not to separate but to integrate them. This was why initial barracks housing was only a temporary emergency measure. As soon as possible the expellees settled amid the indigenous population. Today the integration can be regarded as complete.

From the end of the war until the erection of the Berlin wall in 1961, 3.5 million people moved from the then Soviet Occupation Zone and later German Democratic Republic into the Federal Republic. If their flight was due to some emergency situation they could claim support similar to that given the expellees. They, too, have been absorbed in their new communities. Finally, there are the "later resettlers", Germans who have only recently come to the Federal Republic from East European countries. Much effort is put into their integration which gives rise to special problems, for example the lack of proficiency in the German language.

That integration was successful overall is due to the economic upswing of the 1950's and 60's and to state support programmes.

Burden-sharing. The expellees and other war-damaged first received "immediate support". Then, in 1952, a "burden-sharing" law was enacted. The basic idea of burden-sharing is simple: those who had been able to preserve all or most of their property through the war ceded a part of it to those who had lost everything or almost everything. The administration of burden-sharing is very complicated. Very roughly, it works like this: all natural and juridical persons must pay a levy amounting to half the value of their 1948/49 assets into an equalisation fund, over a span of up to 30 years. From this fund, to which the federal and Länder governments also contribute, compensations, pensions and integration supports are paid to the damaged. Up to the end of 1984 the intakes and disbursements of the equalisation fund totalled c. DM 126,000 millions.

Restitution. From the beginning, compensation for the injustice perpetrated by the Hitler regime was seen as an important task by the responsible politicians of the Federal Republic. In the early 50's several laws were enacted to this end. Anyone who was persecuted because of his opposition to National Socialism or on grounds of race, creed or ideology has a claim to compensation. It is given mainly in the form of pensions, lump sums, capital restitution or loans. More than five million applications have been filed and all but a small number dealt with. In addition, Israel in 1952 was paid integration support for Jewish refugees in Israel and the Jewish Claims Conference a hardship fund for persecuted Jews living outside Israel. The Federal Republic has entered compensation agreements with 12 European states for the benefit of their Nazi-persecuted nationals and their dependents. Compensation disbursements so far total about DM 75,000 millions. It is estimated that approximately DM 17,000 millions will still be disbursed.

Assets for all

Property gives security. In the past millions of people found it impossible, despite lifelong hard work, to acquire assets. Their incomes sufficed for the bare necessities. They were unable to put anything away, to save. Since its foundation, big efforts have been made in the Federal Republic to ease the accumulation of assets for as many people as possible. By the end of the 1950's several laws had been enacted for this purpose. The basic idea was to create incentives for savings through state contributions.

One of the most stable forms of property is one's own home. This is why private housing construction was strongly promoted from the start. Home-savers receive state subsidies or tax concessions. Others get cheap state loans or interest subsidies. Once the homes are built there are tax concessions in the form of higher depreciation allowances and exemption from land tax for a certain period. Also since the 50's there has been a state-bonus savings scheme. That means that anyone depositing a certain sum (up to a fixed maximum) with a savings or commercial bank for six or seven years receives a bonus of 14 % of the sum saved from the state. For each child in a family an additional 2 % are granted.

Millions of people make use of the possibilities of home and bonus saving. The savings promotion through bonuses, as outlined above, is, however, given only to people whose incomes do not exceed a certain maximum. Currently this is DM 24,000 a year for single persons and DM 48,000 for married couples. The bracket increases by DM 1,800 for each child. For employees within these income limits, the aim is to raise not only the will, but also the ability to save. A system to meet this objective was developed in the 1960's. It was improved in 1970 and since then has become popularly known by its abbreviated name of "DM 624 law".

The "DM 624 law". According to the DM 624 law workers with taxable income below the above-named limits receive a "worker savings grant" (Arbeitnehmersparzulage) if they invest DM 624 a year (DM 52 a month) in an "asset-forming manner." Asset-forming investment means that the money is tied down for a longer period. That is the case, for example, in a longer-term savings contract, a homesavings contract or a life insurance policy.

In very many cases — and this is the decisive point — the DM 624 law savings are not, or only partially, paid in by the workers themselves. Most collective agreements contain provisions according to which "asset-forming payments" are wholly or partially made by the employer.

That means that in addition to wages or salaries workers monthly receive a certain sum (DM 52 under the most favourable conditions) which is not paid out to them but credited to an investment account.

Almost all workers are making use of the DM 624 law. In most cases they receive the asset-forming payments under collective agreements wholly or partly from their employers. The annual savings volume, including bonuses and interest, currently amounts to more than DM 12,000 millions.

In 1984 the subsidisable sum for participation in assets (e. g. worker loans, silent participations, shares) was raised from DM 624 to DM 936. Other subsidisable accumulations, such as account-saving, home saving and life assurance, continue to draw subsidies of DM 624 a year.

In 1984 savings deposited with the credit institutions of the Federal Republic totalled DM 576,500 millions, or more than DM 9,400 per inhabitant. This put the Federal Republic at the top of the international savings table. Since 1976 smaller savings deposits have enjoyed increased protection. In the case of a credit institution becoming insolvent there is a fund from which savers are indemnified.

Participation in means of production. An objective of the Federal Republic's market economy is for as many people as possible to acquire ownership of means of production. This purpose is served by the issue of "people's shares" (Volksaktien) which has occured several times in the course of partial privatisation of state enterprises (e. g. the Volkswagen works in 1962). Low-denomination shares were sold at preferential rates to persons with low incomes, each buyer being allowed only a certain number. The same aim is pursued by the issue of "workforce shares". Some 500,000 workers already own stock of the companies employing them.

Another form of worker participation in the means of production (among many others) is a particular system of profit-sharing. In this the workers receive a share of annual profits which is not paid out to them, however, but left — sometimes together with a contribution of their own — in the company in silent partnership.

Worker participation in the means of production is still in an experimental phase in which many forms are being tried. Whether there will one day be a general legislative regulation and what it could look like is not yet evident. Without doubt, however, this is one of the big socio-political tasks of the future.

Housing and urban works

There are 25 million flats in the Federal Republic of Germany. Two thirds of them are rented, the other third are tenant property. Traditionally flats in houses for several families are not purchased but rented in Germany. But the number of owner-units has been growing strongly in recent decades.

Hardly another Western country can point to so comprehensive a housing construction programme as the Federal Republic of Germany. Eighteen million flats have been built since 1949, that is almost three quarters of those now in use. Five million of them are "social housing", that is they were built with government subsidies. Such "social flats" are provided for people with low incomes, families with many children, the disabled and old people. The owners of these flats are allowed to charge their tenants only the socalled "cost rent" which is clearly below the rents paid for new flats on the open market.

The situation on the housing market is now almost balanced. The number of flats corresponds approximately to the number of households. That is why construction of new flats is declining; the emphasis now is on raising accommodation quality by modernisation and rebuilding. Despite this there are still problems on the housing market. For example young married couples, families with many children, low-income earners, pensioners, the handicapped and foreign workers do not always have accommodation matching their needs and ability to pay. On the other side of the ledger there are in some regions surpluses of expensive dwellings. There are also cases of old houses which are still habitable standing empty and being left to decay because owners speculate that their demolition and the use of the land for other buildings — e. g. offices or other business premises – promises higher profits.

Future emphasis will have to be on meeting real needs with new buildings and in respect of old houses to check carefully whether they can be preserved by renovation and modernisation.

Housing quality. In the immediate postwar years the main need was for housing of any kind and its quality was less important. With growing incomes and rapid economic advancement, demands for quality also rose. Thus there is hardly any new dwel-

Modern residential area in Schwalbach

ling nowadays without a bath and central heating. The owners of older housing have also done a lot of modernising. Almost all dwellings are connected to public electricity and water supplies. Almost 90 % of all dwellings satisfy high demands, i. e. they have built-in baths and toilets; more than half have central heating. The rising standard of living is also reflected by the increasing size of dwellings. In 1960 new dwellings averaged 70 square metres of accommodation space, nowadays about 100 square metres.

Nine out of ten households have television and radio receivers as well as telephones. Appliances which ease housework are particularly favoured by German families. Refrigerators, vacuum cleaners, electric washing machines and sewing machines are taken for granted in almost all homes.

Housing subsidy

Year	Recipients	DM millions
1965	395,000	160.2
1970	908,000	600.3
1975	1,660,000	1,643.0
1976	1,585,000	1,615.4
1977	1,467,000	1,472.9
1978	1,549,000	1,788.9
1979	1,518,000	1,856.7
1980	1,486,000	1,834.5
1981	1,609,000	2,432.5
1982	1,611,000	2,666.8
1983	1,422,000	2,567.1
1984	1,383,000	2,430.4

Housing subsidy and tenure protection. All citizens who earn too little to pay for adequate accommodation are helped by housing subsidies from the state. They are paid as a grant towards the rent, or as a subsidy to owners of their houses or flats. The amount depends on size of income, size of family and total outlay for accommodation.

Tenant protection has been improved several times by legislation. Nowadays no tenant need fear unjustified or arbitrary eviction or excessive rent demands. In order to ensure that landlords get a commensurate return on their property and to give private investors an incentive to build new housing the federal government has made further changes in tenancy law. Rents are to re-

Dwellings completed

Year	Dwellings	Year	Dwellings
1949	220,000	1976	392,000
1955	568,000	1977	409,000
1960	574,000	1978	368,000
1965	592,000	1979	357,000
1970	478,000	1980	388,000
1971	555,000	1981	365,000
1972	660,000	1982	347,000
1973	714,000	1983	341,000
1974	604,000	1984	398,000
1975	437,000		

Old-town modernisation in Kreuzberg, Berlin

flect more strongly than hitherto supply and demand on the market.

Home ownership. Most Germans dream of owing a house or flat. This coincides with the socio-political objectives of the federal government which include a broad distribution of assets as well as improving the housing supply, in particular for the socially underprivileged. And so there is a variety of state supports for those wanting to build their own homes, from the moment they decide to do so until completion and beyond.

All these aids notwithstanding, financing a new home, especially in the conurbation areas, means a substantial burden for many years because of inflation and the scarcity of building land. Increasingly important is state support for modernisation of old buildings.

Urban planning. The Federal Republic is one of the most densely populated countries of the world (247 inhabitants per square kilometre). Whereas a hundred years ago by far the majority of Germans still lived in small rural settlements, industrialisation and population increase have reversed this. Most people today live in towns or larger communities.

Almost all towns were severely damaged in the war. The 1950's and 1960's were the time of reconstruction. The emphasis was on economic considerations. In the town centres residential buildings had to make way for commercial premises. The result was that after working hours many town centres were deserted. The rapidly growing motorisation demanded ever wider roads which were ruthlessly driven through residential areas. For a time the "car-suited town" was the ideal striven for by urban planners. One almost forgot that towns are primarily there for the people who live in them. Land prices skyrocketed. It became more and more difficult to assert sensible building and land usage benefiting society as a whole.

Meanwhile a rethinking has begun in urban building policy. Efforts are now made to preserve the grown structures of towns and to fill the centres with life again. Motor traffic no longer gets unconditional priority. In many places pedestrian zones have been established in the busiest shopping areas. New laws have given local governments better instruments for planning and implementing building projects. Citizens are sooner and more intensively brought into the planning process. These are but beginnings. The objective, the "humane town", is still far off.

Protection of the environment

Protection of the natural foundations of life is one the most pressing tasks of our time in the Federal Republic of Germany. Chancellor Helmut Kohl in his policy declaration of 4 May 1983 made clear the high priority of environmental policy: "It is the duty of all of us to preserve for future generations the environment entrusted to us. We do not have the right ruthlessly to exploit nature. Technical progress must take the environment into account."

The people of the Federal Republic of Germany have grown increasingly sensitive to environmental issues. All surveys show how strongly public awareness in this field has grown in recent years. Most civic action groups adress environmental problems. Parties, associations and industry are increasingly addressing environmental questions.

For the highly industrialised Federal Republic protection of the environment makes sense not only ecologically but also economically. Without protection of the air, water and soil, the economy would be deprived of the means of production. But the environmental problems can be solved only with technology, not against it.

Cleaning up the air. Reducing air pollution takes priority. It is urgently necessary to fight the forest damage which has spread alarmingly. Trees are losing their needles or leaves, their growth is retarded and finally they die. Half of the forest area in the Federal Republic of Germany is already damaged. But human health, soil and water, buildings and valuable works of art must also be protected from damage by polluted air.

The federal government pursues the aim of attacking air pollution at source and drastically reducing it. The main task is to cut the pollutants emitted by large firing plants, especially power stations and distant-heating plants, and by motor vehicles. Since 1984 unleaded petrol has been on sale in the Federal Republic of Germany. By the mid-90's all motor vehicles are to be fitted with catalytic exhaust converters for which only unleaded petrol can be used. This is considerably to cut the pollutants in car exhausts.

Air pollution does not stop at boundaries. Half the sulphur dioxide pollution in the Federal Republic comes from abroad and half the sulphur dioxide emitted in the Federal Republic is carried by the wind to other countries. Obviously, keeping the air clean is an international task. Within the European Community the federal government has pressed for further efforts and put forward proposals.

The federal government sees in the international air purity convention which came into force in 1983 within the framework of the Economic Commission of the United Nations for Europe (ECE) an important instrument for developing a joint air purity policy in East and West. Cross-frontier air pollution is also a problem between the two German states. The federal government is engaged in negotiations with the GDR aimed at comprehensive cooperation in environmental protection.

Protection of streams and oceans. The map showing the degrees of pollution of streams in the Federal Republic (p. 284) shows that protection of streams was not able to keep pace with industrial growth. However, the condition of the streams has improved noticeably of late. For example, the oxygen content in a number of especially burdened stretches of the Rhein has risen in 10 years from four to nine milligrammes per litre, a normal level. Such successes have been achieved by building effluent treatment plants and canalisation as well as by industrial programmes. An important role was played in this by an Effluents Act which makes local governments and industry do more about reducing pollutants in effluents.

The federal government wants the discharge of pollutants to be cut or eliminated at source in future. To this end it is most important to improve treatment and filtering techniques and techniques for purifying water for re-use so as to conserve natural water reserves.

Pollution of the North Sea is worrying. Pollutants enter it with the streams and the air. Refuse is tipped in and shipping and oil extraction also add to its burdens. This problem can only be solved in solidarity between all North Sea states. A multilateral North Sea protection conference held in Bremen in November 1984 brought international consensus on practical measures to take against this dangerous development.

Landscape and soil protection. Land is constantly being "consumed" in the Federal Republic of Germany by residential, transport and industrial building. The proportion of residential and traffic land has risen in 30 years from under 8 % to over 12 % of the total. Correspondingly, the area of land not built on has de-

Natural stream in ecologically undisturbed environment

creased. Landscape as near as possible to a natural state is not only an indispensable recuperation area for people, however, but also the main biotope for wild animals and plants. About 350 animal species and 60 flowering plants have already died out in the Federal Republic of Germany. Thirty percent of all animal and plant species are menaced by economic or technical development or by loss of land.

The trend is to be countered by landscape planning provided for by a Federal Nature Protection Act. The law stipulates compensatory action for all unavoidable interference with the environment and provides for the declaration of protected nature and landscape areas.

To ensure the preservation of recuperation landscapes there are already many nature parks, protected larger areas of particular relevance and beauty. To protect the biotopes of animals

A canalised stream devastates the landscape

and plants and to preserve particular types of landscape (such as wandering dunes on the North Sea coast) more than 1,800 nature protection areas have been designated, totalling 2,500 square kilometres.

The use of land for settlement, industry and transportation attacks its structure and its ground water content. Particular threats are heavy metals and certain chemicals which are degradable only with difficulty or not at all and which accumulate in the soil. From there they can get into the food cycle and menace human health.

The federal government has presented a comprehensive soil protection concept to conserve the soil as a storage and filter of water, as a biotope for plants and animals and in all its other many functions. The federal states are also trying to initiate air cleansing and garbage disposal measures to this end.

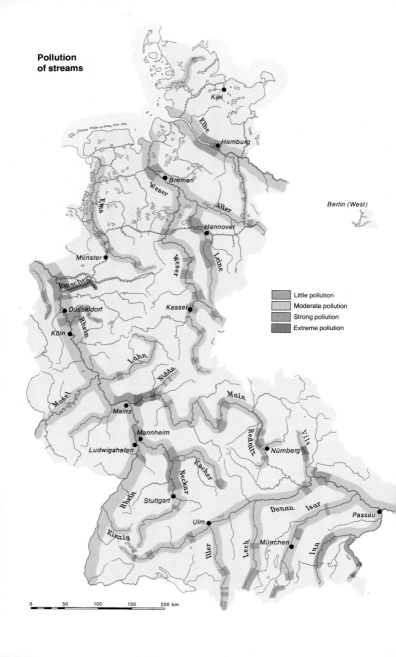

**Pollution
of streams**

Kiel

Elbe

Hamburg

Bremen

Weser

Aller

Hannover

Berlin (West)

Weser

Leine

Münster

Emscher

Düsseldorf

Kassel

Köln

Rhein

Lahn

Nidda

Main

Mosel

Mainz

Mannheim

Redmtz

Ludwigshafen

Nürnberg

Vils

Kocher

Neckar

Rhein

Stuttgart

Donau

Isar

Passau

Ulm

Kinzig

Iller

Lech

München

Inn

	Little pollution
	Moderate pollution
	Strong pollution
	Extreme pollution

0   50   100   150   200 km

Noise abatement wall at Frankfurt airport

Noise and garbage. Economic growth and prosperity have increased the sources of noise pollution. Every second household in the Federal Republic is constantly or intermittently exposed to considerable noise. Most is caused by road traffic. The federal government has worked within the European Community for a uniform tightening up of noise tolerances for motor cars and motor bikes. Noise abatement along roads and railways is to be further improved. Measures are also being taken against aviation and work noise.

The amount of garbage has also risen enormously in the prosperous industrial society of the Federal Republic. Every year more than 30 million tonnes of household refuse and about 100 million tonnes of industrial waste are produced and have to be disposed of. Disposal without harming the environment is an important task of the state and industry. Efficient central installations and technically highly developed special deposits for difficult wastes are available.

Because the Federal Republic of Germany is poor in raw materials, material recycling and energy extraction from waste are especially important. Scrapped cars and old tires are already being almost totally re-used, as are 700,000 tonnes of old glass a year.

Energy is extracted from about 30 % of domestic garbage. One mark of the affluent society is excessive packaging. Used packaging contributes greatly to the volume of refuse. The aim must be to have reusable packaging for as many goods as possible.

Women in society

"Men and women shall have equal rights", says the Basic Law in its Article 3. So why this special chapter and not one about men?

No one would dispute that women in the Federal Republic of Germany have special problems. There are almost three million more women than men, for example. Among the people over 45 years of age the surplus of women is more than three and a half millions. There are three quarters of a million widowers but more than four and a half million widows. The Second World War, although now more than 40 years past, still determines the lives of an entire generation of women in Germany.

But next to that there is also a "women's question" in the narrower sense. Women in German society are subject to discriminations. Old preconceived notions of what women are "entitled to" die hard, even among women themselves. Although much has improved in recent decades, much remains to be done. The problems that await solution concern not only the state but society as a whole.

Equality before the law. In line with the Basic Law women's legal equality is complete. Legal development stretching over decades has almost been concluded. An important advance in this was a 1957 law which introduced, particularly, the equality of woman in matrimonial property law. But there still remained female inequality in marital and family law.

Full juridical equality of women came with a law which has been in force since 1977. The stipulation according to which the woman is responsible for the household and can take outside employment only if this is compatible with her duties in marriage and the family was abolished. Now husband and wife must come to agreement over their household and vocational duties. The family name can by agreement now be either the maiden name of the wife or the man's name. In case of divorce the material security of the economically weaker partner, as a rule the woman, no longer depends on who was blameless. Now the court merely ascertains breakdown of marriage without allocating guilt. The economically stronger partner has to take care of the other until he or she is able to earn their own living again. Furthermore, any pension entitlement or other accumulated old age provisions are split equally.

Women in employment. All education facilities — schools, universities, almost all types of vocational training — are today as open to women as to men in the Federal Republic. Labour law contains special protective regulations for pregnancy. Women are not allowed to be subjected to work beyond their physical capacity. Night work is only exceptionally permissible.

There has been a marked improvement in the vocational training of girls and women. For example, the proportion of female students at all universities in the 1984/85 winter semester was 37.8 % compared with 22.7 % in the 1957/58 winter semester. Of the students who passed the teacher exam in 1983, 60 % were women. Of the 1984 Abitur (senior high school) graduates 45 % were women. In 1957 it was only just under 34 %. The absolute and relative number of girls with completed vocational training (apprenticeships) has also risen substantially since the 1950's.

Every second woman between the ages of 15 and 65 is in employment. Women account for just short of 38 % of the workforce. Their employment in business and industry, health care and education has become self-evident and indispensable.

Despite this women are still discriminated against in many ways in employment. Economic recessions and unemployment strike them disproportionately. The shortage of apprenticeship positions is especially serious for girls. The gross hourly wage of men in private industry in 1984 averaged DM 16.59, that of women only DM 12.00. Even skilled woman workers earned less than untrained men. Average monthly gross earnings of salaried staff in commerce and industry were DM 4,025 for men, DM 2,725 for women in 1984.

Women doing the same work as men or work of equal value have a legitimate claim to the same pay. Discrimination occurs nonetheless in the differing assessments of the types of work "typically" done by women or "typically" done by men. Women's work is generally down-graded as "physically lighter" work.

Discrimination against women is clearest, however, in vocational advancement. Although almost 40 % of the students are women, the number of women concluding their studies with doctorates is just under 20 %. Only 5.2 % of university professorships in the Federal Republic of Germany are held by women. There are hardly any women in top business positions. Much the same applies to the public service, especially to schools. Most of the

Assembly line workers

Doctor

Secretary

Housewife

Taxi driver

Teacher

teachers are women but most of the headmasters are men. However, in the public service the principle of equal pay for equal
work is a reality. All public service workers at federal, state and
communal levels are equally paid in their respective salary or
wage groups.

The reasons for the discrimination of women in work often lie in
women's working lives running differently from men's. Many women train for less qualified vocations because often their employment is regarded as only temporary before they start taking care
of families.

Women in the family. There are about 23 million families in the Federal Republic of Germany. It has been observed for a number of
years now that more marriages than used to remain childless and
that the number of families with three and more children is declining while the number with one or two is growing.

The role of the woman in the family as housewife and mother is
of equal value to working in a job. This is recognised by the law introduced in 1986 providing for childraising benefit and childraising furlough. Under the law the state pays DM 600 childraising
benefit a month for 10 months for children born after 1. 1. 1986. For
this period the parent who gives up his or her job to attend to the
children is under special protection from dismissal. Moreover the
time women spend raising families is to be taken into account in
pensions insurance. These measures aim at strengthening the
social security of women in the family.

Women in politics. Women have had the vote and right to stand for
election in Germany since 1918. Since they comprise more than
half the population they are also in the majority as voters. Although the proportion of politically active women is rising, it is
still remarkably small. There are no significant differences in voting participation.

But all the big political parties have disproportionately few female members: the Free Democrats (FDP) slightly over 25 %, the
Social Democrats (SPD) 24 %, the Christian Democrats (CDU)
22 % and the Bavaria-based Christian Socialists (CSU) 14 %. In
the Greens about a third of the members are women. In the German Trade Union Federation there are 21 % female members. In
the 10th Bundestag only 10 % of the members are women, in the
Länder parliaments the average is similar. At any rate, there has
been at least one woman minister in every federal government
since 1961.

In addition to longer-established women's organisations, in recent years an autonomous women's movement has come into being which tries to fight discrimination. There are meanwhile many clear signs that among women, and also among men, a process of rethinking is taking place which is leading to a noticeable loosening of the roles of the sexes and thereby contributing greatly to the realisation of full equality.

Council of women:
Deutscher Frauenrat
Südstr. 125
5300 Bonn 2

The young

Every fourth inhabitant of the Federal Republic of Germany is below the age of 20. Where there are young people there are youth problems — in all countries. Perhaps in Germany they appear more sharply than elsewhere because recent German history has been so full of divisions. Here people live together who were born at the time of the last emperor, in the Weimar Republic, during the Nazi dictatorship, in the need of the immediate postwar period but mostly in the democratic state after World War II.

Generation conflict. The experiences of the various generations are worlds apart. The older people knew the mass unemployment of the early 1930's and the violent Hitler regime. The middle aged have been marked by war and postwar deprivation; they know what a precarious existence, what loss of all security and the strains of reconstruction mean.

The young generation is growing up in comparative prosperity and a high measure of security. It takes the system of society so much for granted that at times it tends to look down on it.

The unaffected, frank radicalism with which some youngsters criticise their environment is provocative to older people who see what they have achieved at great effort put to question. It is sometimes forgotten that it requires effort to preserve it. Such tensions between the generations are irritating but necessary for the further development of society.

In other respects the young people of the Federal Republic hardly differ in their lifestyle, opinions and appearance from the young people of other Western industrial countries. The specifically German youth movement which played a large part in the first third of our century was practically insignificant in the build-up phase of the Federal Republic. This movement which turned emphatically against the bourgeois world of the adults sought a new closeness to nature and new common experience. With its songs, travel and campfire romanticism it fascinated millions of young people. Some aspects of this German youth movement returned during the student protests of the 1960's which, however, were international in character and occurred in totally different forms. Other elements have gone into the present-day ecology, alternative and peace movement which can also be understood as a protest against the conditions of life in the modern industrial society.

It is not always easy for youngsters these days to find their way in a complex industrial society such as the Federal Republic of Germany. A commission convened by the Bundestag has examined the causes of unease, unrest and protest. They include not only such obvious problems as the destruction of nature, the danger to peace and the shortage of training places and jobs, there are also deeper-lying causes such as the unrequited yearning for caring attention, for security in the incomprehensible and impersonal modern industrial society. The parliamentary report also complains of growing isolation of older and younger people in separate spheres of life. Relations between people of the same age are growing ever more important; this entails the danger of separation from the adult world. The former cohesion between the generations has become looser. Integration of the young is becoming more and more urgent.

Organised and unorganised youth. There are about 80 supraregional youth associations in the Federal Republic of Germany, not counting the sports clubs. Most of these organisations are affiliated to the Federal Youth Ring (Deutscher Bundesjugendring), such as the youth movements of the Evangelical and Catholic churches, the trade unions and the German scouting movement. The youth organisations of the big political parties belong to the Ring of Political Youth (Ring Politischer Jugend). Most youth organisations receive financial support from the federal, state and local governments. Organised and non-organised youth are not rigidly separated from one another. Most organisations also welcome non-members to their events. Youngsters who join no group but wish to be together with others of their age all the same can do so in many types of leisure facilities. There they can talk about their problems, dance and pursue their interests. Usually such establishments employ a social worker they can turn to for help.

In the German town of Altena in Westphalia there is the oldest youth hostel in the world. It was opened in 1912. There are now 564 youth hostels in the Federal Republic. In 1984 they recorded 9.1 million overnight stays; 727,000 of them were by foreigners. The youth hostels are places of encounter between young people from all countries.

Since the late 1970's other forms of cohabitation by youngsters and young adults have grown in importance. These are self-help

Entrant in youth research competition

or initiative groups where social commitment or alternative cultural activities are tried out.

The state and the young. The aim of state policy for the young is to promote their free development. The young people are to learn to shape their lives under their own responsibility. They are to find their place in their work and in society and to be able to develop their personality. In this sense the state wants to help young people to exercise their rights; it wants to support the families and parents in their duties and upbringing tasks. Policy for the young is more than youth policy. It is also always societal and welfare policy. If the young are to feel at home in our everyday world that world itself must get a humane face.

In a free society there are many ways to develop. That is why in the Federal Republic of Germany there is no state youth organisation which has ready answers for the young and shows only one way of shaping one's life. The state takes care of the young with protective laws, with social aids and with offers for voluntary participation; it promotes but does not regiment. It gives preference to clubs, associations, the churches, foundations and other institutions independent of the state in helping the young. In

line with the tasks they have set themselves and with their ideologies they serve the wellbeing of children and juveniles. This
multiplicity of offers and aids is a firm plank in the youth policy of
the federal government.

The state, that is mainly local governments, offers many possibilities of extra-mural youth education, such as youth leisure centres, musical, cultural and political education. Help is also available for needy families and support is given to a great number of
non-statal and welfare organisations. Protection and promotion
of the young by local bodies takes place on the basis of statal
laws. Some, such as the Youth Protection Act and the Youth Welfare Act, are federal, others are state laws.

Most of the funds for youth aid come from state and local governments. In 1983 they totalled DM 5,700 millions. On top of that
there is the public expenditure on schooling and job training, for
employment, for family support and the like.

Youth unemployment is a serious problem. Although it is declining, almost every fourth unemployed person is under the age
of 25. (In most other countries this proportion lies between 30 and
40%.) Worst affected are youngsters with inadequate schooling
or job training. Finding jobs and training places for all these
young people is one of the most pressing tasks the state and the
business community can only solve together.

An important instrument of federal youth policy is the Federal
Youth Plan (Bundesjugendplan). In it the promotion of youth work
by the state becomes effective. Funds from the Plan are spent
mainly for international youth work, the activities of youth organisations and construction of youth support facilities. In 1985 the federal government made available DM 135,000 millions for these
tasks. Finally, the state promotes the "Youth Research" programme with considerable funds. Here young people have the
opportunity to submit scientific findings to an independent panel.
The most original and best works are awarded prizes.

International youth contacts are promoted in the Federal
Republic of Germany as bridges of understanding. The 1985 Federal Youth Plan set aside DM 24 millions for non-school youth
exchange and an additional DM 18.5 millions as the German contribution to the Franco-German youth programme. Over and beyond this the states and local governments promote many international youth encounters.

Intra-German youth exchange serves understanding between
people in the two parts of Germany. The federal government is
particularly concerned about this in order to keep alive the

awareness of a common history and a common responsibility of the Germans.

The will to share responsibility is expressed by the almost undisputed commitment of the young to democracy. Anti-democratic parties on the right or the left find practically no followers among young people. The democratic order of the Federal Republic of Germany is proving open and lively enough to absorb new ideas and impetus from the young.

Youth umbrella organisation:
Deutscher Bundesjugendring
Haager Weg 44
5300 Bonn 1

Health

In the first instance health care is everyone's individual concern. But it is also a task of state and society. Everyone, regardless of financial or social situation, should have the same chances to maintain and restore their health. This objective has not yet been reached in the Federal Republic but much is being done to approach it step by step.

Health is threatened above all in Germany by the so-called "civilisatory illnesses". Half of all deaths are due to heart and circulation ailments. In second place among fatal diseases is cancer. Tuberculosis, still a major risk only a few decades ago, now scarcely occurs.

Doctors and hospitals. There are about 161,000 doctors and 34,000 dentists in the Federal Republic. That is one doctor to every 380 inhabitants, one dentist to every 1,800. This makes the Federal Republic medically one of the best equipped countries in the world. However, access to doctors and dentists is not equally good everywhere. This is especially true of the distribution of the general practitioners who form the backbone of the population's medical care. (Just under half the doctors work in free practice, the others in hospitals or administration.) In rural areas and on the urban peripheries there is often a lack of doctors. Since one cannot force a doctor to open a surgery at a certain place, local government authorities are trying to attract doctors by offering to help them open practices in their areas. Possibilities of distributing doctors better by legislative means are being considered.

There are about 683,000 beds available in more than 3,000 hospitals, or one bed per 90 inhabitants. In this respect the Federal Republic comes off well in international comparisons. Hospitals are operated by the state and local governments (more than half the beds), welfare, mostly church organisations (more than a third of the beds) and private enterprises. The hospitals are financed by the contributions of the patients to their health insurances and from the public budgets. The federation contributes DM 1,000 millions a year to the costs.

Preventive health care. According to the old saying, "prevention is better than cure", preventive health care is becoming increas-

Hydrotherapy for a disabled person

ingly important in health policy. The aim is for every person to learn to preserve health on their own responsibility by avoiding risks such as obesity or lack of exercise. Hence preventive or early detection examinations are being introduced in many fields. Pregnant women are to see a doctor 10 times before delivery to help avoid health hazards to mother and child. From birth to the age of four eight preventive examinations are made of children. Schoolchildren are examined before they begin school; in school they are regularly checked by doctors and dentists. Before youngsters start work they must also submit to a preventive examination.

Since there are good chances of cancer diseases being healed if symptoms are recognised early, tests for early detection of cancer are especially important. Since 1971 the statutory health insurances have been paying for one examination a year for certain types of cancer for their insurants. Unfortunately only less than half the women and only 20 % of the men are making use of this. That is a very unsatisfactory situation. Especially the health insurances are trying to motivate more people to avail themselves of these early detection examinations.

The costs of health. The development of health care costs is caus-
ing grave concern. It reflects the negative side of a positive development. Health protection is better than ever. Doctors and hospitals use the most modern technical facilities. The health insurances which used to pay only for the most necessary things, nowadays cover even very expensive treatment. And such treatment
is more and more taken for granted because people's attitudes to
health have changed. For most inhabitants of the Federal Republic maintenance of health is the number one priority. This in turn
has something to do with everyone having to be at the peak of
health to be able to cope with the demands made on them at work.

All this has resulted in the costs of the health system having risen disproportionately. It now amounts to more than DM 200,000
millions a year. That is why the federal government is trying to cut
costs in the health system without a drop in the quality of services
to the public.

Sport

Every third inhabitant of the Federal Republic of Germany is a member of a sport club. There are some 40,000 public and school sportsgrounds, 25,000 sports, gymnastics and special sporthalls (e. g. for tennis, riding, ice sport) and 7,400 indoor and outdoor swimming pools throughout the country. These figures suffice to show that one can hardly call sport "the most important secondary matter in the world". In the Federal Republic of Germany as everywhere else it has become a major socio-political and economic factor.

Football (soccer) is by far the most popular sport. The German Football Association (Deutscher Fussball-Bund) has by far the largest membership of all sports groupings. Football, moreover, is a spectator sport, attracting many thousands of people every week to professional and amateur games.

The transformation that sport has undergone in the Federal Republic since World War II is illustrated by the example of tennis: once a privilege of the rich, it has become almost a mass sport in recent years. The same goes for horse riding. The people who indulge in sports in clubs and competitively as a rule do this as amateurs. There are professional sportsmen and women above all in tennis, football and riding.

Sport in the Federal Republic is independent of the state. The sports organisations run their own affairs. The state provides funds only where the means of the organisations do not suffice. Partnerlike cooperation with the sports organisations is one of the major tenets of state sports policy.

Sports self-administration is based on about 60,000 clubs grouping about 19 million members. The clubs are organised in 11 state sports federations and many specialised associations. The umbrella organisation is the German Sports Federation (Deutscher Sportbund, DSB). It represents the interests of the individual member organisations vis-à-vis the state and the public at large.

Sport in the service of people. Most people who indulge in sport in the Federal Republic of Germany do not do so because they are out to achieve great things; the joy of taking part in a group is the main motive. The socio-political and health importance of this

National team goalkeeper Harald ("Toni") Schumacher (in blue jersey) in a federal league soccer match

broadly based sports activity is undisputed. Sport serves the preservation of health and offsets the lack of exercise in our highly technical world.

Organised sport has been growing year by year at a fast rate for the past quarter of a century. Especially women and older people have been increasingly joining clubs. The large number of sports lovers is catered for by a broad variety of activities in the clubs. There are, for example, programmes for groups as diverse as the disabled, foreign inhabitants of the Federal Republic and moth-

The 10 biggest sports associations *(members 1985)*

Deutscher Fussball-Bund (soccer)	4,683,857
Deutscher Turner-Bund (gymnastics)	3,495,810
Deutscher Tennis-Bund (tennis)	1,741,622
Deutscher Schützenbund (marksmen)	1,232,841
Deutscher Leichtathletik-Verband (track and field)	787,895
Deutscher Handball-Bund (handball)	764,582
Deutscher Tisch-Tennis-Bund (table tennis)	675,610
Deutscher Skiverband (skiing)	648,781
Deutscher Schwimm-Verband (swimming)	564,427
Verband Deutscher Sportfischer (angling)	511,602

ers with children. There are also offers of sports activities for families and older people.

Popular and leisure sport are also served by the DSB programmes "Trimm Dich" ("Get Fit") and "Sport für alle" ("Sport for all") which include popular competitions in running, swimming, cycling, skiing and hiking in which anyone can take part. Millions of people do every year. Especially popular is the "Sportabzeichen" ("Sports Badge"). It is awarded by the DSB in gold, silver and bronze. About 600,000 Germans do the tests demanded for the badge every year, whereby the individual can choose from a number of disciplines.

Popular sport interacts strongly in the Federal Republic of Germany with competitive sport, with popular sport being the foundation for competitive successes. For athletes to be successful in modern competitive sport they need intensive training, pedagocial and psychological support and not least a measure of financial security. These problems have been addressed by the "Stiftung Sporthilfe" ("Sports Aid Foundation") established in 1967. It regards itself as the social support organisation of sport in the Federal Republic and in exchange for their years of commitment aims to provide sports competitors with at least enough financial

Marathon for all

School sport

security to assure worry-free training. It is not a statal organisation. Its funds come partly from private donors; it also gets funds from a television lottery ("Glücksspirale") and from the sale of sports aid postage stamps which the Federal Post has been issuing regularly since 1975.

State sports promotion. The sports organisations in the Federal Republic of Germany are supported in many ways by the state. Federal sports promotion goes mainly to top competitive sport. The federation gives money in particular for training and competition programmes, for special medical attention for top competitors, for training and employment of trainers, for construction of sports facilities and for scientific sports research. There is also promotion of sport for the disabled and for international sports policy to enable the specialised sports organisations to meet their international commitments.

The aim of effective promotion of top competitive sport is lastingly to influence the development of sport overall in the Federal Republic of Germany. In addition the promotion of competitive sport serves state representation. To this end financial support is provided for the participation of top achievers, both individuals

Boris Becker, Wimbledon singles winner 1985 and 1986

and teams, in international competitions, e. g. European and world championships or the Olympics.

Support of popular sport is mainly the task of state and local governments. The main areas of this support are construction of facilities, school sport and club sport.

From 1961 to 1975 the federation, the states and local governments invested DM 17,400 millions in building recuperation, playing and sports facilities. This has resulted in a standard which is internationally regarded as exemplary. Notwithstanding this there is a need for more sports facilities.

Sports federation:
Deutscher Sportbund
Otto-Fleck-Schneise 12
6000 Frankfurt/Main 71

Leisure and holidays

At around the turn of the century there was as good as no "free time" left to employees after work, sleep and life-sustaining chores. As working hours decreased, so the amount of freely disposable time grew. After World War II the average daily free time of workers in the Federal Republic increased from two and a half hours in 1952 to almost four hours in 1980. There is now enough for one occasionally to hear the slogan of "leisure society".

But that also poses dangers, the disposable free time tempting many to take on extra work at the expense of necessary recreation. Many people do not of their own accord find meaningful ways of spending their leisure time. And so a variety of state, church and communal institutions, clubs and associations are trying to provide leisure activities. This includes sports grounds, indoor and outdoor public baths, libraries, adult education courses, scientific and musical circles and much more. Business has been quick to recognise a promising market and a regular "leisure industry" has grown up. In 1972 an average four-person household spent DM 181 on leisure pursuits. In 1984 it was more than DM 450. Leisure spending is expected to continue rising. Leisure time spending is more and more becoming the object of scientific research, some universities and colleges already offering "leisure pedagogics" as a course of study.

Surveys of people's pastimes are difficult and often produce very disparate findings. Many people name recuperation through sport and walking. But reading books and magazines, watching television and do-it-yourself hobbies are also favourites. There are many others, ranging from entertaining guests to taking part in club gatherings.

One important part of leisure is holidaymaking. Every worker in the Federal Republic has a legal claim to at least three weeks' paid vacation a year. But collective agreements with employers give most workers five weeks or more. More than half of the population make at least one major holiday journey a year. On top of that come short trips over long weekends or public holidays. The most popular foreign holiday destination is Italy, followed by Spain, Austria, France, Yugoslavia and Switzerland. Apart from these favourite destinations, German tourists may be met in any accessible country. In 1976 the Federal Republic for the first time outstripped the United States in the number of holidaymakers going abroad. In 1984 West Germans spent around DM 40,000 millions on foreign travel. Conversely, foreign holidaymakers spent DM 16,000 millions in the Federal Republic.

Germans prefer seaside holidays, 39% choosing to bathe and lie on the beach; 35% are more interested in being together with other people and just as many are keen to make acquaintance with the cuisine of their host country. Holiday sport activities take general priority, according to statements by 52% of vacationers questioned. Swimming, ball games, hiking, sailing, canoeing or rowing, riding, mountaineering and skiing are the preferred activities.

How seriously leisure is taken in the Federal Republic is reflected by the establishment of the German Leisure Association (Deutsche Gesellschaft für Freizeit) in 1971. This grouping concerns itself with basic research into leisure spending, disseminates information and documentation and provides advice. It has as members 33 umbrella organisations from all spheres of society.

Leisure association:
Deutsche Gesellschaft für Freizeit
Niederkasseler Str. 16
4000 Düsseldorf 11

Tourist board:
Deutsche Zentrale für Tourismus e. V.
Beethovenstr. 69
6000 Frankfurt/Main 1

Religion and churches

"Freedom of faith, of conscience, and freedom of creed, religious or ideological (weltanschaulich), shall be inviolable. The undisturbed practice of religion is guaranteed."

This provision of the Basic Law (Article 4) is taken for granted as self-evident by everyone in the Federal Republic.

Denominations. About 90 % of the population belong to Christian churches, almost precisely half each Catholic and Protestant, with a small minority in other Christian confessions. The Protestants are in the majority in the north, Catholics in the south of the Federal Republic. The Länder of Rheinland-Pfalz (Rhineland-Palatinate), Saarland and Bayern (Bavaria) are mainly Catholic, the two major denominations are about equally strong in Baden-Württemberg and Nordrhein-Westfalen (North-Rhine Westphalia). Elsewhere Protestants predominate.

History. The contemporary distribution of Christian denominations dates from the Age of Reformation and there, too, lie the roots of the special German relationship between church and state. After decades of religious warfare the 1555 Religious Peace of Augsburg established the principle "cuius regio, eius religio" (religion according to region) giving regional rulers the right to dictate their subjects' denomination. The 1648 Peace of Westphalia (ending the Thirty Years' War) curbed this right; from then on subjects could continue to adhere to their old faith if their ruler changed his. The close connection between state and church, reflected inter alia by the Protestant temporal princes also being the leading bishops of their regions, was not done away with by this, however. It began to loosen only in the 19th century. The 1919 Weimar Reich constitution implemented the separation of church and state without, however, completely removing historical ties. The legal situation thus created is by and large the one which obtains today, the post-World War II Basic Law having taken over the corresponding provisions of the Weimar constitution in their original wording.

Church and state. There is no state church in the Federal Republic. The state is neutral vis-à-vis religions and creeds. But neither are the churches private associations, they have a special status as corporate bodies under public law which have a partner-like relationship with the state. Apart from the Basic Law, their relationship to the state is regulated by concordats and agreements. To take care of their interests vis-à-vis the federal government and parliament they have high-ranking representatives in the capital.

The churches' property rights are guaranteed. They have a claim to financial allocations from the state which, for example, pays contributions to the salaries of the clergy and assumes, in whole or in part, the costs of certain church facilities, such as kindergartens, hospitals and schools. The churches are empowered to levy taxes on their members which as a rule are collected by state authorities, for which the churches pay the administrative cost. To resign from a church a member must make a declaration to a state authority. The clergy are trained mainly at state universities and the churches have a vested right to influence theological university appointments.

These far-reaching rights of the religious communities and the continuing close links with the state are not undisputed. Despite occasional criticism, the work of the churches in operating hospitals, facilities for the handicapped and problem groups, old people's and nursing homes and schools represents almost irreplaceable social services whose absence from public life would be unthinkable.

The Protestant church. The Evangelical Church in Germany (Evangelische Kirche in Deutschland, EKD) is an alliance of 17 Land churches, each of which is widely autonomous. Church administrative regions are not identical with the territories of the federal states. The EKD's top legislative organ is the Synod, its top executive body the Council of the EKD (Rat der EKD) which also appoints a plenipotentiary in Bonn. Of the 17 Land churches, seven are Lutheran: Bayern, Braunschweig (Brunswick), Hannover, Northern Elbe (Nordelbische Kirche), Oldenburg, Schaumburg-Lippe, Württemberg; two Reformed: Lippe, Westphalia; eight United: Baden, Berlin (West), Bremen, Hessen and Nassau, Kurhessen-Waldeck, Palatinate, Rhineland, Westphalia. "Reformed" is the description for churches based on the teachings of Calvin and Zwingli, "United" the term used for churches formed by mergers between "Reformed" and "Lutheran" groupings.

With the exception of Oldenburg and Württemberg the Lutheran churches are grouped in the United Evangelical Lutheran

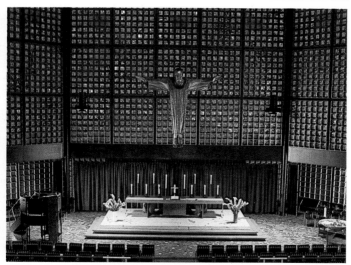

Protestant Memorial Church in Berlin (West)

Church of Germany (Vereinigte Evangelisch-Lutherische Kirche Deutschlands, VELKD), several of the United churches in the "Arnoldshainer Konferenz".

The EKD cultivates close relations with the Evangelical Church in the GDR and, professing a common responsibility, the two churches address the public in both states in joint statements on major issues.

The EKD grouping of Protestant churches was one of the founding members of the Ecumenical Council of Churches (World Council of Churches). The ecumenical movement, in which the EKD participates actively, is growing more and more beyond the institutions and is becoming a matter for the individual Christian. In many local Protestant and Catholic congregations ecumenical exchange circles have been formed.

In line with their denominational affiliations the Land churches also participate in the work of the Lutheran World Federation and the World Alliance of Reformed Churches.

The Catholic church. The five church provinces of the Roman Catholic Church in the Federal Republic of Germany comprise:

Catholic Corpus Christi procession

☐ Cologne archbishopric with the bishoprics of Aachen, Essen, Limburg, Münster, Osnabrück, Trier;

☐ Paderborn archbishopric with the bishoprics of Fulda and Hildesheim;

☐ München (Munich)-Freising archbishopric with the bishoprics of Augsburg, Passau and Regensburg;

☐ Bamberg archbishopric with the bishoprics of Eichstätt, Speyer and Würzburg;

☐ Freiburg archbishopric with the bishoprics of Mainz and Rothenburg-Stuttgart.

Berlin (West) is part of the bishopric of Berlin.

This diocesan division almost totally dates from the 19th century. Some dioceses were established only in the 20th. The archbishops and bishops in the Federal Republic consult together in the German Bishops Conference (Deutsche Bischofskonferenz) which has its secretariat in Bonn. The impetus given by the Second Vatican Council to the involvement of the Catholic laity in church affairs and tasks is translated into action by elected lay representatives. The visit to the Federal Republic by Pope John Paul II in November 1980 brought strong impetus to the ecumenical movement.

Smaller religious groupings. Among the smaller religious communities are in particular the socalled "free churches", i. e. those which perceive themselves as characterised by "voluntarism" rather than allegiance to a popular church. Membership rests on voluntary decision, not child baptism. Two of the largest Protestant free churches, the Methodists and the Evangelical Community (Evangelische Gemeinschaft) joined together in 1968 to form the Evangelical Methodist Church (Evangelisch-Methodistische Kirche). In addition there is the Alliance of Free Evangelical Congregations (Baptists) (Bund Evangelisch-Freikirchlicher Gemeinden [Baptisten]). The Old Catholic Church came into being as a breakaway from the Roman Catholic Church in the 1870's after the First Vatican Council schism over papal infallability. The Mennonite congregations, the Religious Society of Friends (Quakers) and the Salvation Army play a larger part through their activities than the number of their adherents might indicate.

In 1933 there were about 530,000 Jews living in the German Reich. Following their persecution and extermination by the Nazis, there are now about 65 Jewish congregations with about 28,000 members, the largest of which are those of Berlin (West) with 6,500 and Frankfurt am Main with just under 5,000 members. In addition about 15,000 Jews live in the Federal Republic who are not members of the Jewish congregations. The umbrella organisation of the Jewish congregations is the Central Council of Jews in Germany (Zentralrat der Juden in Deutschland).

The presence of the many foreign workers has greatly increased the importance of religious communities which previously were hardly represented in Germany. This is the case with the Greek Orthodox church and especially Islam. More than 1.8 million Moslems, mostly Turks, live in the Federal Republic of Germany.

Joint action. In the period from 1933 to 1945 many Protestant and Catholic Christians fought bravely against National Socialism. Let two be named to stand for them all: Pastor Martin Niemöller on the Protestant and Bishop Clemens August Count von Galen on the Catholic side. The cooperation in this struggle strengthened interdenominational understanding and awareness of common political responsiblity. On the basis of these experiences the churches today exercise a high measure of public responsibility, for example in publishing papers on topical issues and other forms of publicity.

The churches address the public in many ways. Worthy of special mention are the Catholic Days (Katholikentage, since 1848) and the Evangelical Church Conventions (Evangelische Kirchentage, since 1950). Charitable works are carried out by the German Caritas Association (Deutscher Caritasverband) on the Catholic side and the Diaconal Works (Diakonisches Werk) on the Protestant side. Since reconstruction within the country has been completed the churches have put great effort into overseas development aid. Big church aid organisations, funded by voluntary member donations, were set up. Thus the Protestant "Bread for the World" (Brot für die Welt) and the Catholic "Misereor" have together collected thousands of millions of marks for projects throughout the world.

The Christian churches have lately been intervening, including with official statements, in the debate about peace and disarmament, foreign worker and labour market policy and protection of the environment.

Protestants:
Kirchenamt der Evangelischen Kirche in Deutschland
Herrenhäuser Str. 12
3000 Hannover 21

Catholics:
Sekretariat der Deutschen Bischofskonferenz
Kaiserstr. 163
5300 Bonn

Jews:
Zentralrat der Juden in Deutschland
Rüngsdorfer Str. 6
5300 Bonn 2

Clubs, associations, civic action groups

Germans like getting together in all sorts of clubs and associations. When a Lower Saxony farmer emigrated years ago to start a new life overseas, he had to resign from 33 of them. There is hardly a German adult who isn't member of a number of groups.

Clubs and associations. Every third inhabitant of the Federal Republic is member of a sports club, for example. There are 14,500 choral societies with more than a million and a half members. Riflemen and stamp collectors, dog breeders and pigeon racers, local patriots and small gardeners have joined together in thousands of groupings. Most support common hobbies, relaxation and education, or just encourage socialising. Some assume importance in local politics. In local marksmen's or patriot groups people of various political and party leanings come together informally. Here non-partisan contacts are made which may have an impact on the life of a community. But these associations do not play a defined political role.

It is different with groupings which represent concrete material interests of their members. These comprise above all the big worker and employer associations (see pages 251–256). In addition to these there are many other organisations which pursue certain vocational, economic, social or other objectives. Thus house owners, tenants, motorists — to name but a few — have associations, some with very big memberships. These common interest organisations do public relations work to win sympathy for their causes and to influence legislation and administration in their favour. Their influence is indubitably great, but those critics who maintain that the Federal Republic of Germany is "under the rule of the associations" are certainly exaggerating.

Civic activists. A new type of association comprises the civic action groups (Bürgerinitiativen), of which a great number have been formed in recent years. Their outstanding characteristic is spontaneity: a few citizens get together without any large organisational input to work towards removal of a grievance because they feel they have been left in the lurch by the authorities, political representatives, parties and associations. In most cases local issues are at stake, for example the preservation of old trees to be felled for road construction or the installation of a children's playground. Sometimes civic action groups pursue contradictory aims, e. g. campaigning for a detour road to quieten traffic in a residential area, or against such a road for nature conservation reasons. On the whole, however, civic action groups have achieved many objectives, especially at local level, not least because there was readiness to compromise. Meanwhile civic action groups are also operating nationwide. The one which has become most widely known is the widespread movement against the construction of nuclear power stations.

The federal government welcomes and supports the activities of groups which draw attention to and fight malaises in modern industrial society. However, it rejects violence as a means of political pressure, carried into some civic action groups by radical elements. It is important that citizens and civic action groups participate as early as possible in the preparation of all state plan-

Upper Bavarian marksmen's brotherhood jamboree

Farmer demonstration in Bonn; at the microphone is the president of the farmers' federation, Constantin Freiherr von Heereman

ning decisions. Some legislation, e. g. the Federal Building Act, already provides for such civic participation and such possibilities are to be increased. In many cases civic action groups have helped to focus attention on problems, to avoid conflicts and to make decisions by state authorities better.

Mass media and public opinion

The Basic Law guarantees everyone the "right freely to express and disseminate opinion by speech, writing and pictures" and "freely to inform himself from generally accessible sources". Censorship is banned.

Tasks of the mass media. The press — and in the broader sense all mass media — have been described as "The Fourth Estate", next to parliament, government and the courts. The media do, indeed, play an eminently important role in modern society. Their job is to make complicated developments in all fields understandable to the public and to help them comprehend and control the actions of the parliaments, governments and administrations. This task places great responsibility on the media. The Federal Constitutional Court has commented on it in a judgment thus:

"A free press, not controlled by state authority, nor subject to any censorship, is an essential element of the free state; in particular, a regularly published press is indispensable to modern democracy. If the citizen is to take decisions he must not only be comprehensively informed, but he must also be able to know and weigh the views others have formed. The press keeps this permanent discussion going; it procures the information, expresses a considered view on it itself and thus operates as an orientation force in public debate."

Competition in the media. Press, radio and television vie for public attention. In 1984 there were 25 million radio and 22.4 million television receivers registered in the Federal Republic. That means 95 % of all households had radio and 87 % television. More than 21 million newspapers are sold every day. Four out of five West Germans read a newspaper daily.

Only about 5 % of the population are reached by no medium at all. The great majority keep themselves regularly informed from two or even three media. Surveys have found that most people first obtain their political information from television, going on to deepen it from a newspaper.

News sources. The media get their information from their own correspondents and from German and foreign news agencies. In addition to the Deutsche Presseagentur (dpa, Hamburg) and the Deutscher Depeschendienst (ddp, Bonn) there are German-language services of Associated Press (ap, Frankfurt), Agence France Presse (afp, Bonn) and Reuters (Bonn). The churches disseminate through their own agencies — Evangelischer Pressedienst (epd, Frankfurt) and Katholische Nachrichtenagentur (KNA, Bonn) — mainly news on church activities. Important specialised information is provided by Vereinigte Wirtschaftsdienste (VWD, Frankfurt, business news) and the Sport-Informationsdienst (sid, Düsseldorf). The political parties and a large number of organisations, such as those of the employers and workers, also address the media with press and information services.

The 420 German journalists based in Bonn are members of a Federal Press Conference (Bundespressekonferenz), the 315 foreign ones of the Association of Foreign Correspondents (Verein der Auslandspresse). Both groups are totally independent of the authorities. The Press and Information Office of the Federal Government (Presse- und Informationsamt der Bundesregierung) sees its role as a broker between the government and the public. It informs the federal president, the federal government and the members of the Bundestag about public opinion trends at home and abroad. Journalists obtain from it and from the press sections of the ministries information on government activities. The Federal Press Office is headed by a State Secretary who is also the government spokesman directly responsible to the Federal Chancellor.

Opinion research. Opinion expressed in the mass media is often referred to as "published opinion", rather than "public" opinion. This is to say that only the professional opinion formers such as politicians, journalists or associations are able continuously to put forth their views. And these groups could only surmise what the public actually thinks.

To find out real public opinion by scientific means is the aim of public opinion reserach (demoscopy). It is systematically conducted by a number of private institutes and has meanwhile become quite popular. Politicians and the media are equally interested in its findings.

Opinion surveys receive the most public attention in connection with elections. The prognoses of the West German institutes have achieved a high degree of reliability, even though predictions of close election results are quite difficult to make. Election analysts make follow-up surveys after the elections to try to find out why people voted as they did. Parties and politicians draw conclusions from these findings for their future courses of action.

Despite all misgivings about the precision and possible negative side-effects of opinion research, its practical political value is undisputed. Especially important are surveys which attract less public attention than election forecasts but which make clear the necessity of long-term, effective political programmes. The federal and state governments commissioned many surveys in recent years — e. g. about the attitude to nuclear energy, the causes and consequences of unemployment, leisure activities, youth problems and educational ambitions — and their findings influenced policymaking.

The press

Germans are among the world's keenest newspaper readers. Despite the onslaught of television, newspapers have held their own. Statistics prove it: the sale of dailies rose from more than 13 million in 1954 to 20.9 million in 1985.

Subscription and street sales. Up to the early 1950's most German dailies were sold on subscription. Street sale papers circulated mainly in cities like Berlin, Frankfurt, Hamburg, Köln, München and they were the exception rather than the rule. Then the "Bild-Zeitung", started in 1952 by the Hamburg publisher, Axel Springer, ushered in the rapid advancement of the street tabloids. In its first year, "Bild" already achieved a million daily sales. Today sales run to 5.1 million. The largest subscription daily, the Essen-based "Westdeutsche Allgemeine", has a circulation of 675,000.

It cannot be conclusively proved whether the street sale papers attracted new classes of readers. In any event, they have not displaced the subscription ones. Seven out of ten are still sold on subscription. Most street sale papers are taken additionally.

Two nationally circulated subscription papers are "Die Welt" (conservative) and the "Frankfurter Allgemeine Zeitung" (conservative-liberal). Also supraregionally important are the "Süddeutsche Zeitung" (liberal) and the "Frankfurter Rundschau" (left-liberal).

Press concentration. The press in Germany is privately owned. The dailies market is shared by 382 publishers. They circulate about 1,270 editions which vary in local content. Seen historically, that is little, for in 1932 there were 2,889 newspapers — more than twice the present number — in the area now constituting the Federal Republic. Many small local and party papers have disappeared. In many cases it was not possible to assert cost-covering circulation prices, especially as advertising concentrated more and more on the biggest-circulation papers.

This is reflected above all by the fall in the number of "full newsrooms", that is journalistic staffs which produce their newspapers completely independently. They have declined from 225 in 1954 to 116 in 1984. The majority of the dailies are no longer editorially independent, obtaining a greater or lesser proportion of their editorial content from another newspaper or newspaper grouping.

Publishers' moves towards economically viable businesses have resulted in a great many mergers and participations and in the economically and technically leading enterprises pushing competitors out of various regional markets. Hence in many towns people can no longer choose between two or more dailies with different local reporting and political standpoints. Only two thirds of the people of the Federal Republic have that choice. The formation of large publishing conglomerates in recent years has brought the concentration process to a stop.

Internal freedom of the press. Often the view is expressed that the loss of variety and independence the concentration process entails is a threat to press freedom. In this connection the notion of "internal press freedom" has been discussed.

The discussion revolves around questions such as whether the owner of a newspaper should be allowed to intervene at will in its editorial policy and, say, dictate to the journalists a certain political line. The journalists are striving for greater independence from the publisher and want, for example, a say in the appointment of the editor-in-chief. On a number of publications these issues have been resolved by agreed "editorial statutes".

The political weeklies. Readers, viewers and listeners, swamped daily by a deluge of isolated items of information, seek an overall view, evaluation and background orientation in the political weeklies. "Die Zeit" is regarded as liberal, the "Rheinischer Merkur" as conservative, the "Deutsches Allgemeines Sonntagsblatt" follows a liberal Protestant line. Although the party press no longer plays a big part, as it had in the Weimar Republic, there are important party-political weeklies: the "Bayernkurier" of Bavaria's Christian Social Union and the "Vorwärts" of the Social Democratic Party. The German Trade Union Federation publishes "Welt der Arbeit".

The weekly news magazine "Der Spiegel" is unique in the Federal Republic. It was originally modelled on the American "Time". With its "exposures" and sometimes respectless criticism the magazine has made quite a few enemies.

Periodicals. About 9,500 periodicals are published in the Federal Republic of Germany but no exact figure can be given. They cover entertainment, specialised fields, work, housing, customer service, but also include membership journals of small associations and large organisations, with circulations from 250 to the 7.4 millions of the ADAC motoring club magazine.

Sales of major topical printmedia *(1985)*

Daily newspapers

Bild (Hamburg)	5,085,800
Westdeutsche Allgemeine (Essen)	675,000
Express (Cologne)	439,000
Hannoversche Allgemeine (Hanover)*	419,900
Südwest Presse (Ulm)*	404,300
Rheinische Post (Düsseldorf)	393,800
Süddeutsche Zeitung (Munich)	353,100
Augsburger Allgemeine (Augsburg)*	340,900
Frankfurter Allgemeine (Frankfurt)	319,600
B. Z. (Berlin)	317,000
Nürnberger Nachrichten (Nuremberg)	311,800
Hamburger Abendblatt (Hamburg)	281,400
Ruhr-Nachrichten (Dortmund)	227,100
Kölner Stadt-Anzeiger (Cologne)	266,900
Abendzeitung (Munich)	271,400
Westdeutsche Zeitung (Düsseldorf)*	248,500
Stuttgarter Nachrichten (Stuttgart)*	248,400
Die Rheinpfalz (Ludwigshafen)	243,900
Hessische/Niedersächsische Allgemeine (Kassel)	240,800
Münchner Merkur (Munich)*	236,900
Rhein-Zeitung (Koblenz)	225,100
Nordwest-Zeitung (Oldenburg)	215,000
Neue Westfälische (Bielefeld)*	214,900
Westfälische Rundschau (Dortmund)	212,900
Westfälische Nachrichten (Münster)*	204,300
Die Welt (Bonn)	203,000
Saarbrücker Zeitung (Saarbrücken)	201,900

Weeklies and Sunday papers

Bild am Sonntag (Hamburg)	2,252,100
Die Zeit (Hamburg)	421,400
Welt am Sonntag (Hamburg)	321,600
Bayernkurier (Munich)	151,500
Rheinischer Merkur (Koblenz)	130,300
Deutsches Allgemeines Sonntagsblatt (Hamburg)	122,200
Vorwärts (Bonn)	48,700

News magazine (weekly)

Der Spiegel (Hamburg)	900,500

*with regional editions

The biggest public interest is for the entertainment press, a market where the concentration process is stronger than in almost all others. Thus the group of illustrated magazines has shrunk to four titles, selling between one and 1.4 million copies weekly. The biggest circulations are those of "stern" and "Bunte". Altogether the periodicals for the general public have a circulation of about 86.5 million.

Concentration in publishing. As already mentioned, economic development in the press market has led to the formation of large publishing houses and groups which determine editorial, economic and technical trends. In the daily press sector the biggest conglomerate is the Axel Springer AG. Its share of about a fifth of the newspaper market is largely due to the high circulation of "Bild". In the Sunday papers market Axel Springer AG is almost without competition with "Welt am Sonntag" and "Bild am Sonntag". Economic and publicistic power is also concentrated on the publishing groups of the "Westdeutsche Allgemeine Zeitung", Süddeutscher Verlag, Verlag DuMont Schauberg and Societäts-Verlag. Much more important in terms of economic power and publicistic effectiveness are the publishers of periodicals, especially the general interest ones. Leaders in this sector are the Bauer-Verlag and Burda groups as well as Axel Springer AG, mainly with broadcasting programme journals. In this field Axel Springer AG is linked economically with Burda-Verlag. The media corporation with the largest turnover is Bertelsmann which includes book and record clubs, book and periodical publishing (including Verlag Gruner + Jahr), music production enterprises, film and television and printing.

Newspaper publishers:
Bundesverband
Deutscher Zeitungsverleger
Riemenschneiderstr. 10
5300 Bonn 2

Periodical publishers:
Verband
Deutscher Zeitschriftenverleger
Winterstr. 50
5300 Bonn 2

Journalists' trade unions:
Deutscher Journalisten-Verband
Bennauerstr. 60
5300 Bonn 1

Deutsche Journalisten-Union
in der IG Druck und Papier
Friedrichstr. 15
7000 Stuttgart 1

Broadcasting

The broadcasting media in the Federal Republic of Germany are not state-controlled. The broadcasting order and freedom of broadcasting are regulated by law. So far public law corporations have had a monopoly. In 1981 the Federal Constitutional Court ruled commercial broadcasting admissable as long as free expression of opinion is assured and it is open to all relevant groups of society. Several private groups have begun putting out television programmes by cable and satellite which can be received by a slowly but steadily growing number of households.

The public corporations. There are nine regional combined radio-TV corporations, called "Landesrundfunkanstalten", whose legal basis are "Land" laws or inter-"Land" treaties, plus two radio-only corporations set up under federal law, Deutschlandfunk and Deutsche Welle, and a second national television network (Zweites Deutsches Fernsehen, ZDF), based on an agreement between all the Länder.

The regional corporations are linked together in a Standing Conference of German Public Law Broadcasting Corporations (Arbeitsgemeinschaft der öffentlich-rechtlichen Rundfunkanstal-

The public broadcasting corporations

Bayerischer Rundfunk (München, radio and TV)
Hessischer Rundfunk (Frankfurt am Main, radio and TV)
Norddeutscher Rundfunk (Hamburg, radio and TV)
Radio Bremen (Bremen, radio and TV)
Saarländischer Rundfunk (Saarbrücken, radio and TV)
Sender Freies Berlin (Berlin, radio and TV)
Süddeutscher Rundfunk (Stuttgart, radio and TV)
Südwestfunk (Baden-Baden, radio and TV)
Westdeutscher Rundfunk (Köln, radio and TV)
Deutsche Welle (Köln, short and medium wave radio)
Deutschlandfunk (Köln, medium, long wave and VHF radio)
Zweites Deutsches Fernsehen (Mainz, television)

The first nine listed corporations put out a joint, nationally transmitted television evening programme ("Channel One" or "German Television"). The "Zweites Deutsches Fernsehen" ("Channel Two") also transmits its television programme nationwide.

ten Deutschlands, ARD). Each broadcasts several radio programmes and together they operate a nationally-seen television programme officially called "German Television" (Deutsches Fernsehen) but generally referred to as "Channel One" (Erstes Programm). In addition they produce regional "Third" TV programmes. The Mainz-based Zweites Deutsches Fernsehen (ZDF) is a television-only station transmitting the "Channel Two" programme nationwide.

Deutschlandfunk's and Deutsche Welle's task is to convey a comprehensive picture of Germany in their programmes. Deutschlandfunk puts out radio programme for the whole of Germany, other European countries and Germans living in them. It broadcasts in German and 14 other European languages. Deutsche Welle (Voice of Germany) transmits its programmes in 34 languages on short and medium wave throughout the world and with its German-language programme provides a service to Germans living overseas. Both these corporations are members of the ARD conference.

Self-government and freedom in broadcasting. The broadcasting media all have basically the same system of self-government. It is exercised through three main organs:

☐ The Broadcasting Council (Rundfunkrat, Fernsehrat) which is, in effect, the parliament of the corporation. It comprises representatives of all important political, ideological and social groups, although the pattern of representation varies somewhat between regions. The Council deals with fundamental issues concerning the corporation and elects the Director-General (Intendant).

☐ The Administrative Council (Verwaltungsrat) which watches over the day-to-day management of the corporation.

☐ The Director-General (Intendant) who is the responsible chief executive, including control of programme contents.

This self-administration system guarantees the broadcasting corporations' independence from the state. It does not, however, exclude all political influence. Although the supervisory bodies are not totally composed of representatives of political parties, there has grown in them a kind of party-political power distribution which becomes particularly conspicuous when top posts in the corporations — such as those of director-general, programme directors, editors-in-chief and so forth — are up for appointment.

From time to time there are also attempts politically to influence the shaping of programmes. The corporations are duty-bound not to favour any side and to maintain editorial balance. Sometimes this justified demand is misrepresented as supposedly meaning that every broadcast has to be "balanced" within itself and must not contain any decided opinion. If this demand were consistently applied the result would be colourless programmes. Indeed, hardly anyone in a responsible position seriously advocates this. "Internal broadcasting freedom", that is the possibility to express decided points of view, obtains widely. Such efforts must not, however, lead to the freedom of opinion of broadcasting journalists becoming a special privilege. The corporations are required by law to give equal chances to express opinions to all.

Programmes. Each regional corporation runs two to four contrasting radio programmes. This wide choice was made possible mainly by the expansion of the very high frequency network. The radio programmes provide a broad variety of entertainment, music, current affairs, sport, regional reporting, drama, opera, and so on.

Most stations run scientific and literary series. Current affairs magazine programmes have won a large audience. Special programmes for foreign workers are provided in their respective languages. The orchestras, choirs and ballets maintained by the corporations are important on the cultural scenes of many cities.

In the nationally transmitted ARD and ZDF television programmes political reporting, home and foreign affairs documentation, television plays, films and entertainment play a big part. For their foreign coverage both ARD and ZDF have widespread correspondent networks and their own studios in many countries all over the world.

The Third Channel television programmes are transmitted regionally by the ARD corporations. In the 1960's they had the character of minority programmes addressing a more discerning audience. Now their intention is to offer a contrast to the First and Second programmes by putting emphasis on regional affairs, such as state politics and regional culture. The third programmes are also of special significance to the education system. Most ARD corporations regularly transmit television for schools and further-education courses at various levels.

Television in the Federal Republic went into colour in 1967. The German-developed PAL system is used. Only a small proportion of programmes is still transmitted in black and white. More than 80 % of the registered receivers are colour.

1984 television programme

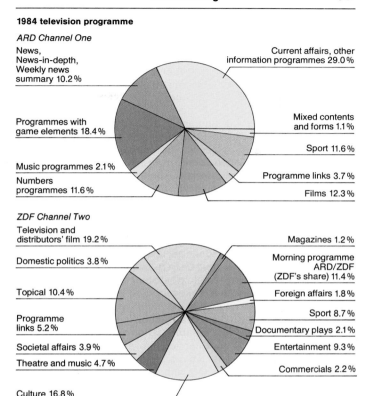

ARD Channel One

News, News-in-depth, Weekly news summary 10.2%

Current affairs, other information programmes 29.0%

Programmes with game elements 18.4%

Mixed contents and forms 1.1%

Sport 11.6%

Music programmes 2.1%

Numbers programmes 11.6%

Programme links 3.7%

Films 12.3%

ZDF Channel Two

Television and distributors' film 19.2%

Magazines 1.2%

Domestic politics 3.8%

Morning programme ARD/ZDF (ZDF's share) 11.4%

Topical 10.4%

Foreign affairs 1.8%

Programme links 5.2%

Sport 8.7%

Societal affairs 3.9%

Documentary plays 2.1%

Entertainment 9.3%

Theatre and music 4.7%

Commercials 2.2%

Culture 16.8%

Finances. The broadcasting corporations obtain most of their funds in the form of listener-viewer subscription fees. In 1984 there were 25 million registered radio listeners and more than 22 million television viewers. Television licence revenues are split 70:30 between the ARD corporations and the ZDF. Since transmission areas vary in size, the larger ARD stations contribute to the budgets of the smaller to offset their disproportionate costs.

A smaller share of the stations' revenues comes from commercial advertising. In 1983 more than 20% of the ARD's and just under 50% of the ZDF's revenues came from advertising. This is limited in time, however, and transmitted in blocks, i. e. one spot after another, not as inserts in programmes proper.

Big changes in the media landscape. Fundamental changes have taken place in the media system of the Federal Republic in recent years. In the late 1970's the Federal Post began to connect households to broadband cables. Now more than 1.5 million households are connected and the number is to increase to four million by 1987. The system enables reception of an incomparably larger number of radio and television programmes. Whereas with a conventional aerial one can now choose between at most five television and five radio programmes, a cable connection provides a choice of more than 20 television and just a many VHF radio programmes. Private companies in particular are making use of this technology. Their revenue comes from advertising broadcast.

With the aid of parabolic aerials which have a diameter of three to four metres one can receive with a cable connection television programmes transmitted via satellite. Such reception "dishes" are being installed by the Federal Post in increasing numbers in the centres of larger cable networks. In future it will also be possible to receive radio and TV programmes directly from satellites with the aid of smaller parabolic aerials. Other types of new communication technologies have been moving into households on a considerable scale. The "Teletext" system which requires an additional piece of equipment makes it possible, for a fee, to call in the stock exchange report, for example, or sports news. Conversely one can make a direct transaction in one's bank account. The "Videotext" system, available nationwide, works similarly but in one direction only. It carries information in writing, e.g. news and weather reports. Above all, however, Videotext provides viewers hard of hearing with the spoken content of programmes.

All these systems, once established, can make a tremendous impact on the life of society and on media policies. The federal government intends to work towards them being used for multiplicity of opinion. To this end it will draw up a comprehensive concept for the promotion of information and communication technologies.

Education
Science
Culture

Cultural diversity
Schooling
Vocational training
Universities
Research
Adult education
Zeitgeist: spiritual trends of recent decades
Literature
The book trade and libraries
Fine arts
Architecture
Museums, collections, exhibitions
Music
Theatre
Cinema
Festivals

Cultural diversity

Germany has never been a unitary state. It has always consisted of a number of more or less autonomous territories. The federative structure is traditional in Germany. There is hardly a sphere of life which it has not affected. This is why the theme crops up in so many places in this book. But in no field has this German peculiarity remained so marked as in culture which has been most successful in withstanding the centralistic tendencies which also occurred in Germany.

In contrast to neighbouring countries, Germany has never had a real metropolis, one predominant centre in which the nation's entire public life was concentrated. Berlin was the Reich capital for only just over seven decades, too short a time to attain the dominant position of Paris or London. The lack of such a centre has been a gain for cultural life, making Germany a country with many centres.

To become aware of this one need only note how the various cultural institutions and activities are distributed. The central library of the Federal Republic of Germany is in Frankfurt, where the book trade is also concentrated. Hamburg has the largest concentration of press publishing. The most theatres are in München (Munich). The central state archives of the Federal Republic are in Koblenz. There are scientific academies in Düsseldorf, Göttingen, Heidelberg, Mainz and München. The major museums are in the old Reich capital, Berlin. The largest literary archives are in the small Württemberg town of Marbach on Neckar.

It is due to such cultural polycentrism that there is hardly anything like the remote, desolate "provinces" in the Federal Republic. One need not travel hundreds of kilometres to see good theatre or hear good music. In medium-sized towns one sometimes finds astonishingly valuable libraries or interesting art collections. Be it because the princes of the age of absolutism had the ambition to make their residences centres of culture or because self-confident bourgeoisie patronised the arts and sciences within their walls — Germans today profit from their efforts and enjoy a wide variety of cultural amenities.

The establishment and maintenance of most cultural facilities in the Federal Republic of Germany is the responsibility of local government. Legislation in cultural matters — with few exceptions — is the prerogative of the federal states. Each has a large measure of autonomy in organising its schools system. And here it becomes apparent that there are also negative aspects to cultural federalism. Since some schools' curricula and graduation levels vary widely from state to state, problems can arise when families move and the children have trouble adjusting. At other levels of the education system the federative structure also causes difficulties.

Instruments to assure the necessary coordination are therefore very important. A Permanent Conference of Länder Ministers of Education (Ständige Konferenz der Kultusminister der Länder) has long had an important role to play in this area. It is the major clearing house for cultural policy. In some fields, particularly tertiary education, the federation has been empowered to issue guiding regulations which the Länder have to obey. A joint Commission for Educational Planning and Promotion of Research (Bund-Länder-Kommission für Bildungsplanung und Forschungsförderung) has been set up by federation and Länder, specifically with an eye to future tasks. All these measures and efforts serve the objective of assuring the degree of standardisation necessary for a modern, efficient education system without abandoning the fruitful diversity to which German cultural life owes so much.

Schooling

School issues are always of high public interest in the Federal Republic and get much media attention. Interest is focused on the structures of the school system, the learning contents and the methods of instruction.

Fundamentals. According to the Basic Law the entire schools system, including private schools, is under state supervision. The federal states (Bundesländer) are mainly responsible for school matters, which is why the systems vary across the country. The necessary levelling-out is provided by joint agreements concluded by the Länder and for deliberation of issues of common concern a Permanent Conference of Länder Ministers of Education is regularly convened. A federal-state commission works towards coordinated education planning and research promotion.

School attendance is compulsory from the ages of six to 18, i. e. for 12 years, during which fulltime attendance is required for nine years and part-time attendance at vocational school thereafter. In some Länder there is already a 10th compulsory year. Attendance at all public schools is free. Study materials, in particular school books, are also put at the pupils' disposal partly free of charge. Needy pupils can receive support under a Federal Education Promotion Act (Bundesausbildungsförderungsgesetz, BAFöG for short) if too great distance forces them to live away from home.

The Basic Law demands that religious instruction be a regular subject. From the age of 14 any pupil can decide whether or not to continue to take part in it. Denominational schools — i. e. those which orientate their entire programme to a certain religious creed — have lost importance in the past decades. Here, too, things differ from state to state. Most states have "interdenominational schools oriented to Chistian principles", that is schools based on Christian culture in which only religious instruction is given in denominationally separate classes. As a rule girls and boys are in mixed classes; in older classes sport is taken separately.

Kindergarten. Kindergarten is a German institution adopted by many countries — the very word, in fact, has become assimilated in many languages. Kindergarten supports and supplements the upbringing of the three to six-year-olds in the family. It focusses on encouraging the ability of children to express themselves fluently, developing children's personalities, teaching them to become useful members of society, and on play. Mostly children spend only the morning in kindergarten. But there are also many all-day kindergartens, important to families where both parents are in employment. A special form is the school kindergarten which tries to prepare children of school-age who are not yet mature enough for full school entry.

The kindergartens are not part of the state school system. Attendance is voluntary and usually parents have to contribute to the cost. Most are operated by local government, churches, associations, firms or private people. More than 80 % of all three to six-year-olds attend kindergartens; the aim is to have places for all children in this age bracket.

The school system. At the age of six children enter primary school (Grundschule). In general it lasts four years, in Berlin (West) six years.

All children attend primary school together. Thereafter their ways separate as they choose between several possibilities. Nowadays, however, many pupils first go into orientation grades (classes 5 and 6), leaving their options open for a later choice.

Most children — just under half of this age group — subsequently attend a short-course secondary school (Hauptschule).

Schools providing general eduction

	1966		1984	
	Schools	Pupils	Schools	Pupils
School kindergartens and prep classes	623	12,300	3,001	58,100
Primary and short-course secondary	29,217	5,710,900	18,276	4,006,400
Special (for handicapped)	1,614	198,800	2,784	284,600
Intermediate	1,660	590,000	2,627	1,132,200
Senior high	1,968	1,038,100	2,483	1,851,200
Comprehensive	—	—	301	220,100
Evening	269	16,700	262	41,500
Total	35,351	7,566,800	29,734	7,594,100
Teachers		255,500		501,300

Schematic depiction of the education system

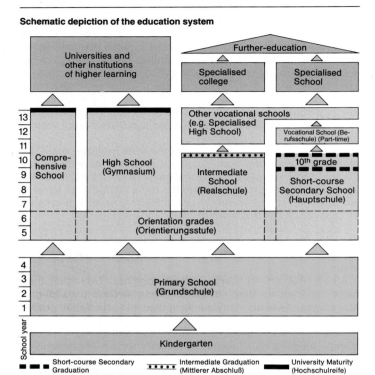

Most who leave it at the age of 15 go into vocational training (attending part-time vocational school until the age of 18, see page 339).

Successful graduation from Hauptschule opens the way to many occupations for which formal training is required. The range of subjects taught at Hauptschule has been substantially improved on what it used to be. For example, nowadays almost every pupil is instructed in a foreign language, mostly English, and gets vocational orientation to ease the transition after leaving school.

Intermediate School (Realschule) as a rule takes six years, from fifth to 10th grades. Realschule leads to a graduating certificate at intermediate level between Hauptschule and Senior High School (Gymnasium). The intermediate certificate qualifies children for attendance at a technical school (Fachschule or Fachoberschule), specialised schools offering vocational training at upper secondary level. The intermediate graduation is also regarded as a prerequisite for a medium-level career in business and administration and in general improves the young person's starting chances in employment. A third of all pupils attains the intermediate graduation.

The nine-year Gymnasium (5th to 13th school years) is the traditional grammar or senior high school in Germany. The former classification into ancient language, modern language and natural sciences Gymnasium is only very rare nowadays. Today the socalled "reformed upper phase" (11th to 13th years) is the rule in which a course system has replaced the conventional classes. In the courses the students are to concentrate on the subjects they are most interested in. This is to ease the transition to university. In addition to the Gymnasium with the reformed upper phase there are special forms such as business Gymnasium or technical Gymnasium.

Graduation from the Gymnasium, the so-called "maturity certificate" ("Reifezeugnis") or "Abitur" is the entitlement for study at university. However, the number of Gymnasium graduates has increased so greatly — from 50,000 in 1965 to almost 310,000 in 1984 — that not all those who wish to study can get university places. Certain restrictions have had to be introduced (see pages 346, 348).

In addition to the three basic general forms of school education — Hauptschule, Realschule and Gymnasium — there are many special schools. Physically or mentally handicapped children can attend special schools (Sonderschule), for example, where account is taken of their disability and existing capabilities are promoted as far as possible.

The triple-category school system has often been criticised. It is argued that for many children the direction is determined too early and that it is too difficult later to correct wrong decisions. These problems are to be avoided by comprehensive schools, a from of schooling which remains in dispute. Its critics maintain that it brings down the average standard of achievement. These group the hitherto seperate school forms together and as a rule keep the children from the 5th to the 10th grades. Some comprehensive schools have their own senior grades akin to those of the "Gymnasium". According to ability, pupils have the option of taking courses with higher or lower demands. Vocational familiarisation instruction is part of the syllabus. The graduation certificates of comprehensive schools are recognised in all federal states.

A break for senior high school students

Anyone who for any reason has missed out on education opportunities can catch them up in a "second education route". Evening class grammar schools give workers the chance to work for Gymnasium graduation in courses lasting three to six years, which they attend in addition to their daily work. In the same way one can achieve Hauptschule or Realschule graduation in evening classes. But it is a hard row to hoe and demands great sacrifice from the student.

Teachers. For every type of school there are especially trained teachers in the Federal Republic. Academic study is obligatory for all but its contents and duration vary. Generally speaking the future Grundschule and Hauptschule teachers study for six semesters, in some Länder still at special teachers' training colleges (Pädagogische Hochschulen), but mostly at universities. Longer university study is required for Realschule and Gymnasium teachers.

All applicants for the teaching profession have to sit an exam after completion of their studies. This is followed by a period of practical training and a second exam. After that the teachers are as a rule appointed civil servants for life. Their incomes ar from one and a half to two times the average of all workers. In this they are better off than their colleagues in most European countries.

Teacher training is being debated as hotly in the Federal Republic as is the entire schools system. Here, too, more permeability is being demanded. In most recent years, however, another, more pressing problem has come to the fore. Whereas for many years there was an acute shortage of teachers, there is now a large number of jobless teachers, posing difficult problems for those in political responsibility.

Vocational training

Ninety percent of the youngsters who end their general schooling at primary (Hauptschule) or intermediate (Realschule) level go into vocational training, most of them in the "dual system". This comprises practical, on-the-job learning with theoretical instruction in vocational school. That means private enterprise and the state are jointly responsible for vocational training. On the state side, the federation is responsible for vocational Training Orders, while the vocational schools are the responsibility of the Länder governments. Currently 1.9 million youngsters are in vocational training.

There are about 430 recognised occupations for which formal training is required. Their popularity with young people varies. Almost 60 % of the male trainees are concentrated in 20 preferred vocations and among the female trainees it is more than 75 % (see pages 339/340). Most boys want to become motor mechanics, electricians and fitters and turners, most girls hairdressers, sales clerks or office clerks.

On-the-job training. The practical on-the-job training, usually called apprenticeship (Lehre), takes from two to three and a half years, depending on the occupation, but in most cases three years. The apprentice is paid "training money" (Ausbildungs-geld) which increases annually. What has to be learned, and finally examined, for a vocation is set out in Vocational Orders. These are issued by the responsible federal ministers based on proposals from the business associations and trade unions. The training concludes with an examination held by the self-governing business organisations, such as chamber of industry or crafts or other institutions prescribed by the state. On the examination board are representatives of the employers, labour and vocational schools.

Large enterprises have their own training workshops. But a large part of the training takes place on the job. More than half the trainees learn in smaller firms with up to 50 employees, most of which are too specialised to be able to impart all the necessary knowledge. This is why since 1973 inter-firm training centres (überbetriebliche Ausbildungsstätten) have been set up where trainees can broaden their vocational skills. At the moment these

Technical high school laboratory

centres offer 73,000 such training places. It is intended to increase their number to 77,000.

Vocational schools. In addition to on-the-job learning, the trainee has to attend vocational school on one or two days a week for three years. The schools give instruction in general subjects — e. g. social studies, politics — and the specific vocational theory which a young person is better able to learn in a school than at the place of employment. Vocational schools are, however, not only attended by trainees. They are also obligatory for all under 18-year-olds who attend no other form of schooling. Large enterprises have vocational schools of their own which, after inspections, are recognised and financially supported by the state.

Other ways of vocational training. Apart from apprenticeship and vocational school there is a number of other vocational training systems being used by ever more young people. A few are referred to here.

There is the full-time specialised vocational school (Berufsfachschule) which has to be attended daily. It prepares young people for various occupations, predominantly clerical work, home economics, social work and administration. The duration of this schooling is at least one year. Where it is longer, part of the

The most popular occupations requiring formal training *(1983)*

Boys		%
1	Motor vehicle mechanic	7.7
2	Electrician	5.4
3	Fitter and turner	4.5
4	Cabinet maker	3.7
5	Painter and varnisher	3.5
6	Mason	3.3
7	Gas and water installer	3.2
8	Baker	2.6
9	Wholesale and foreign trade clerk	2.6
10	Bank clerk	2.3
11	Works maintenance mechanic	2.3
12	Mechanic	2.2
13	Butcher	2.1
14	Toolmaker	2.1
15	Industrial clerk	2.0
16	Cook	1.8
17	Sales clerk	1.8
18	Farmer	1.6
19	Central heating and air conditioning mechanic	1.6
20	Energy electronics technician	1.6
	Total	57.7
	All occupations subject to formal training	100.0

time spent can be credited as apprenticeship, or replace this altogether.

The specialised secondary school (Fachoberschule) admits pupils with intermediate graduation. It covers the 11th and 12th school years. In the 11th year practical occupational training is given, partly in school-owned workshops, partly in practical trainee placement firms. The 12th year is only for scientific and theoretical instruction. Those who have concluded a vocational training in the dual system and have graduated from intermediary school do only the 12th class. Successful graduation from the Fachoberschule qualifies young people for study at specialised institutions of higher learning (Fachhochschule).

An ambitious goal. In principle, no youngster is to begin his working life without vocational training. Almost 90 % of the youngsters in the Federal Republic now get it. Of the other 10 % — that is 100,000 young people every year — some do not want to take up

Girls		%
1	Hairdresser	9.2
2	Sales clerk	8.9
3	Sales clerk in the food crafts	6.6
4	Office clerk (industry and commerce)	6.0
5	Doctor's assistant	5.8
6	Industrial clerk	5.3
7	Bank clerk	4.1
8	Dentist's assistant	4.0
9	Retail clerk	3.6
10	Office assistant	3.1
11	Wholesale and foreign trade clerk	3.0
12	Tax and business consultant's assistant	2.9
13	Domestic economist	2.1
14	Lawyer's and notary's assistant	1.9
15	Lawyer's assistant	1.9
16	Hotel economist	1.8
17	Office clerk (crafts)	1.7
18	Administrative clerk	1.6
19	Pharmacy assistant	1.5
20	Technical draughtswoman	1.3
	Total	76.6
	All occupations subject to formal training	100.0

vocational training for various reasons. In 1983, however, 50,000 youngsters could not find training places, no matter how hard they tried.

Juveniles without proper school graduation, the children of foreign workers and those who are not prepared to train in vocations other than those of their choice or far from home have the most difficulties finding qualified training places. The problem is all the greater in structurally weak regions where there have never been enough job training opportunities.

Some relief has come to these groups in recent years from numerous programmes and pilot schemes launched by state and federal governments. Important for the promotion of under-achieving pupils and their placement in traineeships is longer obligatory schooling by a vocational preparation year.

Apart from this, there is the possibility in all Länder to do a "Basic Vocational Training Year" (Berufsgrundbildungsjahr). This is also open to youngsters who have not yet decided on a vocation or found a traineeship position in the vocation of their choice. The Basic Vocational Training Year counts towards the later traineeship duration. The introduction of a Basic Vocational Training Year, in which a broader training than in the traditional vocations is offered, is one of the vocational training improvements striven for. Vocational training is to prepare more than hitherto for possible changes in the working world. One of the main requirements for this is to motivate the youngsters to further learning later and to lay the foundations for this.

Universities

German universities have a long history. The Federal Republic's oldest university, at Heidelberg, was founded in 1386. Several others have had 500-year jubilees. But apart from these venerable institutions there are very young universities, more than 20 having been founded in the past 15 years. Tradition and modernism are very close together.

For more than a century the educational ideal of German universities was that which Wilhelm von Humboldt tried to realise at the Berlin University he founded in 1810. The Humboldt type of university was conceived for a relatively small number of students. It was to be a place of pure science, non-purposive research and teaching, and only secondarily serve vocational preparation. In our day and age this ideal clashes more and more with the requirements of a modern industrial society which strives for equal educational opportunities for all.

Whereas in 1950 only 6 % of the school leavers of an age group took up academic studies, nowadays every sixth seeks a study place. The number of students has risen from 511,000 in 1970 to more than 1,300,000 in 1984.

The state tried to meet this increased demand by expanding existing universities and building new ones, doubling teaching staff and quadrupling university funding in 10 years. New courses of study were introduced and efforts were made to orientate study more than before to later vocational practice. But no system of study has yet been found to cope optimally with the large number of students.

University organisation. The Federal Republic's universities (apart from the church universities) are the responsibility of the Länder. The federation controls only the general principles of the university system and research financing, contributing funds to university construction and research projects.

The universities have a large measure of autonomy in their own affairs. Of fundamental importance is the freedom of research, the state not being permitted to influence teaching content. Within the framework of the law, each university draws up its own constitution. Consequently there are wide differences in structure and organisation.

Some universities have the conventional categorisation into a few large faculties, with a wide range of scientific disciplines collated in each. More frequent, however, is the categorisation into many small departments (Fachbereiche). The head of the traditional university is generally the "Rector", elected from the staff of professors. Depending on the university's constitution the period of office is up to four years. Many rectors continue to teach and research while in office. Since many universities nowadays have attained the dimensions of large enterprises and require tight management, modern university constitutions often provide for a President, who is elected for seven or eight years, does the job fulltime and does not have to come from the ranks of the academic staff.

The self-government of the universities used to be in the great majority of cases in the hands of the ordinary professors who also provided most of the academic instruction. In recent decades many other teaching staff with various functions and qualifications have been added. One objective of the reform efforts of the past decade and a half was to involve these staff as well as the students in the universities' self-government. Satisfactory forms for this kind of involvement have not yet been found everywhere. There is much complaint that the work in the many self-governing bodies takes up too much time and effort which are then lacking for teaching and research.

Types of universities. The major pillar of the tertiary education system of the Federal Republic are the academic universities, including technical and a number of other specialised universities, as well as teacher training colleges (Pädagogische Hochschulen) at which teachers for primary and short-course secondary schools are trained. In most Länder the teacher training colleges have been integrated in the universities. Studies at academic universities culminate in a Master's degree, a Diploma, a Doctorate, or the so-called "State Examinations".

Another type of tertiary college are the "Fachhochschulen", specialised institutions of higher learning (corresponding approximately to the Technical Colleges of some other countries). They provide scientifically based practical education in numerous fields, concluding with diplomas and in most cases leading directly into employment.

In some Länder comprehensive universities (Gesamthochschulen) were established in the early 1970's or existing tertiary facilities regrouped as such. The comprehensive university is to

Universities

- ● Universities, Comprehensive Universities and Teacher training colleges
- ▲ Art academies
- ✚ Theological colleges

Flensburg

Kiel

Lübeck

Hamburg

Oldenburg

Bremen

Lüneburg

Vechta

Hannover

Berlin (West)

Braunschweig

Osnabrück

Bielefeld

Hildesheim

Münster

Bethel

Detmold

Clausthal

Duisburg Bochum

Soest Paderborn

Höxter

Dortmund

Göttingen

Essen

Witten-Herdecke

Düsseldorf Hagen Meschede

Wuppertal Correspondence University

Witzenhausen

Köln

Kassel

Aachen

Siegen

Bonn

Marburg

Vallendar

Gießen

Fulda

Koblenz

Oberursel

Trier

Mainz Frankfurt

Bamberg

Offenbach

Würzburg

Bayreuth

Darmstadt

Kaiserslautern

Mannheim

Neuendettelsau

Erlangen

Speyer

Nürnberg

Saarbrücken

Heidelberg

Landau Germersheim

Karlsruhe

Ludwigsburg

Regensburg

Stuttgart Esslingen

Eichstätt

Hohenheim Schwäbisch-Gmünd

Tübingen Reutlingen

Weihenstephan

Passau

Ulm

Augsburg

München

Freiburg i. Br.

Trossingen

Neubiberg

Weingarten

Konstanz

Benediktbeuern

0 50 100 150 200 km

combine the various tertiary forms under one roof and make it easier for students to move from one type to another. It is a model which has not spread widely.

Also new in the Federal Republic is the comprehensive multimedia university in Hagen, Westphalia, which began operation in 1975. Since it conducts its teaching programme mainly by correspondence through 23 regional study centres it needs only a minimum of buildings.

Courses and students. Some 1,300,000 students are enrolled at the Federal Republic's universities — ten times as many as in 1952. Seventy thousand are foreigners. A few figures may show how successful efforts to open tertiary study to all strata of the population have been. In the 1952/53 winter semester 4 % of the freshman students came from wage earner families, compared with 17 % in the 1983/84 winter semester. In 1952 one fifth of the students were women, today it is about two fifths.

Traditionally students are quite free to shape their own courses of study. Although for many studies curricula are recommended and interim examinations are obligatory, in many courses students still have the choise of certain subjects and lectures.

As a group, the students administer their own affairs in most federal states. Student self-government is as a rule practised through the student parliament as the "legislative" and the General Student Council (Allgemeiner Studentenausschuss, ASTA) as the "executive".

No study fees are charged at the Federal Republic's universities. If neither the students nor their parents are able to pay for their living expenses the state helps. Under the 1971 Federal Education Promotion Act (BAFöG) students can draw benefits on loan. The amount is subject to a test of the parents' means.

To improve the students' material situation, the state gives financial subsidies to university canteens or for the construction of student hostels. Today there is a place in a hostel at relatively low rent available for every tenth student.

Since 1971 all students have been in the statutory accident insurance scheme. Since 1975 they have been able to claim the services of the statutory health insurance in exchange for moderate contributions.

Problems of mass study. Despite considerable expansion of the university system the enormous growth in the number of people wanting to study has led to admission restrictions (numerus clau-

Tübingen University (Alte Bursa, built 1479)

Bochum University

sus) having to be introduced for some subjects. The available study places are distributed by a central authority in Dortmund (Zentralstelle für die Vergabe von Studienplätzen, ZVS). For the particularly attractive studies such as medicine, dentistry and veterinary science a selection procedure is planned taking into account the average high school graduation mark and the time waited for admission. Special consideration is given to hardship cases. For medicine, the results of an admission test and an interview are also taken into account.

In study courses such as economics, business, law or informatics distribution procedures are used, that is applicants are allocated places at a certain university, often different to the one of their choice.

Refined admission criteria will only ameliorate, not solve the problems mass study poses, however. Most important will be to change the content of courses and thereby also to cut study times. Today more than 31 % of students are older than 25. Each spends an average of 12 semesters, that is six years, at university, which is decidedly too long.

German tertiary students by vocational status of their fathers *(in %)*

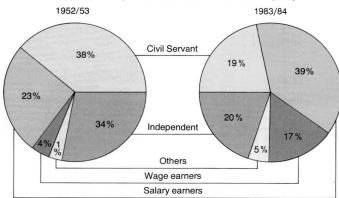

University students by fields of study 1984/85

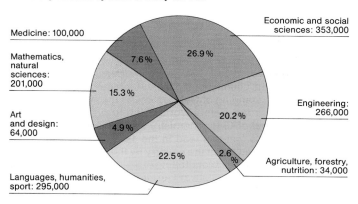

Medicine: 100,000

Mathematics, natural sciences: 201,000

Art and design: 64,000

Languages, humanities, sport: 295,000

Economic and social sciences: 353,000

Engineering: 266,000

Agriculture, forestry, nutrition: 34,000

26.9%
7.6%
15.3%
4.9%
22.5%
2.6%
20.2%

But the continuing entry pressure on the universities and the much less favourable job prospects for graduates force society to rethink the tertiary study system and the question of how much priority to give to academic study in our age.

Standing conference of university rectors:
Westdeutsche Rektorenkonferenz
Ahrstr. 39
5300 Bonn 2

Research

Germany ranked for a long time as a land of scholarship and science. Its universities were world leaders in many fields. People came to the country for the most advanced research. Some indication of the standing of German science was the number of Nobel Prizes awarded. Before World War II 10 out of 45 awards for physics and 16 out of 40 for chemistry went to Germans.

German science lost this lead in the 1930's. Many of its best scholars were driven out of the country by the Hitler dictatorship. The war brought another bloodletting of talent and the situation in vanquished and divided postwar Germany was anything but conducive to research. The Federal Republic was hard pressed to catch up with world standards and to produce scientific peak achievements in some fields again.

Who does research? Research goes on in three big sectors in the Federal Republic: the universities, non-university institutions and industry.

Research by university teachers has a long tradition in Germany. "The unity of research and teaching" has been a pillar of German academic life since Wilhelm von Humboldt reformed the Prussian universities in the early 19th century. At the universities one still frequently finds the traditional type of scientist working alone or with a small team of assistants on a subject of his choice. He will always be indispensable.

But certain research undertakings, especially in the natural sciences, are too vast for this type of approach. Only team work and large-scale equipment can cope with them. Their finance requirements run into the millions. The German Electron Synchrotron (DESY) in Hamburg, for example, has a staff of more than 1,000 and costs more than DM 100 millions a year. Such modern large-scale researches are best done in non-teaching institutions outside the universities. Among them are the federally financed nuclear energy, aerospace, medicine and molecular biology research centres. In the arts and social sciences the tendency towards largescale research is less marked, but it does exist. The Mannheim-based Institute for the German Language, for example, is using electronic data processing to analyse German vocabulary.

Effelsberg radio-telescope

The third branch is industrial research. Generally speaking, re-
search-intensive industries are able to hold and expand their
market positions. Not only large enterprises do industrial research. There are also notable achievements by medium-sized
ones. Practical competitiveness and a high level of production
are particularly important. Both can be achieved only by research
and the use of the most modern technology, the prerequisites for
sophisticated products and efficient manufacture. Notwithstanding the high efficiency of the German economy, the widespread
notion of the country's being a "blueprint exporter" is not quite
correct. Although the Federal Republic of Germany does export a
lot of technical know-how, it imports more. In 1983 the Federal Republic had to pay more than DM 3,000 millions in foreign license
fees, taking in only DM 1,500 millions.

More than 375,000 people work in the sciences and research in the Federal Republic. One third each are scientists, technical and other personnel (administrators, manual workers, etc.).

Wo pays? Spending on research and development has almost doubled in the Federal Republic of Germany from 1975 to 1983, from DM 23,000 millions to DM 43,000 millions. More than half of this amount is raised by industry, just under half is from the state. "State" in this case is no central authority but a large number of more or less autonomous agencies. Almost 70 % of the research spending is in industry, the remainder in non-university and university research. The Land-financed universities are self-governing and the mainly federally-financed big science centres work by and large independently.

Public funds flow into research in a number of other ways, for example via the German Research Society (Deutsche Forschungsgemeinschaft, DFG). The DFG is a self-governing scientific organisation. It is allocated more than DM 900 millions annually from Land and federal budgets to distribute to research projects. Any scientist can apply for support for a project. He must be prepared to submit it to critical appraisal by a select body of experts and to publish his findings.

In contrast to the DFG as a pure fund-distributing organisation the Max Planck Society for the Advancement of Science (Max-Planck-Gesellschaft zur Förderung der Wissenschaften, MPG) runs 55 institutes of its own. Most do basic research in the natural sciences and many have for decades been world renowned. The MPG is financed mainly by the federal government and by Land governments.

An important link between research and the application of its findings in the economy and administration is the Fraunhofer Society for Advancement of Applied Research (Fraunhofer-Gesell-

Spending on research and development (in DM 1,000 millions)

Area of research	Research spending				
	1975	1977	1979	1981	1983
Non-university					
research facilities	3.8	4.1	4.9	5.5	6.0
Universities	4.6	4.8	5.7	6.5	6.0
Industry	14.6	17.3	21.1	26.4	30.2
Total	23.0	26.2	31.7	38.4	43.0

Industrial laboratory

schaft zur Förderung der angewandten Forschung). In 32 institutes of its own it carries out commissioned researches in the natural sciences and technology.

An important part is also played by the large scientific foundations in the Federal Republic. Most prominent of these are the Volkswagen Foundation, the Fritz Thyssen Foundation and the Donors Association for German Science (Stifter-Verband für die Deutsche Wissenschaft). With their private funds they can often initiate new developments which are later taken over by state-financed agencies.

Research policy. "Art and science, research and teaching shall be free", says the Federal Republic's Basic Law. The state cannot dictate to any scientist the object and direction of his researches. But research is so important to society in general that the state cannot remain indifferent to it. It must ensure that the limited funds are spent as productively as possible, it must foresee what fields of research will become particularly important in future and it must assess the consequences of technical developments. The Federal Ministry for Research and Technology (Bundesministerium für Forschung und Technologie) in Bonn is responsible for this forecasting and planning. It goes without saying that it can only fulfil these tasks in close cooperation with the researchers themselves. Areas of particular emphasis in state support — beside basic research — are projects for ensuring energy and raw material supplies, environmental and safety research, humanisation of work, health research, marine and polar research, information techniques, electronics, space and aviation research and traffic research.

Aims of the state's promotion of research and technology are in general: expansion of scientific knowledge, raising economic efficiency and competitiveness, sparing use of resources and preservation of the natural prerequisites to life, improvement of working and living conditions, improving knowledge about the chances and risks of technologies and promoting young scientists and technicians. In addition to these tasks, research in the 1980's will have to contribute increasingly to sparing use of raw material and energy reserves and avoiding or reducing environmental burdens from technology and industry.

All these efforts in research and technology help the Federal Republic, a central European country with a great cultural heritage, to maintain and expand its scientific standards. But they also help maintain the competitiveness of an exports-oriented economy and thereby the standard of living in a highly industrialised and densely populated country.

Adult education

In the Federal Republic of Germany it has been generally accepted that in a modern society people have to keep educating themselves throughout their entire lives. The demands of work are becoming ever greater and changing all the time. Many people have to change occupations several times in their lives. But continuous learning is also necessary for other reasons. In order to be able to use their growing amount of leisure time meaningfully people's creative abilities must be developed and new fields of interests opened up. And finally, the citizen is called upon everywhere to become involved and to make a contribution to society. He can follow this call only if he is knowledgeable and capable of judgment in many fields.

This is why the state, local government, the churches, the trade unions, the political parties and business organisations provide a great number of facilities which are used today by more than 10 million citizens — more than all the pupils at general education schools.

Adult education centres. The first thing that comes to mind in connection with adult education in the Federal Republic are the Adult Education Centres (Volkshochschulen). Based on the Scandinavian model, they were set up at the end of the 19th century. Although from the outset they conveyed knowledge which could be put to practical uses, their work was for a long time characterised by the ideal of neo-humanistic education which laid emphasis on the non-purposive acquisition of spiritual values. Nowadays the modern Volkshochschulen perceive themselves as part of an overall system of further-education.

There are some 950 Volkshochschulen in the Federal Republic with about 4,000 branches. Operators are generally communal or local governments or registered associations, with the Länder contributing funds. The Volkshochschulen are non-partisan and non-denominational. There are two types: evening class adult education centres — by far the greatest number — and residential adult education centres, where courses lasting several days or weeks are held. The programme offered is more varied than those of all other comparable facilities. From astronomy to shorthand and broadcasting technology to Zen meditation there is hardly a subject one would not find there. In 1983, 311,000 courses were held for 4.6 million enrolled students. In 1965 there were only 78,000 courses with 1.7 million enrolled. In addition 3.2 million people took part in 68,000 one-off events. The finance involved was DM 639 millions, of which DM 210 millions was brought in by student fees. For a number of years certificates have been given in 15 subject areas — languages, mathematics, natural sciences, technology — with more than 8,000 participants receiving such certificates in 1983. In addition more than 12,000 people took exams for various levels of school graduation. More than 26,000 people took the examinations of chambers of industry and crafts and vocational organisations.

This widely varying education work is done by some 4,000 full-time staff and about 115,000 part-time course leaders. Only few Volkshochschulen have permanent buildings of their own. Since 1953 all Volkshochschulen have belonged to the Federation of Adult Education Centres (Deutscher Volkshochschulverband) which has a congress every five years. Exchange of experiences with similar institutions in the USA, Great Britain and Scandinavia is being intensified.

Wide diversity of facilities. The trade unions also run a large further-education programme. The Volkshochschulen and the German Trade Union Federation (Deutscher Gewerkschaftsbund, DGB) are linked in a working group called "Arbeit und Leben" (Work and Life). This provides workers with courses in economic and social policy, works constitution, insurance and labour law and much more. The DGB runs five Federal Schools for its members. Young people can participate in programmes arranged at the House of Trade Union Youth at Oberursel (Hessen). Works Councillors and other labour representatives can take courses at special DGB colleges and academies.

The business community spends several thousand million marks a year on the further-education of its employees. It runs 11 supraregional education schemes and 30 further-education institutes. Large enterprises run additional courses of their own for their staff. Participants want to achieve either higher vocational qualifications, refresh occupational skills or learn completely new trades. Three quarters of the participants claim to have enhanced their vocational positions as a result. Government authorities support participation in vocational further-training by considerable financial contributions. If the employee is not earning while attending the further-education or retraining course, the

Language laboratory in adult education

state pays a grant which can be as high as 80 % of the last net income. The learner can also be partially or wholly relieved of the cost of the course and study materials (see also pages 172/173).

An important contribution to further-education is made by the armed forces. There are 29 craft training schools (Bundeswehrfachschulen) for the further-education of soldiers. They can catch up on various school qualifications from short-course secondary school to senior high school. The armed forces vocational promotion service provides initial and retraining and offers many possibilities for further-education in crafts. Up to now well over 300,000 craft qualifications were achieved.

The churches also work in the field of adult education. The Protestant Church maintains 15 academies where it holds seminars on topical issues, e. g. youth problems or development aid policy, in which about 80,000 people take part every year. Local working groups and excursions are also very popular. In the foreground of Catholic further-education work are family and marriage problems, and theological and cultural themes. The umbrella organisation is the Catholic Federal Adult Education Working Group (Katholische Bundesarbeitsgemeinschaft für Erwachsenenbildung) in Bonn. Finally, there is also a number of foundations, closely allied to the political parties, which have further-education programmes (Friedrich-Ebert-Stiftung, Friedrich-Nau-mann-Stiftung, Konrad-Adenauer-Stiftung, Hanns-Seidel-Stif-tung).

Well over 100,000 people take part in about 1,000 correspond-ence courses offered by private enterprises. A Central State Of-fice of Education by Correspondence (Staatliche Zentralstelle für den Fernunterricht), set up in 1972, controls the quality of the stud-ies offered.

Zeitgeist:
spiritual trends of recent decades

If one does not shrink from the accusation of over-simplification one can define a succession of predominant ideas in the history of the Federal Republic of Germany to date. Of course, the most varied philosophies, schools of thought and ideologies have always coexisted. What is meant here are those ideas which penetrated beyond the small circle of the philosophically interested into the public at large and influenced thinking in many fields where each in its way for several years determined the "Zeitgeist", the spirit of the times, the drift of thought and feeling in a period.

Existentialism. The immediate postwar years belonged to existentialism. This school of philosophy (mostly referred to as "Existenzphilosophie" in Germany) is linked above all with the names of Martin Heidegger and Karl Jaspers. The main works of both had appeared decades previously, but only now met with a broader response, whereby no doubt misunderstandings and over-simplification occurred. In the time of crisis and period of deprivation following total defeat in 1945, where often enough the issue was mere survival, many could identify with a philosophy whose main precepts were "Angst" (anxiety), "Sorge" (worry), "Scheitern" (failure), "Geworfenheit" (being cast down) and which radically threw the human being back to that innermost core which is preserved even in the face of death. As the nation with all its members stood in a make-or-break situation the moment had come for this teaching to prove its worth. Thus it is no coincidence that among the many who in philosophical seriousness pronounced on the question as to the blame for the crimes of the Hitler regime, Karl Jaspers had the weightiest utterances to make.

Rejection of ideologies. With the economic rise of the Federal Republic the attractiveness of existentialism paled. In fact, occupation with "ultimate questions" in general receded into the background. From the early 1950's the public philosophical awareness in the Federal Republic was becalmed. The democratic state was consolidating, prosperity and social security advanced year by year and there appeared to be no limits to their growth. In such a climate one readily tended to think that fundamental questions

Martin Heidegger   *Karl Jaspers*

such as the meaning of history or human coexistence had lost their importance, that the only thing which still mattered was finding pragmatic solutions to individual problems. Nor did the fact that on the other side of the intra-German frontier, in the GDR, the closed ideology of communism had taken power in theory and in practice challenge many philosphers to fundamental debate. The majority wanted nothing to do with such problems. Sociologists of the time spoke of the "sceptical generation" and of a process of "de-ideologisation" which they regarded as irreversible.

Criticism of society and utopia. They were proved wrong when in the latter 1960's interest in Marxism reawakened after it had for two decades been a matter for small circles in the Federal Republic. When with the formation of the grand coalition government in Bonn between the conservative Christian Democrat parties and the Social Democrats in 1966 all ideological struggle for "the right way" appeared to be buried, the protagonists of fundamental criticism of this state again found a greater audience. As in the case of existentialism, thinkers came to the fore whose works had long been in existence. One should mention here above all the founders of the "Frankfurter Schule" (Frankfurt School), Max Horkheimer and Theodor W. Adorno, whose "critical theory" fused Marxist criticism of society with the findings of psychoanalysis. They had great influence on the student movement which began in 1966 and at the beginning saw itself as anti-authoritarian. Also

Max Horkheimer   *Ernst Bloch*

important, albeit less direct, was the impact of Ernst Bloch, probably the most original Marxist philosopher of recent decades. At the centre of his work fed from many sources, including religious, lay the concept of utopia.

Not only Marxist, but many other societal analyses were the subject of lively discussion. "Society" became the fashionable word of the time. The interest in sociological inquiry was in large measure prompted by doubts being articulated more frequently than previously as to whether the social system of the Federal Republic was really as complete as one had thought. Too high, sometimes simply utopian hopes were placed in reforms begun in the late 60's. They were not fulfillable on the scale hoped for, especially when the economic crisis beginning in the 1970's greatly curbed the material means available. Thereupon disappointment, disillusionment with reform and an anti-utopian mood spread. Many observers saw in this a turn of the tide, a return to conservatism.

Change of trend? Probably this interpretation is too superficial. It is true, however, that the belief in simple theories which claim to offer an explanation of all social phenomena, has become shaky, as has the idea that society could be changed quickly. One testimony to this is the growing following attracted by critical rationalism, a school of thought whose leading representative is Sir Karl Popper. But beyond this, new problems have arisen which seem

Werner Heisenberg   *Carl Friedrich von Weizsäcker*

to fit into none of the inherited ways of perceiving the world. They can be summarised under the catchword "environment" which then began to dominate discussion. This has created altogether new fronts.

One of the first indications of this development was that natural scientific and socio-scientific thinking moved closer together again. When Werner Heisenberg, one of the great nuclear physicists of our century, published his "unitary theory of elementary particles" — popularly known as "world formula" — in the 1960's, it met with respectful recognition amongst the interested public but hardly influenced the philosophical thinking of his contemporaries.

Half a generation later things already looked different. Heisenberg's pupil, Carl Friedrich von Weizsäcker, an outstanding physicist himself, turned away from natural science towards peace research and the study of living conditions in our industrially shaped world. By addressing questions which the established sciences had not yet posed he was representative of a whole new generation of thinkers. In the 1970's many people began to doubt the sense of continuous economic growth and constant technical advancement. The number of critics of unbridled industrialisation grew. They warned that it was bound to destroy the natural environment and thus humanitiy's future life base. An ecological movement grew which demanded a change of attitude, a change of course: away from one-sided growth-thinking back to sensible human behaviour vis-à-vis nature. These ideas have been widely attractive and are still gaining ground.

Some radical followers of this movement sought to withdraw from the pressure of the industrial world altogether by "dropping out". They gave up their jobs, made do without the usual standard of living and joined groups of like-minded people to try out "alternative" lifestyles, often in communes on the land, but not just there. But they remain a small minority. The "alternative movement" could not exist without the industrial society around it and probably has passed its peak.

The change of awareness of which it is an extreme expression extends far beyond the original themes and circles, however. More and more people are again espousing values which were long held to be old fashioned. There is again appreciation of the simple, natural, enduring things. Vis-à-vis huge anonymous systems more value is again being attached to the small, the comprehensible: one's home district, the neighbourhood, the family. People are putting their own subjectiveness up against "objective compulsions", instead of bureaucratic efficiency they seek human warmth. Concepts such as "progressive" or "conservative" are no longer readily applicable to this new life-feeling. In any case, unless one is grossly misreading the trend, this will dominate the zeitgeist of the years ahead. The industrial society is not to disappear but the yearning of more or less everyone is that it change into a "society with a humane face".

Literature

German literature comprises all literature written in the German language. It has never been confined by state frontiers, nor is it so today. No state can lay any kind of claim to the German literature of the past or present. Regardless of whether a writer is at home in the Federal Republic, in the German Democratic Republic, in Austria or in the German-speaking part of Switzerland, his works are a contribution to German literature. With the exception of the GDR, the spoken and written word is freely exchanged within the German-speaking region. The influences, intertwinements and cross fertilisations are innumerable. Although in the GDR literary life is tightly regimented, it is not completely cut off from that of other German-speaking countries. There is mutual recognition, albeit with restictions.

The subject of this chapter, however, is the literary life of the Federal Republic of Germany, not German literature as a whole. Some development trends can be shown. Where names are mentioned, they are meant only as examples representative of dozens of others.

Phases and newer trends. The year 1945 was to literature, as to all other spheres of life, a complete break with the past. Following the isolation enforced by the Hitler regime new literary currents from abroad, such as the neo-realism of Hemingway and the existentialism of Sartre, were greedily absorbed in Germany. Starved readers reached for the works then becoming available again of writers who had been driven out of the country by the dictatorship in 1933, such as Thomas and Heinrich Mann, Alfred Döblin, Carl Zuckmayer, Bertold Brecht and Anna Seghers.

But manifold as this impetus was, the predominant feeling, especially among the younger generation of writers, was one of a radical new beginning. There was talk of "zero hour" and the need for a literary "clean sweep".

A "literature of ruin" came into being which tried to work in the experiences of the dictatorship, the war and the post-war misery. Its basic tenets were often already discernible in its titles, such as "Inventur" (Inventory), by Günter Eich, "Draußen vor der Tür" (Outside the Door), by Wolfgang Borchert, "Bericht eines Überlebenden" (Report by a Survivor), by Hans Erich Nossack. All their despair notwithstanding, these writers had great social commitment, they wanted to work politically with their literary means.

In the 1950's and early 60's this approach disappeared almost completely. That is not to say that there was a lack of morally founded social ciriticism, however. The disquiet over the negative aspects of the economic upswing, egotism and materialism of the "affluent society" found articulation, for example, in the novels of Wolfgang Koeppen, Heinrich Böll and Marin Walser. But most writers were sceptical about the ability of literature to stir society. There was mention of literature becoming again a "private affair". Problems of form came to the fore. The conventional forms of storytelling were put to question (Uwe Johnson, Peter Härtling). Experiments were made with the possibilities of language, indeed, language was made the actual theme of literature (Peter Handke).

A new turning point came in the late 60's. The literature of the Federal Republic became politically aware again. The trigger for this was above all provided by the student movement of the years 1967/68. The most radical proponents of the new trend simply declared literature dead, wanting to recognise only practices which could change society.

They soon refuted themselves. What remained lastingly important was that many writers overcame their contempt for "dirty" workaday politics and, for example, even actively took part in electioneering. The distrust of "fiction" which arose for a time gave birth to a documentary phase which resulted in interesting works of recording and commentary.

However, there soon followed another withdrawal into the private sphere. Lyricism as the "most private" of literary genres enjoyed a new flowering which persists. In addition to established names like Karl Krolow or Peter Rühmkorf, unknowns like Karin Kiwus, Ludwig Fels or most recently Peter Maiwald and Ulla Hahn made their appearance. Other authors tried to work the student revolt into their novels. Reflections on their own person and the family (Christoph Meckel, Elisabeth Plessen) also showed that the literary climate had changed.

Since the mid-1970's, starting with the growth of women's lib, there has been women's literature which is producing remarkable results. Apart from Margot Schroeder and Verena Stefan special mention must be made here of Gabriele Wohmann. She tries in her stories, often with distant irony, to expose the hierarchical relations between the sexes.

In recent years several well known writers from the GDR have settled permanently or temporarily in the Federal Republic. Common to these very different personalities was a critical attitude to the regime in that state. The GDR government granted the bothersome critics a privilege it refuses its other citizens: they were allowed to leave the country. Apart from Jurek Becker, Karlheinz Jakobs, Sarah Kirsch, Guenter Kunert, Erich Loest and Rolf Schneider particular reference must be made here to Reiner Kunze who throws a critical light on everyday life in the GDR in his poems and short prose pieces.

Contemporary literature, when it addresses general themes, is marked by scepticism and dark pessimism. One even occasionally hears the word "depressionism" used. Representative of this are the works of Fritz Zorn or Nicolas Born's novel "Die erdabgewandte Seite der Geschichte".

Individuals. There have, of course, been many other trends apart from these in the Federal Republic. Everything always existed concurrently: in times of scepticism there was commitment, and in times of political excitement there was dreaming and escapism. (Arno Schmidt, for example, kept almost completely out of the literary scene until his death in 1979.) Next to the avantgarde the conventional always exists, next to the dissolution and fusion of forms always the strict adherence to form.

Above all, however, individuality can rarely be straight-jacketed as the common denominator for a trend. A literary life's work of some standing is always complex and richly-faceted. Take as examples works of storytellers like Alfred Andersch or Wolf Wondratscheck, or of lyricists such as Hilde Domin, Hans Magnus Enzensberger and Sarah Kirsch. Here only some of the most outstanding writers can be briefly portrayed.

Heinrich Böll, who died in 1985, was indubitably the best known author at home and abroad who ever wrote in the Federal Republic of Germany. In 1972 he was the sixth German to be awarded the Nobel Prize for Literature. A central theme of his novels and short stories is Catholicism and its role in society. As a rigorous moralist he depicts the problems and anxieties of ordinary people low on the social scale. His worldwide success is also due to the simplicity of his language which makes his works easy to translate.

Günter Grass enjoys equal renown. If possible, he is even less politically compromising than Böll. Several times he has even been proposed for high political office. His language, however, is of a baroque fullness, and an inexhaustible imagination popu-

Gabriele Wohmann

Reiner Kunze

Heinrich Böll

Günter Grass

Walter Kempowski

Siegfried Lenz

lates his novels with fanciful characters. All the same, his books deal with problems of our time.

In the 1970's Walter Kempowski attracted attention. In six strongly autobiographically coloured novels he traced the history of his family from the Kaiser era to the 1950's. Characteristic of his style is a preciseness of detail. All his novels were bestsellers, not least because of the humour in his portrayal of some characters.

Siegfried Lenz is another of the German authors best known internationally. Identifying strongly with his East Prussian homeland, where many of his novels and short stories are set, he often addresses the causes of human failures and doubts. Like Heinrich Böll, he does this in quite an uncomplicated style. Lenz, who is also strongly engaged politically, has also written a number of radio plays.

Writer organisations. For 20 years the "Gruppe 47" (Group 47) played a big part in the Federal Republic's literary life. It was not an organisation with a programme and statutes, but a loose association of writers and critics who, on the initiative of Hans Werner Richter, met annually from 1947 onwards. These meetings, with readings and discussions, became a focal point of contemporary literature. The annually awarded prize of the group almost always went to young writers who later made an impact. The last formal meeting of the grouping took place in 1967, a last informal get-together in 1972. The "Gruppe 61" (Group 61), from which has split a "Working Circle on the Literature of the Working World" (Werkkreis Literatur der Arbeitswelt) had set itself more closely defined aims. The authors of this grouping dealt mainly with the modern working environment. Its importance in literary life is also waning.

As a rule writers have to live off what they earn with their literary work. They have material interests just like anyone else. But because of the individualistic nature of their work, they are less well-equipped than other groups to assert these interests. Although there have always been various regional writers' associations in the Federal Republic which concerned themselves with the social interests of their members, they proved ineffectual. In 1969, under the slogan "an end to the modesty", the Association of German Writers (Verband deutscher Schriftsteller, VS) was founded, with the participation of leading authors. It saw itself from the outset as a trade union-like organisation. In 1974 it joined as a specialised sub-group with the Printing and Paper Workers'

Union. The association has made some headway with its objectives.

Mainly due to its pressure a library levy was enacted in 1972.
For every lending by a public library — there are about 160 millions a year — the library operators must remit DM 0.10 to a fund
which, inter alia, finances writers' old age welfare. Furthermore,
in 1974 the possibility was introduced for freelance contributors to
the mass media to regulate terms with their employers according
to agreed tariffs. That means they no longer face those employing
them as isolated "independent" individuals, which in reality they
are not. One of the next objectives is a similar arrangement for relations between authors and book publishers.

The book trade and libraries

The first book to be printed with movable type was published in Mainz in 1455. The inventor, Johannes Gutenberg, was printer and publisher in one. Thus, with the hour of birth of the new technology there also began the history of German book publishing and selling. For a long time the leading publishing centre was Frankfurt am Main. In the 18th century it was surpassed by Leipzig (now in the GDR) which held the position until World War II. Now several cities share the leadership of publishing in the Federal Republic of Germany, including München (Munich), Berlin (West), Hamburg, Stuttgart, Frankfurt and Köln (Cologne).

The Federal Republic's book production is the third largest in the world after the USA and the Soviet Union. In 1980, the record year so far, 67,176 titles were published — four times as many as in 1951. Paperbacks accounted for 11.6% of this. In autumn of 1985 there were more than 400,000 German-language titles available.

There are more than 2,000 publishers in the Federal Republic. About 75 have an annual turnover of DM 10 million or more. But none dominates the market. The greatest publishing enterprise, Verlagsgruppe Bertelsmann, a grouping of small and medium-sized publishing houses, accounts for 5% of the industry's turnover. Beside the large enterprises there are many quite viable small publishers whose products are an important contribution to literary variety.

After World War II, book clubs developed into a particularly important form of bookselling, introducing wide fields of new readers to books. They have their origin in popular strivings for education, such as the "Gutenberg Books Guild" (Büchergilde Gutenberg), founded by the trade unions. Today there are 10 book clubs with about six million members. Most belong to the Bertelsmann and Holtzbrinck companies.

The 1984 turnover of the Federal Republic's book trade was c. DM 9,000 millions, book clubs accounting for 6.6% and department stores for 5.1%. The book trade is the only branch of commerce in the Federal Republic still permitted to dictate retail prices. Book stores have to sell every book at the price set by the publisher. This exceptional regulation, which is not undisputed, is claimed to be justified by the special cultural mission of the book trade. The view is taken that without it the existence of many book shops would be in jeopardy.

Translations. In 1984 publishers in the Federal Republic of Germany brought out 6,457 titles translated into German from 53 languages, two thirds of them from English and 13 % from French. More than a third of the translations were belles lettres. Publishers in the Federal Republic in the same year sold 2,160 licenses for translations to foreign publishers. The biggest single category, 12.6 %, were into English. Other big categories were Dutch (10.6 %), Spanish (10.5 %), Italian (10.5 %) and French (9.6 %).

Book production by subject areas (1984, first and reprints)

Titles		%
577	General, book and writing, universities	1.1
2,598	Religion, theology	5.0
1,946	Philosophy, psychology	3.8
2,555	Law, administration	4.9
4,668	Economic and social sciences, statistics	9.0
964	Politics, defence	1.9
1,817	Linguistic and literary science	3.5
9,386	Belles lettres	18.1
3,098	Juvenile	6.0
1,737	Education, instruction, youth care	3.4
513	School text books	1.0
2,189	Fine arts, applied arts	4.2
979	Music, dance, theatre, film, broadcasting	1.9
1,771	History, cultural history, folklore	3.4
1,335	Geography, anthropology, travel	2.6
2,897	Maps, cartography	5.6
2,558	Medicine	4.9
2,171	Natural sciences	4.
1,690	Mathematics	3
3,493	Technology, industry, manufacturing	6
346	Transportation	
1,734	Agriculture and forestry, home economics	
550	Gymnastics, sport, games	
33	Others	
128	Calendars and almanacs	

...al library of the medium-sized town of Gütersloh, Westphalia

Association and Book Fair. The organisation group-
...lishers and sellers is the Börsenverein des Deut-
...ndels in Frankfurt. It was instrumental in launching
...Book Fair which takes place every autumn and
...presentational as well as commercial ends. In
...hers from 79 countries exhibited there. The high
...ery year is the awarding of the Peace Prize of
...Trade. Recent prizewinners included Gunnar
...éopold Sédar Senghor, Ernst Bloch, Max

Frisch, Leszek Kolakowski, Astrid Lindgren, Yehudi Menuhin, Ernesto Cardenál, Lev Kopelev, Manès Sperber, Octavio Paz and Teddy Kollek. In 1986 the prize was awarded to Władysław Bartoszewski. The trade journal of the association is the twice weekly "Börsenblatt für den Deutschen Buchhandel".

Libraries. In contrast to many other countries Germany has no large national library, hundreds of years old. A start was made only in 1912 with the foundation of the Deutsche Bücherei in Leipzig. That library — launched by the book trade — was given the task to collect all German-language literature which appeared from 1913. The division of Germany after World War II made it necessary to establish a corresponding institution for the Federal Republic. This is the Deutsche Bibliothek in Frankfurt, founded in 1946. It, too, was launched by the book trade and since 1969 has been operated by the federal government. In addition to all German-language literature published since 1945, it collects the so-called "exile literature", that is the works German writers who fled the country during the Third Reich produced from 1933 to 1945.

The biggest libraries are the Bayerische Staatsbibliothek (5.2 million books) in Munich and the Staatsbibliothek Preussischer Kulturbesitz (more than 3.5 million books) in Berlin (West). Most of the other libraries with large stocks are national, state and university libraries. In addition to these general scientific libraries there are specialised ones, most of which are attached to research institutes and museums — for example the Central Medical Library in Köln.

There are some 15,000 public libraries with more than 30 million volumes in the Federal Republic. They serve the reading and education wishes of broad strata of the population and are operated mainly by local governments and churches.

Book trade association:
Börsenverein des Deutschen Buchhandels
Grosser Hirschgraben 17 — 21
6000 Frankfurt/Main 1

Fine arts

If one surveys the post-World War II art scene one becomes aware that there is really no such thing as specifically German art. Naturally this has something to do with the increasing internationalisation of the arts in general, but also with Germany's specific situation. The Hitler dictatorship suppressed most modern art trends as "degenerate", which for more than a decade cut Germany off from international trends. With the end of the war came the division of Germany. The new beginning led in widely disparate directions in the two parts of the country. Whereas artists in the Federal Republic of Germany were decisively influenced from Western countries — partly by Germans who had emigrated there — those of the German Democratic Republic had "Socialist realism" foisted on them. It took until the 60's for a broader development to begin in the GDR, which cannot be dealt with here.

Painting. The figurative expressionism in the first third of this century, which was predominantly a German manifestation, had lost its impact. Oskar Kokoschka had left Germany. Painters like Emil Nolde and Otto Dix lived away from the mainstream. After 1945 development linked up with Paul Klee and Wassily Kandinsky who had already moved towards abstractionism before World War I. The abstract expressionism which grew in France under the influence of the Germans Wols and Hans Hartung asserted itself. Its major exponents, after the death in 1955 of Willi Baumeister, were Ernst Wilhelm Nay and Fritz Winter, the central figures of the München group "Zen 49", to which Julius Bissier, Emil Schumacher and Rupprecht Geiger were also close. In the Frankfurt group centred on Bernard Schultze the so-called "tachism" which, taking up surrealistic ideas, put the spontaneous creation process in the centre of artistic effort, experienced its decisive breakthrough in Germany. Schultze went on to develop into one of the most fascinating figures of the German arts scene with his "migofs" which penetrate with fantasy into the three-dimensional.

By its very choice of name the Düsseldorf group "Zero" proclaimed a new beginning. It no longer saw art as a platform of pathetic humanity but turned to neutral phenomena and directed attention to an awareness of the objective, technologically influenced environment and its significance to mankind. The best

Oskar Kokoschka: Cologne from a fairgrounds tower
(Wallraf-Richartz-Museum and Museum Ludwig, Cologne)

known of these artists are Otto Piene, Günther Uecker and Heinz Mack. Whereas one can still see Piene's fire and smoke pictures and Uecker's nail pictures within the framework of traditional board painting, the light steles and light dynamos of Mack, in their relationship to Op-Art, can still just be categorised as painting, but in their kinetic manifestion as sculpture. In their large-surface components which aim at changing the world about them (Sahara project) they belong to Environmental Art and, in a broad sense, also to Land Art.

The Pop-Art which emanated from Great Britain and America found little response in Germany, while Hard-Edge painting, limited to signal-like colour signs, was taken up by painters like Günter Fruhtrunk, Georg Karl Pfahler and Winfred Gaul.

Surrealism, which Max Ernst embodied in a uniquely personal way, is proving astoundingly long-lived. The movement is represented in Germany by Edgar Ende, Mac Zimmermann and above all Richard Oelze with his end-of-the-world visions. An eccentric variant of fantastic art developed within the strict medium of graphics. Such extraordinary draughtsmen as Horst Janssen and Hans Bellmer belong here, as do Peter Ackermann, Uwe Bremer and Friedrich Meckseper. Apart from this, the hyperrealism originating in America in the early 70's, which is not so alien to the "magic realism" or "new objectivity" of the 20's, was also adapted in the Federal Republic of Germany. Here one should name particularly Konrad Klapheck with his symbolically intended machine pictures and Dieter Asmus, the founder of the group "Zebra". Lambert Maria Wintersberger and Peter Nagel vary the theme of wounding. Away from all schools, Horst Antes created for himself a cyclopean art style by which his pictures are easily recognisable. He and Klapheck are the best known German painters abroad.

In the early 80's the "Neuen Wilden" ("the New Wild Ones"), also called "Junge Wilde" ("The Young Wild Ones"), made their appearance. With uninhibited subjective painting they linked up with expressionist forerunners. They are centred on Köln (Cologne), Berlin (West) and Hamburg. The main representatives of this direction who have meanwhile scored successes abroad are Elvira Bach, Jörg Immendorff (who also works as a sculptor), Helmut Middendorf, Markus Lüppertz and Salomé.

Sculpture. No clear development is discernible in German postwar sculpture. Figurative and abstract works are coming into being side by side as in the 20's when, apart from the expressionism of Ernst Barlach and Wilhelm Lehmbruck, there were already ab-

Jörg Immendorff with his sculpture "Brandenburg Gate"

Dieter Asmus: Holiday skier

stact sculptures by Hans Arp and Rudolf Belling. The first postwar decade was still shaped by artists of the older generation, such as Ewald Mataré who began teaching at the Düsseldorf Academy in 1946 and Gerhard Marcks who taught in Hamburg and Köln from 1946. Both were unequivocal exponents of abstracted objectivism. In Berlin (West) Karl Hartung's work was trend-setting; he taught in the city since 1951 and — himself pupil of Bourdelle and Maillol — brought to the fore the qualities of material in his monumental figures. His most important pupil, Rolf Szymanski, created fragmentary figures of religious fervour. The abstract school with constructivistic works which are, however, oriented to the laws of natural structure, is also represented in Berlin (West) in the person of Hans Uhlmann.

In the southwest German region there concentrated around artists such as Otto Herbert Hajek, Emil Cimiotti and Wilhelm Loth an approach to sculpture which one can conceive as the counterpart to the informal, tachistic painting. Part of this circle is also Erich Hauser, who has become known through his room pillars and who today is the best known sculptor, recognised also abroad (Grand Prix of the 10th Biennale in Sao Paulo). Symptomatic of the work of Frankfurt-based E. R. Nele is her transition since the mid 60's from expressive figurativeness to ornamental play objects.

Joseph Beuys in one of his actions

A third centre of contemporary German sculpture lies in the west between Köln and Dortmund, where experimental tendencies are most clearly articulated. Norbert Kricke creates from steel wire weightless sculptures; Jochen Hiltmann with his burst spheres emphasises the process of forming; Horst Egon Kalinowski constructs leather-spanned objects ("caissons"). Exponents of kinetic art have already been named in connection with the group "Zero". In addition there is an object art in which the element of movement plays a part. Thus, Günter Haese makes fragile housings of brasswire in which the balance wheels of clocks are ranged, which begin to vibrate at the slightest excitement, and Günter Weseler constructs shaggy "breath objects" which derive their effect not only from movement but also from the spatial context.

Action art, Arte Povera. The dissolution of the traditional concept of art in the 1960's led to the action art of the flux and happening movement whose main exponents were Wolf Vostell and Joseph Beuys († 1986). The flux actions were more destructive displays in the spirit of Dadaism, while the happening-actions such as Vostell's "in Ulm, um Ulm und um Ulm herum" (1964) quite consciously involved the public as actors. Beuys, controversial in Germany, attracted much interest abroad. In his actions and in his objects Beuys dispensed with all material extravagance. His use of fat and felt places him in the "Arte Povera" context, that is the art form using poor materials, as e. g. Reiner Ruthenbeck with his heaps of ash. The "tracking techniques" as pursued, for example, by Nikolaus Lang who presents unassuming lost-and-found objects in display cases also belong in this context.

Environment, textile objects. Just as the wall picture emerged out of two-dimensionality and ultimately developed into environmental architectorial planning in the train of Pop-Art (in Germany with Michael Buthe) so textile art also conquered the dimension of space. The impetus for this came above all from Poland (Magdalena Abakanowicz). In Germany it was taken up by textile artists such as Inge Vahle, Else Bechteler and Susanne Hepfinger.

Applied art. One of the main applied arts is handicrafts. In it wood, metal, glass and ceramics and all kinds of other materials are worked. As in painting and sculpture, to which it has always been related, its craft and art products reflect trends of the time. The same can be said about commercial art and poster art. To raise artistic quality in these fields efforts are made by the Federal Handicrafts Association and various specialised museums. They run exhibitions and competitions which aim to give these art forms new impetus.

Architecture

When considering the contemporary state of architecture in the Federal Republic one must keep in mind the conditions left by World War II. The rush to rebuild the towns and re-house millions of homeless left little scope for urban building concepts and architectural quality. Now that these elementary needs have been met, there is increasing complaint about the carelessness of brutalistic building, as reflected in monotonous satellite housing estates or inner-city department stores and office buildings. Awareness is also growing that more than any other art form, architecture shapes the people's life-feelings because they cannot withdraw from it and that because of this it has special responsibility.

But there are also in Germany outstanding examples of modern, yet humane architecture. Much of it derives from a style of building which originated in the 1920's in Dessau. The Dessau Bauhaus — whose leading exponents, such as Walter Gropius and Ludwig Mies van der Rohe were persecuted by the Hitler regime and had to emigrate after 1933 — with its fundamental idea of a synthesis of art and expert craftsmanship disseminated the idea of functionalism worldwide. Functionalistic masterpieces with emphasis on the material used and on the constructive elements are to be found today all over the globe.

Important individual achievements. While little use was made in housing construction of the opportunity offered by the new beginning, some outstanding individual achievements were made in representational building. The skeleton high-rise, all-glass construction type, as exemplified by Mies van der Rohe's Seagram Building in New York, found variants in Germany in the high-rise building of Phoenix-Rheinrohr (Thyssen house) in Düsseldorf (Helmut Hentrich and his group, 1957 — 1960) and in the administration building of the Hamburg electricity works (Arne Jacobsen and Otto Weitling, 1969). That company buildings do not only have to follow the principle of verticality but that dynamic building can arrive at adequate solutions for any given task is demonstrated by the head office of the Bayerische Motorenwerke in München (Munich) with its conspicuous quadri-cyclindrical form (Karl Schwanzer, 1972) or the Bahlsen biscuit factory in Hannover with

Office building of the BMW motor company in Munich (Karl Schwanzer)

its cubistic boxing (Dieter Bahlo, Jörn Köhnke, Klaus E. Stosberg and Partner, 1974).

A representational building which is not only an urban building milestone but in which the public at large can also participate is the television tower in Stuttgart (Fritz Leonhardt, 1954 − 1956), often imitated since. It is moreover, convincing proof that architectural art does not necessarily have to be a losing business. Although it cost several times as much as the alternative which provided only for the antennae carriers it quickly paid for itself with its restaurants and viewing terrace. That may take longer in the case of the München Olympics installations (Günter Behnisch and Partners, 1972) but it remains a stroke of luck that the airy tent

Pilgrimage church in Neviges (Gottfried Böhm)

roof construction could be achieved which, embedded in an attractive park, keeps in touch with the environment and gives opportunities for leisure use even after the Games.

Original ideas have also been realised in cultural buildings in
the narrower sense — places of communication such as theatres,
museums and libraries. The best known are the new Philharmo-
nie in Berlin (West) by Hans Scharoun (1964), with its vineyard-
like auditorium terracing, facing the central orchestra — a building conceived from within — and the Staatsbibliothek Preussischer Kulturbesitz, also erected in the city according to his plans.
For the Stadttheater in Münster (1954 — 1956) a classical ruin was
incorporated into the building itself. The Stadttheater of Gelsenkirchen (1963) with its glass front became the model for many
other theatre buildings. Stuttgart's Liederhalle and the Multihalle
in Mannheim's Herzogenriedpark are further examples of gen-
erously conceived public auditoriums. A Mönchengladbach museum, superbly fitting local conditions, was completed in 1982 by
the Vienna architect, Hans Hollein.

There have been some happy solutions to the special planning tasks posed by education and research buildings. Thus the university at Konstanz whose building masses are asymmetrially assimilated in the terrain is a pleasing contrast to an "education factory" such as in Bielefeld. Exemplary of how organically a clinic can be built into a landscape is the Filderklinik in Filderstadt-Bonladen (1972).

Several thousand churches have been built since the war, with great scope left to architectural experimentation. Apart from a great number of buildings which tend more just to serve the church's representational function, some also came into being which aesthetically meet the challenge to be places of encounter with a divine presence.

Worthy of mention in this respect are the Berlin Memorial Church (Gedächtniskirche) by Egon Eiermann (1963) with its transparent glass facades whose blueness creates an aura of transcendency; the massive, fortress-like pilgrimage church at Neviges by Gottfried Böhm (1967); or the pyramid construction of the Catholic church centre "Maria am Wege" at Windach (Josef Wiedemann with Rudolf Ehrmann and Karlheinz Scherrer, 1971).

Town planning. The most pressing tasks in contemporary architecture, however, concern urban building in the broadest sense. Large-scale ready-made solutions, such as the crossing-free Sennestadt of Bernhard Reichow have so far remained exceptions. The destruction of historical building substance is being stopped. Efforts are made to reverse the uninhabitability of the town centres caused by traffic getting out of hand. This is increasingly being done by the construction of pedestrian malls and bypass roads. New buildings are integrated in the historical substance, as in the case of Neustadt in Hamburg. Here historical ensembles were not only preserved but even rebuilt. The designs for the Schneider store in Freiburg (Hein Mohl, 1976) or for the Würzburg Kaufhaus by Alexander von Branca, which carefully merge with their historical surroundings, show that there is a move away from the acceptance as beautiful of box-like department stores in historical town centres. How a new town hall can be welded into a medieval urban core was shown by Gottfried Böhm in Bensberg in 1964.

Museums, collections, exhibitions

There are more than 2,000 museums of the most varied types in the Federal Republic of Germany: Land, town, association, folk and private museums, treasure chambers, diocesan, cathedral, residence, castle, palace and outdoor museums. They faithfully mirror the federal structure of Germany and grew over the centuries out of royal, church and later civic collections. This is why one will seek in vain for a centre of national representation, such as the Louvre in Paris. Berlin (West) has the greatest concentration of museums, the Prussian Culture Foundation (Stiftung Preussischer Kulturbesitz) set up by federal legislation in 1957. It looks after the cultural collections of the former state of Prussia. A museum of German history is to be completed by 1987.

The themes the museums serve are as varied as the different types. They collect art, natural objects, objects of technology and cultural history; there are museums devoted to a single artist (e. g. the Kolbe Museum in Berlin [West]) or a single art genre (e. g. the Museum Alter Plastik, Liebieghaus in Frankfurt); nor is there lack of specialised museums such as one for playing cards in Bielefeld or bread baking in Ulm. Strict specialisation is rare, however, most museums being mixed types, with natural science and art collections often being under one roof (Hannover, Wiesbaden).

Especially important are the historical art and anthropological museums which in the broad scope of their displays have something to offer every visitor and are correspondingly popular. Thus the Deutsche Museum in München (Munich) displays originals and models showing the development of technology and science, while the Germanisches Nationalmuseum in Nürnberg (Nuremberg) has the greatest collection on the history of German art and culture from prehistory to the 20th century. Also unique is the large number of ethnological museums in a country which exercised hardly any colonial power but produced many major discoverers and researchers of distant cultures. In addition to the Berlin (West) museums, the Linden Museum in Stuttgart deserves special mention in this field.

Museum variety. The traditionally broad scope of the German museums system has advantages and disadvantages. An advantage of decentralisation is that the museums are accessible to many people. Indeed, nine out of ten West Germans have been to a museum at least once. There is no disadvantage in the museums' frequently regarding each other as competitors. Every large one is out to offer everything from Rembrandt to Picasso if it can. Yet specialisation can be quite attractive. Anyone who wants to see Rubens will just have to make his way to München.

Important museums

Art

Berlin (West): Gemäldegalerie, Nationalgalerie
Bonn: Städtische Kunstsammlungen
Braunschweig (Brunswick): Herzog-Anton-Ulrich-Museum
Essen: Museum Folkwang
Frankfurt: Städelsches Kunstinstitut
Hamburg: Kunsthalle
Hannover: Niedersächsisches Landesmuseum, Kestner-Museum
Hildesheim: Roemer-Pelizaeus-Museum
Karlsruhe: Staatliche Kunstsammlungen
Kassel: Staatliche Kunstsammlungen
Köln (Cologne): Wallraf-Richartz-Museum und Museum Ludwig
München (Munich): Alte Pinakothek, Neue Pinakothek
Stuttgart: Staatsgalerie

Cultural history

Bonn: Rheinisches Landesmuseum
Köln (Cologne): Römisch-Germanisches Museum
Mainz: Gutenberg-Museum
München (Munich): Bayerisches Nationalmuseum
Nürnberg (Nuremberg): Germanisches Nationalmuseum
Würzburg: Mainfränkisches Museum

Science and technology

Berlin (West): Museum der Weltluftfahrt
Bochum: Bergbau-Museum
Bonn: Zoologisches Forschungsinstitut und Museum Alexander Koenig
Braunschweig (Brunswick): Staatliches Naturhistorisches Museum
Dortmund: Museum für Naturkunde
Frankfurt: Natur-Museum und Forschungsinstitut Senckenberg
München (Munich): Deutsches Museum
Stuttgart: Staatliches Museum für Naturkunde

Anthropology

in: Berlin (West), Frankfurt, Göttingen, Hamburg, Kiel, Köln (Cologne, Rautenstrauch-Joest-Museum), Lübeck, München (Munich)

A "centrally guided museums policy" as advocated by some experts is never likely to come about. But doubtlessly there are many fields in which they can and must work together — for example questions of restoration and museum security, central documentation, coordination of research and the development of fundamental methodology.

This joint specialised work is served by the German Museums

Römisch-Germanisches Museum, Cologne

Museum für Völkerkunde (anthropology) in Dahlem, Berlin

Association (Deutscher Museumsbund) set up in 1957, in which all the museums of the Federal Republic of Germany are grouped.

A very large proportion of the museums is owned by the Länder and communes (Gemeinden). The directors and custodians are public servants. This gives rise — in comparison with, say, the U.S. museums system — to a certain ponderousness while on the other hand securing the continuity of the work and the independence of research.

Buildings and presentation. Also widely varied are the museum buildings, ranging from the preserved 19th century museum temples to the new constructions of our age. Many museums were destroyed in World War II but most of their holdings were evacuated in time. War damage has still not been completely re-

paired. Thus it took more than 30 years before the Neue Pinakothek in München was able to emerge again in a completely new
shape.

The newer museum buildings are quite varied in their design.
The Völkerkundemuseum (anthropology) in Berlin (West), for example, is wholly artifically lighted, lamps spotlighting individual
objects, whereas in München's Neue Pinakothek paintings can be
seen in natural light. In most museums the lighting is mixed; in
others, e. g. in Bielefeld's Kunsthalle (art gallery) there is day-
light, artificial lighting and mixed lighting. Not all new museum
buildings have proved completely suited to their purpose. Thus
the glass facades of the Nationalgalerie in Berlin (West), designed by Mies van der Rohe — although it is a beautiful and representational building — endanger the pictures because sunshine
makes temperature regulation difficult (quite apart from the security risk). By contrast, the Mainfränkische Museum behind the
thick walls of Marienberg fortress near Würzburg does not have
that kind of problem.

One of the most remarkable new museums is the Römisch-Germanisches Museum in Köln which links in extraordinarily successful form the requirements of modern museum technology
with public-oriented presentation. Here the visitor is not left alone
and bewildered as in the scholarly museum of the 19th century,
but can make use of numerous aids, from readable brief descrip-
tions to push-button audiovisual presentations. The success of
this new museum gives an indication of the advances made in attracting new sections of the public.

Modern museum practice tries to break down the pseudo-
sacred atmosphere of the traditional museum by making it a
place of encounter and discussion and placing the displayed objects into juxtaposition with present reality.

A number of techniques, some of which have come from the
U.S., aim at making museums more attractive. Most museums
these days have a cafeteria, are open in the evenings and give
free guided tours; some even have children's departments.

Exhibitions. There has also been a heartening increase in exhibition activities. Since limited space frequently precludes showing
a museum's entire stocks, which would only be tiresome anyway,
specialised showings are made from time to time. Historical exhibitions such as "Die Welt der Staufer" (commemorating the medieval imperial Staufer or Hohenstaufer dynasty) in Stuttgart in
1977 or "Preussen — Versuch einer Bilanz" (Prussia — Attempt

at an Appraisal) in 1981 in Berlin (West) enjoyed response from far beyond their own regions.

Comprehensive retrospectives such as the Darmstadt Jugend-stil (Art Nouveau) exhibition "Ein Dokument deutscher Kunst" in 1976 and the 1977 European Exhibition "Kunst der Zwanziger Jahre" (Art of the 20's) in Berlin were extraordinarily popular. Kassel's "documenta" is an international forum of contemporary art held for the first time in 1955 and attracting about 400,000 visitors in 1982.

In recent years various museums succeeded in bringing important international mobile exhibitions to Germany, e. g. the Tutankhamen exhibition and an exhibition, "Der Schatz von San Marco in Venedig".

That art from non-European countries is being increasingly displayed (e. g. "Palastmuseum Peking: Schätze aus der 'Verbotenen Stadt'", Berlin [West] 1985), is all the more meritorious, since many museums no longer send their most valued pieces on tour, when transport endangers the art works to such a degree.

Association of museums:
Deutscher Museumsbund
Colmantstr. 14 – 16
5300 Bonn 1

Music

The outstanding achievements of German composers, performers and ensembles past and present are undisputed. The great composers in German musical tradition are known throughout the world. In a relatively compact area there is a wealth of musical activities. It is therefore not surprising that many foreign musicians were able to gain artistic experience and start their world careers here.

Opera and orchestras. Of the many opera houses the Hamburger Opernhaus, built in 1678, is the oldest. Under its head of many years, Rolf Liebermann, it had many premieres. Other important opera houses are in Berlin (West), Munich, Stuttgart, Frankfurt, Cologne and Düsseldorf.

Lately Hamburg, under the leadership of the American, John Neumeier, has been developing into a ballet metropolis. New forms of ballet were developed in Wuppertal by the choreographer Pina Bausch and her ensemble. The Stuttgart ballet long enjoyed world renown under its English director, John Cranko, who died in 1973.

The best known orchestra is the Berliner Philharmoniker under Herbert von Karajan. Also worthy of mention are the Münchner Philharmoniker and the Bamberger Symphoniker. Most orchestras perform in concerts and opera. Among the institutionalised orchestras are also the highly qualified orchestras of the broadcasting corporations. In the Federal Republic of Germany there are 82 orchestras which receive statal or municipal subsidies, 13 radio orchestras and 58 musical stages with permanent ensembles; in addition there are high-quality chambre orchestras, some in their own right and some comprising members of the large symphony orchestras.

Great musical variety. People interested in music have a wide choice of possibilities to hear it. The range is particularly broad in the cities and covers all types of music. Many theatre and concert subscriptions are offered. There is a wealth of special events such as guest concerts by international soloists and orchestras. Annual festivals add to the variety. Especially attracitve are the many concerts given in summer in old palaces and convents.

Various regular events of a workshop nature serve the promotion of modern music, such as the "Donaueschinger Musiktage" (Festival of New Music), the "Internationale Ferienkurse für Neue Musik" in Darmstadt, the "Tage der neuen Musik" in Hanover and the "Wittener Tage für Neue Kammermusik". A number of special ensembles also cultivates old music, some using historical instruments. Worth mentioning here are the "Collegium Aureum" and the "Musica Antiqua Köln". The most prominent chambre music ensembles are the Melos Quartet, the Kreuzberger Streichquartett, the Cherubini Quartet, the Odeon Trio and the Klavierduo Kontarsky.

Anyone living too remotely to be able to visit concerts has a wide choice of music broadcasts on radio and television. The broadcasting stations have also done much to promote contemporary music. Without the experience and technical facilities of the broadcasting studios experimental electronic music and its mixed forms would hardly be thinkable. The Westdeutscher Rundfunk in Cologne was the first broadcasting corporation to set up an electronic studio which has served as a model for similar facilities around the world. But the other broadcasting corporations also feel committed to furthering contemporary music, co-sponsoring many concerts and series. Every year they commission works from German and foreign composers and broadcast and record them.

Also part of the richness of German musical life are music publishers of world renown (Breitkopf & Härtel, Wiesbaden; Bärenreiter, Kassel; B. Schott's Söhne, Mainz) and instrument makers (Schimmel in Braunschweig; Moeck in Celle; Hohner in Trossingen).

Music teaching and talent promotion. Those who want not only to hear but also to make music can do so in countless lay ensembles (choirs and orchestras of various kinds). There is a correspondingly great demand for qualified instruction as is shown by the existence of almost 700 public music schools.

The conservatories and music academies train professional musicians and music teachers. There are conservatories inter alia in Berlin (West), Bremen, Detmold, Essen, Frankfurt, Hamburg, Hanover, Karlsruhe, Saarbrücken, Stuttgart and Würzburg.

Young soloists are promoted by several competitions and prizes, starting with the national contest, "Jugend musiziert" ("Youngsters make music"), going on to the "Deutscher Musikwettbewerb" ("German Music Competition") in Bonn and going

Scene from "Lear" by Aribert Reimann (Bayerische Staatsoper)

up to the "Internationaler Musikwettbewerb der Arbeitsgemein-schaft der öffentlich-rechtlichen Rundfunkanstalten" ("Internatio-nal Music Competition of the Public Broadcasting Corporations") in Munich.

Soloists, conductors, composers. Among the younger generation of musicians who have been able to make names for themselves are the pianists Christoph Eschbach, Herbert Henck and Chri-stian Zacharias, the violinists Anne-Sophie Mutter and Ulf Höl-scher, the viola-player Tabea Zimmermann, the trumpeter Mar-kus Stockhausen, the organist Edgar Krapp, to name but a few of them.

Internationally known are the composers Gerd Albrecht, Chri-stoph von Dohnanyi, Michael Gielen, Wolfgang Sawallisch, Horst Stein, Klaus Tennstedt, Helmut Rilling, Eugen Jochum and Hans Zender and the singers Hildegard Behrens, Wolfgang Brendel, Brigitte Fassbaender, Dietrich Fischer-Dieskau, Peter Hofmann, René Kollo, Hermann Prey and Edda Moser.

Several modern German composers who have since died achieved international importance. Carl Orff with his scenic can-tatas ("Carmina Burana") and stage works ("Antigone", "Oedi-pus der Tyrann") renewed musical theatre in the classical spirit. Karl Amadeus Hartmann continued the tradition of the German symphony. Boris Blacher, the inventor of the "variable metres" gained prominence as an opera composer. With his "Soldaten"

Bernd Alois Zimmermann created one of the most important contemporary operas.

Wolfgang Fortner is one of the best known twelve-tone composers and most outstanding teachers. Karlheinz Stockhausen as well as Dieter Schnebel, Helmut Lachenmann and Hans-Joachim Hespos have become known internationally as trailblazing experimenters. Hans Werner Henze who lives in Italy is an influential opera composer. Aribert Reimann gained attention with the opera "Lear" (1978) and Wolfgang Rihm with his ballet "Tutuguri" (1982).

In connection with the musical avant garde it must also be mentioned that three of the internationally most renowned representatives are foreigners who have lived in Germany for years: the Hungarian György Ligeti, the Argentinian Mauricio Kagel and the Korean Isang Yun (the latter two have taken German citizenship).

German jazz made a name for itself mainly in Free Jazz (Peter Brötzmann, Manfred Schoof, Alexander von Schlippenbach). Albert Mangelsdorff is regarded as one of the best trombonists in the world. In rock and pop music German groups like "Tangerine Dream", "Nena" or Klaus Doldinger were able to achieve successes abroad. Udo Lindenberg and the Cologne group "BAP" use German lyrics, a growing trend in this field. Chanson and protest song are mainly associated with Wolf Biermann, Franz Josef Degenhardt, Hannes Wader, Klaus Hoffmann and Reinhard Mey. In hit music the singer Nicole gained attention in 1982 by winning

Karlheinz Stockhausen

the Grand Prix de la Chanson. Dance and entertainment bands such as those of James Last, Max Greger and Paul Kuhn have won followings beyond the borders of the Federal Republic of Germany.

German Music Council:
Deutscher Musikrat
Am Michaelshof 4 a
5300 Bonn 2

Theatre

The German theatre landscape is rich and varied. There is no "theatrical capital" which attracts all the best talents. Berlin was able to play such a role for only a few decades. The German theatre has always had several equal-ranking centres and good productions can be seen in many places. This is because Germany was late in becoming a unified nation. In the 17th and 18th centuries many of the then sovereign German princes set up splendid court theatres in their capitals. It is out of these that today's "Staatstheater" have grown. In the 19th century the citizens of prosperous towns followed by founding municipal theatres. To this day the "Staat" and municipal theatres with permanent ensembles form the backbone of theatrical life in the Federal Republic of Germany. In addition there are theatres serving the public in other forms. Only just short of a quarter of the approximately 360 theatres is privately owned. Traditionally, theatre in Germany is regarded as a community service.

The theatres. That applies in particular to funding. In the 1983/84 season the expenditure of all theatres in the Federal Republic amounted to more than DM 2,000 millions. Less than a sixth of this was recouped by admission charges, while about five sixths came out of the public coffers — about DM 90 for every theatre ticket issued. These subsidies went mainly to the publicly owned theatres, but private ones also received some.

Public subsidisation enables German theatres to be guided more by artistic than commercial considerations in drawing up their repertoires. All the "Staat" or municipal theatres are repertory theatres, that is in every season they have a number of works on the programme which they play in daily rotation. Many of them have a "big house" and besides that a smaller theatre or studio stage, so that they can usually offer the public plays, operas and operettas, and sometimes even ballets performed by their own ensembles. One special type of public theatre are the so-called "Landesbühnen" (country stages) which, operating from a central house, play in medium-sized and smaller centres of a region. Some medium-sized towns have a municipal theatre building but no staff ensemble and these are played in only by visiting troupes.

Cuvilliéstheater in Munich

The permanent private theatres, with few exceptions, are fairly small. Some still hail from the immediate postwar era, when everywhere in the bombed-out cities "room" or "cellar" theatres came into being. These small stages have done much to assert modern works. Another important type of private theatre are the touring companies. These engage actors, in most cases including one or more stars, for only one set piece which, similarly to the Landestheater, they take to small and medium towns.

Theatregoers. In the 1983/84 season more than 21 million people went to the theatre in the Federal Republic. Most did not buy their tickets at the evening box office but came as subscribers. The subscription system is very widespread in Germany: one books in advance for an entire season of a series of 10 or 12 performances. In some theatres the subscribers comprise up to 90 % of the audience. Apart from this form of attendance, organised by the theatres themselves, there is also an indirect one: large groups of theatregoers buy complete performances or ticket contingents for an entire season. The oldest and largest of these theatregoing organisations is the "Volksbühne" (People's Stage), founded in 1890 and originally connected with the labour movement, with a current membership of about 600,000. In addition there are the

Christian-oriented "Bund der Theatergemeinden" (Association of Theatre Communities) with about 130,000 members, as well as youth organisations.

Some critics take the view that the German theatre system with its peculiarities — public subsidies, subscription, visitor organisations — is detrimental to artistic daring and favours boring routine. That is surely wrong — or at least grossly exaggerated. Granted, in drawing up his programme a superintendent has to take account of the more conservative among his subscription audience who do not only want to see avant-garde works. And from time to time there are attempts by local politicians to prevent the performance at "their" municipal theatre of pieces they dislike for one reason or another. But there can be no talk of any serious jeopardisation of artistic freedom. And the courage to experiment is greater if one does not under all circumstances have to look to commercial success.

Works. What works, then, are seen on the stages of the Federal Republic? The most performed writers in the past 30 years have been Shakespeare and the German classical authors Schiller, Lessing and Goethe. The most produced dramatists of our century have been Bernard Shaw, Bertolt Brecht and Jean Anouilh, who have also in their way meanwhile become classical. The greatest stage success of a German author after the war was Rolf Hochhuth's "Stellvertreter" (The Representative), a work which found little praise from the critics but which triggered off impassioned discussions because of its gripping subject matter, the at-

Major theatres and their heads *(1985/86 season)*

Berlin (West): Schiller-Theater mit Schloßpark-Theater and Werkstatt (Heribert Sasse), Freie Volksbühne (Kurt Hübner), Renaissance-Theater (Friedrich von Kekulé), Schaubühne am Lehniner Platz (Jürgen Schitthelm, Klaus Weiffenbach)
Bochum: Schauspielhaus (Rolf Paulin, Claus Peymann)
Bremen: Schauspielhaus (Tobias Richter)
Düsseldorf: Schauspielhaus (Günther Beelitz)
Frankfurt: Schauspiel (Günther Rühle)
Hamburg: Deutsches Schauspielhaus (Peter Zadek), Thalia-Theater (Jürgen Flimm)
Köln: Schauspiel (Klaus Pierwoß, Horst Siede, Alexander von Maravić)
München: Bayerisches Staatsschauspiel (Frank Baumbaur), Münchner Kammerspiele (Dieter Dorn)
Stuttgart: Württembergisches Staatstheater (Ivan Nagel)

"Schaubühne am Lehniner Platz" in Berlin;
scene from "The Park" by Botho Strauss

titude taken by Pope Pius XII to Hitler's extermination of Jews.
Other German dramatists of recent time are Botho Strauss, Franz
Xaver Kroetz, Martin Walser, Patrick Süsskind, to name but a few.
Also worth mentioning are Peter Hacks, Heiner Müller and Ulrich
Plenzdorf, three authors living in the GDR, whose pieces have
been successfully played in the Federal Republic.

Association of theatres:
Deutscher Bühnenverein
Quatermarkt 5
5000 Köln 1

Cinema

German films once enjoyed world renown. In the 1920's and the early 30's, the time of the Weimar Republic, filmmaking reached a level of achievement still remarkable by present-day standards. Names like Fritz Lang, Ernst Lubitsch, F. W. Murnau and G. W. Pabst testify to the impetus which the cinema received from Germany at the time.

Little has remained of this accomplishment. The Hitler dictatorship put an end to free artistic development. Most of the great directors and many important actors had to flee abroad. After World War II Germany was initially artistically and economically isolated; it could not immediately catch up with international developments.

Consequently filmmaking in the Federal Republic fell short of international standards. A few respectable achievements notwithstanding, superficial entertainment films dominated. In the early 60's competition from television was increasingly making inroads, withdrawing much of the cinema's public. This not only threw the film industry into a crisis, it also strengthened the trend to run-of-the-mill entertainment films.

Filmmaking crisis. Whereas in 1956 the cinemas still attracted a public of more than 820 millions, in 1976 there remained only 115 millions. In the meantime half the cinemas had had to close down. In 1956 there had been 6,438, in 1976 only 3,100 were left. Hardest hit were the cinemas in rural areas, in small towns and at urban peripheries. The approximately 300 premiere-showing cinemas in city centres which were always able to show the newest films got off relatively unscathed. The 100 biggest made 15% of the 1978 turnover.

There is tough competition for this greatly diminished market. In 1976 German films had only 11.4% of it (compared with 46.8% in 1955) while U.S. films were able to increase their share from 32.3% in 1955 to 43.1% in 1976.

For a while it looked as if the trend might change. While economic recession cut cinema attendance in many countries, it rose in the Federal Republic. So did cinemas' turnover, from DM 655 millions in 1977 to DM 905 millions in 1980. But meanwhile it appears that a new film crisis is in the offing. The filmgoing public dropped from 143 millions in 1980 to 125 millions and cinema turn-over to DM 872 millions in 1983.

The young German film. In the mid-60's a new development began which is summarised under the heading "Junger deutscher Film" (the young German film). Supported by public funds and television contracts some younger directors were able to make names for themselves with formally attractive, in part contemporaneously critical feature films. Suffice it to name here Alexander Kluge ("Abschied von gestern"), Volker Schlöndorff ("Der junge Törless") and Rainer Werner Fassbinder ("Katzelmacher"). They were later joined by Werner Herzog ("Jeder für sich, Gott gegen alle"), Hans Jürgen Syberberg ("Ludwig II"), Bernhard Sinkel/Alf Brustellin ("Lina Braake") and Wim Wenders ("Der amerikanische Freund"). With his "Die verlorene Ehre der Katharina Blum" (after a novel by Nobel Prize-winning Heinrich Böll) Volker Schlöndorff achieved a big commercial success which he even bettered with his next literature adaptation, "Die Blechtrommel" (after a novel by Günter Grass). This film won him the "Golden Palm" in Cannes in 1979 and the "Oscar" for the best foreign film in 1980. Such productions prove that films of a high standard have big chances not only with the critics but also at the box office.

With his later films (e. g. "Die Ehe der Maria Braun") R. W. Fassbinder, who died in 1982, became one of the commercially most successful directors. He was awarded the "Golden Bear" at the 1982 Berlin film festival for "Die Sehnsucht der Veronika Voss". In the same year Wenders won the "Golden Lion" in Venice for "Der Stand der Dinge". In Cannes Werner Herzog was awarded the prize for the best direction for "Fitzcarraldo". In 1984 Wenders was awarded the Cannes "Golden Palm" for "Paris, Texas". Edgar Reitz won wide acclaim for his series, "Heimat". Wolfgang Petersen was commercially successful with "Das Boot" and "Enemy Mine — Geliebter Feind". Among the women directors the most prominent is Margarethe von Trotta ("Rosa Luxemburg"). Werner Schroeter made a name for himself with the film "Der Tag der Idioten".

State supports. Since 1951 the Federal Minister of the Interior annually awards prizes and grants for outstanding film achievements: for the best full-length feature film the "Goldene Schale" ("Golden Bowl") with DM 500,000 as well as "Film Bands" in gold and silver up to DM 400,000. In addition the minister grants funds for raising the artistic reputation of German films in the form of

Scene from "Rosa Luxemburg", directed by Margarethe von Trotta

production and exhibition subsidies as well as grants for talented young filmmakers.

A Film Promotion Act was passed in 1968 which runs initially up to 1986. Under it, cinemas are levied to support film production, distribution and cinemas. Most of these funds (70%) go into promotion of feature films. Not to be underestimated, either, is the contribution of the public television corporations. They share the costs of feature films and in return acquire the right to show them later in their programmes. A "Kuratorium junger deutscher Film" (Young German Film Trust), an institution of the Länder, supports primarily young artists.

New impetus has come to West German filmmaking from the establishment of two film schools, at Berlin (West) (1966) and München (Munich) (1967), which offer a limited number of students the possibility of theoretical and practical film training.

A "Film Ratings Agency" (Filmbewertungsstelle) established in 1951 by an agreement between the Länder, awards to feature and short films the ratings "wertvoll" (valuable) and "besonders wertvoll" (especially valuable). These ratings result in tax exemption or tax cuts as well as subsidies under the Film Promotion Act.

Major film festivals are the "Berlin International Film Festival" (Internationale Filmfestspiele Berlin, main prize "Golden Berlin Bear"), the "International Mannheim Films Week" (Internationale

Mannheimer Filmwoche, prize: "Film Ducat") and the "West German Short Film Days" (Westdeutsche Kurzfilmtage) in Oberhausen. A number of smaller festivals also give insights into specialised areas of German filmmaking.

Umbrella organisation of the film industry:
Spitzenorganisation der Filmwirtschaft
Langenbeckstr. 9
6200 Wiesbaden

Festivals

In the Federal Republic one never has far to go to the nearest art festival. It goes without saying that big cities have them. But there are also very attractive small towns able to offer something special, such as Schwetzingen with its rococo theatre. Thematically, too, every taste is catered for, from the Oberammergau Passion Play to the Bayreuth Richard Wagner festival to the workshop-style Donaueschingen Music Days.

Berlin (West) can serve as an example of the concerted festival activities of the larger cities. In the 1920s Berlin was for a short time a real centre of cultural life in Germany, attracting serious artists from everywhere. After the division of the city in 1948 danger of isolation threatened a regression into provincial mediocrity. In the western part of the city there has been an attempt ever since 1951 to counteract this by organising festivals. Nowadays they go

Bayreuth festival hall

From the Oberammergau passion play

on there almost throughout the year. Major functions are the "Berliner Festwochen" in September/October (about five weeks), in which a wealth of musical events from solo concert to opera and ballet are offered, and the "Berliner Jazztage" (from 1964) in November, which although lasting only five days, rank with the most important jazz functions of the world. Many soloists have been discovered here, such as the virtuoso Al Jarrau in 1976. The "Internationale Filmfestspiele" in February/March dates from 1951. The prizewinning works in this competition of the latest films from all over the world are rewarded with the Golden and Silver Berlin Bears. Since 1964 the "Theatertreffen Berlin" has presented selected theatre productions from German-speaking countries. "Horizonte", the festival of world cultures, started in 1979 and has taken place three times so far. It brings together in Berlin European culture and cultures from other parts of the world.

Other cities and towns keep their festivals completely in the musical field, such as München (Munich) with its Opera Festival (July/August) or Kassel with its Music Days (September/October). Frequently the work of a single composer is featured. In München, homage is paid to the local genius Richard Strauss;

Würzburg and Augsburg specialise in Mozart, Ansbach in Bach, Bonn in Beethoven. The Richard Wagner festival at Bayreuth is probably Germany's best known abroad and, some might say, also the most venerable. In 1976 Wagner's tetralogy "The Ring of the Nibelung" enjoyed a controversial jubilee production on the occasion of the 100th anniversary. Also in Bayreuth there is the "Internationales Jugend-Festspieltreffen" (youth festival) inaugurated in 1950. Since then more than 10,000 young people from more than 70 countries have taken part in it.

There are also festivals devoted to the music of a certain period, such as the "Tage alter Musik" in Herne, or to a certain instrument, such as the "Internationale Orgelwoche Nürnberg — musica sacra" (organ). Surprisingly, there is no piano festival in the Federal Republic of Germany.

This list is enough to show that in Germany musical festivals dominate. Dramatic theatre is offered mainly at the festival in the Carolingian monastery ruin of Bad Hersfeld (Hessen). The same goes for the Ruhrfestspiele in Recklinghausen which, domiciled in the middle of the industrial Ruhr region, tailors its classical and modern repertoire mainly to a worker public.

The oldest festival is the Passion Play at Oberammergau (Upper Bavaria), which takes place every 10 years on a 1634 pledge to God for deliverance from the plague, for the last time in 1980. To mark the 350th anniversary of the pledge the passion play was put on additionally in 1984. The play productions always attract about half a million visitors, two thirds of them from the United States of America.

Bibliography

Michael Balfour, *West Germany,* London 1968

Klaus von Beyme (ed.), *German Political Systems. Theory and Practice in the Two Germanies,* London 1976

Gerard Braunthal, *The West-German Social Democrats, 1969 – 1982,* Boulder, Colo. 1983

J. Brueckner and G. Doeker, *The German Democratic Republic in International Relations and the Federal Republic of Germany,* New York 1979

Charles Burdick et al. (ed.), *Contemporary Germany – Politics and Culture,* New York 1984

Honoré M. Catudal, *The Berlin Agreement of 1971,* Berlin 1976

Sebastian Cobler, *Law, Order and Politics in West Germany,* London 1978

David P. Conradt, *The German Polity,* New York 1978

Gordon Craig, *Germany – 1866 – 1945,* Oxford 1978

Donald S. Detwiler, *Germany. A Short History,* London and Amsterdam 1977

Deutscher Gewerkschaftsbund (ed.), *The German Trade Union Federation,* Düsseldorf 1981

Raymond Ebsworth, *Restoring Democracy in Germany. The British Contribution,* London 1960

Lewis S. Edinger, *Politics in West Germany,* Boston 1977

Edition Rainer Kledrowski, *The Federal Republic of Germany Today,* Ratingen 1983 (mainly pictorial)

Ludwig Erhard, *Prosperity through Competition,* London 1958

Constantine Fitzgibbon, *Denazification,* London 1969

Henry W. Flannery and Gerhart H. Seger, *Which Way Germany?,* New York 1968

James Furlong, *Labor in the Boardroom. The Peaceful Revolution,* Princeton 1977

Hans W. Gatzke, *Germany and the United States – a "Special Relationship"?,* Cambridge and London 1980

Hildegard and Reinhold Geimer, *Research Organisation and Science Promotion in the Federal Republic of Germany,* München 1981

German Centre of Gerontology, *Report on the Situation of the Elderly in the Federal Republic of Germany,* Berlin

German Information Center, *Germany's Contribution to Western Defense. The Role of the Federal Republic of Germany in Nato,* New York 1984

John Gimbel, *The American Occupation of Germany. Politics and the Military, 1945 – 1949,* Stanford 1968

Guido G. Goldmann, *The German Political System,* New York 1974

Laszlo Gorgey, *Bonn's Eastern Policy 1964 – 1971. Evolution and Limitations,* Hamden 1972

Wolfram F. Hanrieder (ed.), *West German Foreign Policy 1949 – 1979,* Boulder, Colo. 1980

Arnold Heidenheimer and Donald P. Kommers, *The Governments of Germany*, New York 1975

Richard Hiscocks, *Democracy in Western Germany*, London 1957

Richard Hiscocks, *Germany Revived. An Appraisal of the Adenauer Era*, London 1966

Viola Herms Draht (ed.), *Germany in World Politics*, New York 1979

Peter Hoffmann, *The History of the German Resistance, 1933 – 1945*, Cambridge, Mass. 1977

Walter Kempowski (ed.), *Did you ever see Hitler?*, New York 1976

Rüdiger Klessmann, *The Berlin Museum*, New York 1972

H. Krausnick and M. Mau, *German History 1933 – 1945*, London 1973

Walter Laqueur, *Germany today – a Personal Report*, New York 1985

Robert Gerald Livingston (ed.), *The Federal Republic of Germany in the 1980s – Foreign Policies and Domestic Changes*, New York 1983

Prinz Hubertus zu Loewenstein, *Nato and the Defense of the West*, Westport 1975

Golo Mann, *The History of Germany since 1789*, New York 1968

Peter Hans Merkl, *The Origin of the West German Republic*, New York 1963

Roger Morgan, *The United States and West Germany, 1945 – 1973*, London 1974

Rolf Neuhaus, *Social Security: How it works in the Federal Republic of Germany*, Bonn 1979

Arnold H. Price, *The Federal Republic of Germany. A Selected Bibliography of English-Language Publications. 2nd revised edition*, Washington, D. C. 1978

Terence Prittie, *The Velvet Chancellors. A History of Post-War Germany*, London 1979

Hans Rothfels, *German Opposition to Hitler*, London 1978

C. C. Schweitzer et al. (ed.), *Politics and Government in the Federal Republic of Germany. Basic Documents*, Leamington Spa 1984

Kurt Sontheimer, *The Government and Politics of West Germany*, New York 1973

R. B. Tilford, *Federal Germany, Political and Social Order*, London 1969

Roger Tilford (ed.), *The Ostpolitik and Political Change in Germany*, London 1975

H. G. Peter Wallach and George K. Romoser (ed.), *West-German Politics in the Mid-eienties – Crisis and Continuity*, New York 1985

Index

[D] = Diagram · [M] = Map · [P] = Picture

PICTURE SOURCES

Colour: Anthony Verlag, Starnberg − Fischer (1) − Storck (1); Dieter Asmus, Hamburg (1); BASF AG, Landw. Versuchsstation, Limburgerhof (1); Bertelsmann LEXIKOTHEK Verlag GmbH, Gütersloh (3); Bibliothèque Royale Albert Ier, Brüssel (1); Bildarchiv Preußischer Kulturbesitz, Berlin (3); Klaus Barisch, Köln (1); Bavaria-Verlag, Gauting (1) − Adam (1); BMW, München − Ott (1); Bongarts, München (1); Bundesminister f. d. Post- u. Fernmeldewesen, Bonn − Gierig (1); Deutsche Bundesbahn, Frankfurt (1); dpa, Frankfurt (6) − Dürrwald (1) − Ossinger (1); FAG-Foto M. Skaryd, Frankfurt (1) − Freig. Reg.-Präs. Darmstadt Nr. 1995/79; Manfred Grohe, Kirchentellinsfurt (1); GTZ, Eschborn − Michler (1); Bildarchiv Huber, Garmisch-Partenkirchen (1); Dr. Konrad Karkosch, München (2); Gerhard Klammet, Ohlstadt (1); Kraftwerk Union AG, Erlangen (1); Kreissparkasse, Köln (1); Landeshauptstadt, München (1); Klaus Lehnartz, Berlin (1); Photo Löbl, Bad Tölz (1); Luftbild Klammet & Aberl, Germering (2) − Freig. durch d. Reg. v. Oberbayern unter Nr. G 43/408 bzw. G 43/970; Fritz Mader, Hamburg-Barsbüttel (3); MAN-Werke, Augsburg (1); Bildagentur Mauritius, Mittenwald − Grasser (1) − Hansson (1) − Kalt (1) − Lorenz (1) − Siska (1) − Schmidt-Luchs (1) − Werner (1); Werner H. Müller, Stuttgart (1); Horst Müller, Düsseldorf (1); NATO, Brüssel (1); Maria Otte, Melle (1); Joachim Peters, Sulzbach (1); Presse- und Informationsamt der Bundesreg. Bundesbildstelle, Bonn (18); Wilhelm Rauh, Bayreuth (1); Rheinische Braunkohlenwerke AG, Köln (1); RWE, Essen (1); roebild, Frankfurt − Ege (1) − Röhrig (2) − Schuster (1); Günter Rossenbach, Wuppertal (1); Sven Simon, Essen (2); Achim Sperber, Hamburg (2); Susanne Schapowalow, Hamburg − Ligges (1); Toni Schneiders, Lindau (1); Georg Stiller, Gütersloh (2); Foto Felicitas Timpe, München (1); VISUM, Hamburg − Meisel (1); VW-Fotozentrale, Wolfsburg (1); Wallraf-Richartz-Museum und Museum Ludwig, Köln ./ © COSMOPRESS, Genf (1); Ruth Walz, Berlin (1); ZEFA, Düsseldorf − Anatol (1) − Buchner (1) − Geissler (1) − Grebe (1) − Idem (1) − Kerth (1) − Praedel (1).

Black and white: Bertelsmann LEXIKOTHEK Verlag GmbH, Gütersloh (1); dpa, Düsseldorf (7); Foto-present, Essen − Vollmer (1); Hanns Hubmann, Kröning (1); Keystone Pressedienst GmbH, Hamburg (2); Klaus Lehnartz, Berlin (1); Erica Loos, Pforzheim (1); Isolde Ohlbaum, München (1); Presse- und Informationsamt der Bundesreg. Bundesbildstelle, Bonn (2); roebild, Frankfurt − Röhrig (1) − Schindler (2); STERN, Hamburg − Schmitt (1) − Scheler (1); Stiftsbibliothek St. Gallen, Zumbühl (1); Ullstein GmbH Bilderdienst, Berlin (5).

Envelope pictures: Bundesbahn Zentralamt, München (1); Henning Christoph, Essen (1); laenderpress, Düsseldorf − Martzik (1); ZEFA, Düsseldorf − Adam (1).